D1600444

THE OWNER'S AND MANAGER'S GUIDE TO CONDOMINIUM MANAGEMENT

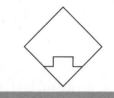

Contributing Authors

Joseph T. Aveni, CPM®
Steven P. Bloomberg
R. Bruce Campbell, CPM®
Aaron M. Chaney, CPM®
John N. Gallagher, CPM®
R. Don Larrance, CPM®
Robert W. McLallen
W. Donald Sally, CPM®
Thomas A. Scapillato, CPM®

Editorial Consultants

Michael Cousins, CPM®
Richard M. Goldberg, CPM®
Michael E. Packard, CPM®
John J. Smolenski, CPM®
M. Vince Turner

Keith F. Levine,
Publishing Manager

THE OWNER'S AND MANAGER'S GUIDE TO CONDOMINIUM MANAGEMENT

REVISED EDITION

INSTITUTE OF REAL ESTATE MANAGEMENT

of the NATIONAL ASSOCIATION OF REALTORS®

430 North Michigan Avenue, Chicago, Illinois 60611-4090

International Standard Book Number: 0-912104-61-9
Library of Congress Catalog Card Number: 83-81899

Printed in the United States of America

CONTENTS

Contents

PREFACE

Although the growth of residential condominiums has slowed since the condominium boom of the 1970s, the outlook for condominium housing remains bright. For a number of widely recognized reasons, including the long-term trends toward increasing numbers of small families, working couples, older people, and singles, demographic groups to whom condominiums particularly appeal, most experts anticipate the continued growth of residential condominiums in the coming decades. While condominiums probably will never fully replace traditional single-family homes, they have become viable and attractive alternatives to home ownership in many areas.

Condominium ownership involves a person's exclusively owning an individual dwelling unit and sharing ownership of areas used commonly by all residents, such as hallways, swimming pools, and parking lots. Unfortunately, while more people have grown familiar with the condominium concept or have gained direct experience with it, this complex form of real-property ownership still is often not fully understood by people who buy condominium homes or by those who become involved in the governance of their condominium community.

Usually a condominium unit owner's problems begin when he or she purchases a unit without being informed about the meaning of condominium ownership, basic condominium law, condominium management, maintenance problems and costs, rights and restrictions and obligations, and the condominium association that governs the community. The new owner also may not be prepared for living with others in an often densely populated community, usually consisting of many units in a single building, which relies on social interdependence and practices self-government. It is essential to the overall success of the condominium form of home ownership that people who have bought and will buy condominium units and become responsible for making decisions affecting their condominium community understand what they are doing and why.

Although the condominium concept of home ownership initially was greeted with skepticism, acceptance and a construction boom soon followed. According to some professionals in the real estate industry, however, this occurred much too quickly. They theorize that not enough research and thought had gone into condominium planning, and many problems arose, leading to confusion, misapprehension, and more skepticism. The main difficulties were poor construction, lack of suitable insurance coverage or an income tax system for this residential arrangement, shoddy selling techniques, unworkable governing documents, and inexperience on the part of both professionals and unit owners with condominium management and association administration. The condominium image became blemished.

But time has been a good teacher. Many problems have been recognized, and steps have been and are being taken to eliminate them. A second wave of state condominium legislation—in some states, even a third wave—is providing improved guidelines for developing and governing condominiums, and consumer standards are being set to eliminate sales abuses, leading to greater satisfaction with condominium living. Based on the experiences of the first two decades of condominium ownership, the future can bring together the best of the individual home and the best of multifamily living. New condominium unit owners can benefit from earlier owners' experiences to widen their knowledge and enable them to set the proper balance for working with professionals.

Experience has shown that the association form of government is a practical and desirable method for maintaining a condominium's open spaces and recreational facilities and enforcing the legal covenants. A set of governing documents gives the association its authority and provides its legal framework. Serious difficulties and problems are not as likely to occur in associations where a sound legal foundation is created through these documents. However, while this legal basis is important, the success of an association's ability to govern a community hinges on the people who live there. With effective leaders who understand their obligations and how to fulfill them, the association should operate smoothly through its board of directors—the official policy-making body of the association—and a network of complementary committees.

The Institute of Real Estate Management (IREM), aware of the problems connected with managing a condominium and running an association, recognized the need for a comprehensive, up-to-date textbook to be used as a reference for persons involved with condominiums. Therefore, *The Owner's and Manager's Guide to Condominium Management*, a thoroughly revised, updated, and expanded edition of IREM's popular text *The Condominium Community: A Guide for Owners, Boards, and Managers*, was developed—like its predecessor—to assist all condominium unit owners, especially those involved in the governance of their condominium associations, and all property managers involved with condominiums.

This book should help the new board of directors that is accepting the transfer of control from the developer, and should provide suggestions for the ongoing board that wants to improve its operation so the condominium can become a more stable community. It should benefit small associations of only a few units that manage themselves, and should assist large associations that use total professional management. Equally important, it should be a useful reference for property managers faced with having to develop unique skills and solutions in order to successfully meet the distinct challenges and opportunities of condominium management.

The Owner's and Manager's Guide to Condominium Management is not an operational manual. It does not intend to describe the "only" way or the "right" way to finance and operate a condominium association and maintain the physical plant. For one thing, the size of a condominium development plays an important part in determining the way it can function most effectively. Also, because condominium legislation is made by states—and in some areas, even by local governments—not centrally by the federal government, associations in different states and localities may have different legal obligations. Given the size and statutory variations, however, there are common managerial and operational premises upon which most condominium associations may make decisions, and there are certain problems with which most condominiums will be confronted.

The Owner's and Manager's Guide to Condominium Management outlines these premises and suggests ways of solving the problems that will be common to most condominiums. It defines condominium ownership and explains the powers and responsibilities of the association and the board of directors. It deals with accepting control of the association from the developer, creating an effective administrative system, conducting effective meetings, deciding on a condominium management plan, maintaining the common areas, providing security and life-safety systems, establishing lines of communication, instituting sound fiscal procedures, insuring the condominium, and understanding the tax status of the association and the unit owners.

Of course, condominium ownership is not the only form of multifamily ownership, nor is the condominium association the only organization designed to govern a community of home owners. Other kinds of residential community associations, such as cooperatives, planned unit developments, homeowners associations, and timesharing associations, are found in many areas. Although these other kinds of community associations are not governed by the same laws that govern condominiums, their general operations and the requirements of their covenants may be similar. In all of these associations, all owners automatically belong. All rely on assessments of owners as the principal means of funding their operations. All have similar problems in the areas of government, management, and human relations. Consequently, many of the operational and administrative guidelines provided here could be applied to other kinds of community associations.

Similarly, there are kinds of condominiums other than the residential one, on which *The Owner's and Manager's Guide to Condominium Management* is focused. The condominium concept is also used in office buildings, shopping centers, warehouses, mobile-home parks, camping grounds, marinas—even parking spaces. Again, although each form of condominium will have specific legal requirements and unique problems, some of the concepts that apply to residential condominium operation may be applied to the operation of condominiums created for other uses.

The Owner's and Manager's Guide to Condominium Management was developed as a means of exchanging experiences by making available to condominium unit owners, association leaders, and property managers the lessons that have been learned about living in and working with condominium communities. This was accomplished by compiling research materials, ideas, theories, documents, forms, personal accounts, and suggestions that have come out of the contributing authors' and editorial consultants' long experience assisting condominium associations.

The contributing authors are grateful to a number of people who helped to make this book possible. We wish to thank the editorial consultants, who reviewed the manuscript prior to publication and made thoughtful criticisms and suggestions; M. Vince Turner, in particular, provided especially extensive and helpful input. Eight of our team of nine contributing authors would like to extend special thanks to the ninth member of our group, John N. Gallagher, CPM®, for his tireless efforts and dedication beyond the call of duty.

We wish to thank Joan A. Grygel for her expert editing of the manuscript and Norman Baugher for his outstanding designs for both the interior and the cover of the book. We are especially grateful to Keith F. Levine, IREM's publishing manager, who coordinated the entire project, and who did so with efficiency and care. We hope and trust that the reader will share our belief that all of these individuals helped us to make *The Owner's and Manager's Guide to Condominium Management* accessible, enjoyable, and useful.

1

WHAT IS
A CONDOMINIUM
ASSOCIATION?

*T*raditionally, the United States has been the "land of plenty"—with plenty of land. Part of the American dream has been to own a home and some of that land. In the past, millions of people have realized that dream, but now the dream is fading quickly for many. The harsh reality is that land is becoming increasingly scarce in the more heavily populated areas of the country. Today, few families can afford the luxury of a large rambling house set amid several grassy acres. For that matter, even a modest split-level house on a quarter-acre lot is beyond the reach of many. As a result, alternative forms of housing that use the land more economically are increasing in popularity.

The dwindling land supply and its consequent rising cost, along with high interest rates and construction costs, have had profound effects on the housing market. There are other factors that also have had significant impact. Most important, personal attitudes about lifestyles are changing and significantly influencing the country's housing industry.

Attitudes about ownership responsibilities are changing. Many people want to own a home, but do not want to be tied to houses that require a lot of time and money to maintain. These people are looking for ways to enjoy the benefits of ownership without being burdened by the maintenance responsibilities that usually accompany home ownership.

Attitudes about families are changing. Several decades ago families with three or four children were common. Today many families have only one child or remain childless. As a result, although more households are being formed, their average size is smaller. Thus, while more housing units are needed, these units are not as large as they once were.

Attitudes toward renting versus buying housing are changing. From 1976 through the first half of 1979, approximately a million households who should have been renters (according to the demographics) became buyers instead. The 1980s will witness the gradual aging of the housing market. The number of people under 25 forming households will remain steady and then decrease. The number of households in the next older bracket, 25 to 29, will increase slowly and could start decreasing before 1990. The fastest growing age group will be the 35 to 44 group. The number of households in this group is expected to increase 50 percent. Over-65 households will increase sharply and should outnumber the under-25s from 1986 on.

Attitudes toward careers are changing. It is no longer unusual for both husband and wife to work, increasing the average couple's total income. Such increases in income are usually accompanied by an increase in the desire for home ownership and the status that goes with it. The Equal Credit Opportunity Act has given new mortgaging power to these couples and to singles.

Attitudes of older persons are changing. Many retired men and women choose to live in warmer climates. They want recreational facilities near at hand to help them enjoy their later years. "Empty nesters," parents whose children have grown up and left home, no longer need large houses. They often want smaller, more conveniently located residences that require less work.

Attitudes of unmarried men and women are changing. People who are single, divorced, or widowed want the security and tax advantages of owning a home but not the problems of maintaining one. Singles increasingly want to invest in homes but do not want accompanying responsibilities or suburban living. They tend to prefer more informal surroundings and conveniently located recreational facilities.

All of these—small families, working couples, older people, and singles—have needs and desires that promise to be met by multifamily housing developments commonly known by the umbrella term of *community associations.*

What Is a Condominium?

Contrary to general belief, condominiums are not created under federal law. They are actually created by state statute in each of the 50 states where they are located. The law defines "condominium" as a form of ownership. By derivation, the word *condominium* is actually a Latin term that combines *dominium,* meaning "control" (over a piece of property), with *con,* meaning "with" (other individuals). This form of ownership may apply to residential buildings, boat docks, aircraft hangers, burial vaults, safety deposit boxes, office buildings, and other physical entities where ownership can be clearly defined by measurement or survey. This book will limit the topic of condominium ownership to residential associations.

The condominium unit and the common areas

If you own a condominium, exactly what do you own? The buyer of a condominium receives a "bundle of rights." That is, when title is transferred the buyer receives two things: exclusive ownership of that specific unit of property and an undivided percentage interest of ownership in the *common areas.* The common areas are areas and facilities that are used by all owners as tenants in common with other owners, such as walkways, driveways, courtyards, and all other property of the development. A condominium owner has exclusive ownership and control of all the space and improvements within the walls of the unit. From the legal point of view it is no different than ownership of a single-family house in any residential subdivision. If you live in a high-rise building, you might think of it as a vertical subdivision. Your unit can be given away, sold, leased (if permissible by the association), taxed, mortgaged, deeded away, and insured.

The distinctions between condominium unit ownership and single-family home ownership may be described as follows: the owner of a single-family home usually owns and has virtually unrestricted use of a house and the land on which it is built. By contrast, a condominium unit is most often legally defined as a space of air or a three-dimensional area located within the walls, floor, and ceiling of a condominium structure, be it vertical or horizontal. The owner of the unit rarely has exclusive title to the walls, roof, and floors that enclose this cube of air. If constructed horizontally, the unit could be a zero lot line house or even a single-family house where the ownership of these components would be different.

Condominium owners have an *undivided interest* in the balance of the property shared with all other unit owners. This common area (as it is called) may consist of the hallways, basements, elevators, lobbies, stairways, boilers, pipes, conduits, air vents, exterior walls, and any other structural or mechanical elements, especially in multistory buildings. It may also include the land on which the building is built and any other buildings or facilities that are not part of the individually owned units, such as swimming pools, tennis courts, parks, playgrounds, and parking areas. The term "undivided interest" means that ownership cannot be divided. For example, if there are 50 units in a project that covers 100,000 square feet of land, all of the unit owners own the land in common, but the land cannot be divided among them. No one owner can claim ownership of a specific 2,000-square-foot area of that land. Common areas are owned jointly by all of the unit owners, and all owners have joint responsibility for the common areas.

Ownership of a condominium unit and the undivided portion of the common areas is defined as a *fee simple absolute interest*. Fee simple absolute interest gives the title holder ownership of the property without restriction (although this is not always true), as well as the right to use it and dispose of it as he or she chooses.

Some condominium buyers may acquire a *leasehold inter-*

est, which means they are leasing the estate for a definite, usually very long, period of time. This gives them the right to possess, use, and enjoy their property for a certain period of time, during which they may transfer the title of the unit to others, mortgage it, or do anything else with it that the owner who has a fee simple absolute interest can. However, when the lease expires, the leasehold interest terminates, and the use and possession of the property is returned to the owner of the estate.

A person who holds title to a condominium unit and the undivided interest in the common areas is customarily referred to as a *unit owner,* and sometimes as an apartment owner or a co-owner. The term "unit owner" may refer to one person or to a combination of persons, such as a married couple, a corporation, a trust, or a partnership. For simplicity, this book will refer to the unit owner as though he or she were one individual. The reader should keep in mind, however, that this is not necessarily so in all cases.

The trend to conversion

There is, then, no "typical" condominium. A condominium may be a new or an old structure. It may be large or small. It may include as few as two units or as many as thousands. A condominium may be a luxury or a low-income development. It may contain one building or several buildings. It may come complete with a swimming pool, tennis courts, and even medical services, or it may offer no recreational or other amenities. Therefore, a condominium cannot be defined as any one particular type of building. It can only be defined as a form of ownership of a building or development that is becoming increasingly popular.

One significant trend in condominium development is the conversion of rental properties to condominiums. Conversions, as these condominiums are called, may involve any kind of multifamily development that originally consisted of rental apartments. From a legal standpoint, a conversion occurs when the grantor/developer files with the proper state official the Declaration of Condominium that establishes the property as a condominium, thus establishing a different form of ownership. This should occur before the units are offered for sale or during the sales program. It should be done no later than when 50 percent of the units are sold.

The primary reason for converting rental apartments to condominiums is a financial one. For example, the owner of a rental property may decide to dispose of his or her property because of a poor return on investment. This poor return may be the result of rent controls, increased maintenance costs, increased real estate taxes, high interest rates, loss of depreciation, or other economic factors. Converting the rental property to a condominium is often risky. In spite of the risk, however, conversion may be more profitable than selling the property to a single investor. In today's economics, selling the apartments one at a time as condominium units yields a higher return than would be realized if the entire apartment building were sold for continued use as a rental property.

Conversions have other advantages. A condominium conversion usually is accompanied by improvements to the property. The tax base is increased since, although condominiums usually are assessed at a lower rate than rental buildings, the assessment is on a per unit basis. This assessment method, together with the increased value, raises the tax base, thereby helping to stabilize a neighborhood.

Conversions can also create problems. Although a condominium theoretically can take any physical form, some existing apartment buildings simply are not designed for condominium use. Many lack the amenities commonly associated with newly constructed condominiums. Conversions also cause serious social problems for tenants who cannot or do not want to buy their apartments. This is especially true of older persons who may have difficulty obtaining long-term mortgages or who prefer not to own at all.

In the 1970s, 366,000 rental apartment units in the United States were converted to condominiums. Of these conversions, 71 percent occurred during the last three years of the decade. From 1980 through 1985 approximately 1.1 million additional rental units are expected to be converted to condominiums. A condominium/cooperative study published by the United States Department of Housing and Urban Development (HUD) in 1976 stated that 50 percent of our nation's population would be living in some form of community association housing by the turn of the century.

Kinds of Community Associations

There are many kinds of residential community associations. Some are distinguishable by size or configuration, others by the limits or extent of ownership. Community associations include condominiums, cooperatives, timesharing associations, planned unit developments, and homeowners associations.

Condominiums

Condominiums vary in architecture and residential type. Common types of condominiums are referred to as high- and mid-rise garden, and townhouse condominiums.

A *high-rise condominium* is a vertical arrangement of units. Although high-rise condominiums can be as many stories high as is structurally possible, most range from 11 to 30 stories. This architectural concept utilizes land with maximum efficiency and density. Therefore, it is popular in locations where land is at a premium.

A recent variation of high-rise condominiums is the multiuse concept, as found in Water Tower Place in Chicago. The 80-story building contains commercial/shopping areas on the lower floors, a hotel immediately above the retail area, and condominiums above that.

The *mid-rise condominium* ranges in height from 4 to 10 stories. Typical characteristics of the mid-rise are a single front entrance and lobby, common corridors, and similar apartment plans on each floor. The architectural design is usually similar to that of the high-rise.

The *garden condominium*, also called the *low-rise condominium*, is usually no more than 3 stories tall and is an arrangement of units attached horizontally as well as vertically. The garden condominium is usually built around a courtyard or lawns. The garden condominium is the type of structure that has been most commonly converted from rental to condominium.

A *townhouse condominium* is an arrangement of units attached side by side, usually consisting of single-family rowhouses with individual entrances and private patios or yards for each resident. Townhouses could be referred to as zero lot line houses.

In yet another condominium concept, one building may include several types of units. These are referred to as *duplex, triplex, quadraplex,* and even *fiveplex* condominiums. Primarily conceived to keep costs low and make better use of existing land, these units are usually good "starter" homes for younger couples. They are most often designed as a mixture of single-story, two-story, and three-story buildings. Housing units range in size from efficiency to three-, or more, bedroom units.

The condominium concept is now often applied to manufactured home parks, recreational parks, and groups of single-family houses whose owners have undivided interest in common areas. In fact, the structural and design possibilities are endless.

Cooperatives

In a *cooperative* (co-op) more than one household owns a multifamily development. The cooperative is a residential property in which the residents form and are shareholders in the corporation that owns the building. The residents hold proprietary leases on their apartments by virtue of their being shareholders. Cooperative owners are responsible for paying the lease on their apartments (their portion of the ownership), plus a share of the costs for upkeep and maintenance of the entire building. Total costs include mortgage payments, insurance, real estate taxes, and personnel costs.

The cooperative concept is most popular in New York and nearby eastern communities, but is also found throughout the country. Since the corporation owns the property there is only one mortgage on the entire property and a mortgage cannot be placed on the apartment. Purchases of co-op units generally require a higher cash down payment because it may be difficult to finance a co-op unit, especially after the initial sale. Administration of the property is quite similar to a condominium regarding policies, rules, and management. Like condominiums, cooperatives can take any physical form.

Timesharing associations

The *timesharing association* is a relatively new community association concept. Timesharing associations offer vacation homes at affordable prices to buyers who purchase a "slice" of time for one or more weeks a year. The two basic types of timesharing are *fee timesharing*, where the purchaser acquires an actual real property interest, and *non-fee timesharing*. Many professionals recommend only fee timesharing.

Non-fee timesharing takes several forms, the most common of which is *timesharing ownership* (TSO). Purchase of an interest in the association involves taking title of a vacation home as tenants in common, and signing an agreement that sets aside a specific time interval for use. This method has certain legal ramifications that should be thoroughly studied and understood. Other forms are interval ownership, leasehold, and right-to-use.

Interval ownership means that a purchaser acquires a revolving tenancy for a specific number of years. For example, one could buy the month of December for 30 years. At the end of that time, the "interval estate" would cease to exist.

The remaining types of non-fee timesharing are *leasehold* and *right-to-use*. Under a leasehold agreement the owner leases a time period of a week or two for a specified number of years, paying for them all in a lump sum in advance. A right-to-use agreement involves a vacation license to use the property, but no formal interest in real property, and is structured very much like a country club membership. The vacation club license is usually for shorter time periods of from 10 to 20 years.

Planned unit developments

The *planned unit development* (PUD) is utilized when large tracts of land are going to be developed over a period of several years. This development may consist of various forms of housing, such as single family, townhouses, multifamily rentals, and recreational, commercial, and industrial facilities. These may be formed under an "umbrella" homeowners association, which is responsible for maintaining such common areas as parks, streets, lawns, and even some utilities. Created by the use of a master plan, these communities usually result in a better balance of housing, fewer traffic problems, and a more orderly development.

Homeowners associations

The *homeowners association* (HOA) is best described by distinguishing "What is owned and by whom?" In a townhouse development that is established as a homeowners association, you purchase a lot with an improvement (house) on it. The association has title to all common areas and the responsibility for maintaining them. The association may or may not have responsibilities for maintaining the exterior of the buildings. The purchaser of the "lot and improvements" becomes an automatic member of the homeowners association and owns the home in fee simple title. Usually homeowners associations are also planned unit developments.

How Did It All Begin?

The condominium form of property ownership is neither unique to the United States nor a creation of the twentieth century. Its history goes back to the time of the Roman Empire, when Rome's leaders, faced with a shortage of land, solved their housing dilemma by passing a law that permitted Roman citizens to own individual dwelling units in multifamily structures. Although there is some question about the details of this Roman law, it is generally believed to be the predecessor of the condominium concept as it exists today.

Condominiums became popular again for a time during the Middle Ages when many cities in what is now Western Europe feared attack by outside enemies. This fear drove people to live within defensive walls. As populations grew, the land within these enclosed cities became increasingly scarce and valuable, and the idea of dividing a single building into many separately owned homes reemerged.

The condominium concept lay dormant until the early

years of the twentieth century. At that time it was revived in Europe and became an increasingly popular form of home ownership in Spain, Italy, Germany, Belgium, France, and Great Britain. However, the United States did not adopt the condominium idea from Europe. The concept first spread from Europe to South America. In 1928 Brazil became the first South American country to pass a law permitting the sale of horizontal property, as condominiums were known there. Several decades later, Puerto Rico, troubled by a booming population, a housing shortage, and a scarcity of appropriate land on which to build new homes, looked to its South American neighbors and passed the Horizontal Property Act of 1958. This act defined the ownership of real property under the condominium concept.

The situation in Puerto Rico set the immediate precedent for enactment of condominium legislation in the United States. The first action to stimulate interest in condominiums came in 1961. In that year the National Housing Act was amended to include Section 234, which extended to condominiums government mortgage insurance provided by the Federal Housing Authority (FHA) of the Department of Housing and Urban Development. While the Act did not empower the FHA to actually lend money, it did permit it to insure loans made by private lenders for the construction, rehabilitation, and/or purchase of single-family or multifamily housing for rent or ownership. This protection by FHA insurance made it easier for developers to obtain loans to build condominiums and for buyers to obtain loans to purchase them.

Real estate laws are under the jurisdiction of the individual states. Thus, following the adoption of Section 234, the FHA in 1962 drew up a condominium statute based on the Puerto Rican Horizontal Property Act and intended as a model for state use in drafting condominium legislation. By 1968 all states had enacted legislation that enabled condominiums to be created and constructed.

Acceptance of this form of ownership was not immediate. However, by 1970 a total of approximately 4,000 community associations had appeared throughout most areas of the country. A representative of the Community Associations Institute (CAI), an educational research nonprofit organization based in Arlington, Virginia, stated that more than 65,000 condominium and homeowners associations were in existence by 1983.

According to the 1976 HUD study, acceptance has varied with sections of the country, with 80 percent of all condominiums in the United States located in 11 states: Arizona, California, Florida, Illinois, Maryland, Michigan, New York, Ohio, Pennsylvania, Texas, and Virginia. One-half of the 80 percent are concentrated in California, Florida, and New York.

Making a Choice

The increasing popularity of the condominium concept in the United States has been attributed in large measure to the advantages that condominium ownership offers. Although condominium ownership does have its drawbacks, many people feel that they are outweighed by its benefits. In effect, condominium living combines the convenience of an apartment environment with the financial advantages of single-family home ownership.

Condominium or rental unit?

Condominium unit owners enjoy several benefits that typical apartment tenants do not. Tax advantages are a major benefit. Since unit owners are homeowners under federal income tax statutes they enjoy the same advantages as owners of conventional single-family homes. Specifically, unit owners can subtract from their taxable incomes the amounts paid for property taxes and mortgage interest on unit mortgages through the itemized deduction process.

As real property owners, unit owners also enjoy the economic benefits of equity accrual and capital appreciation. *Equity* is the owner's interest in the property (the value of the unit less the amount of any mortgage on it), and *equity accrual* is the increase in this interest. For example, a person who obtains a $60,000 mortgage to purchase a condominium unit and reduces it by payments over a period of time to $40,000 has $20,000 ($60,000 less $40,000) worth of equity.

Equity accrual increases as the mortgage principal gets paid off, and it grows at an even greater rate when the market value of the unit increases. To continue with the example, assume that the market value of the unit increases in value from the purchase price by $10,000 over a period of time. The owner's equity has then increased by $10,000. Added to the earlier mortgage pay down of $20,000, equity would be $30,000.

Security of occupancy is another advantage of condominium ownership, since unit owners know they cannot be evicted by a landlord. Also, the monthly mortgage payment should be stable over time. If not, the owner will at least know in what increments the mortgage will increase. This has a distinct advantage over renting, where rents may increase dramatically with little warning.

People who own condominium units can participate in the operation of the association through an organization of unit owners. Each owner has a voice in how the development is run, something a tenant is less likely to have. This does not mean that one should buy a condominium unit solely to avoid the rules and regulations imposed by a landlord since a condominium also imposes rules and regulations. In fact, since many condominium rules and regulations are based on state law, they may be more readily enforceable than those of a rental property. Nor should a person buy a condominium expecting more privacy than is available in a rental community. The average condominium usually offers no more privacy than comparable rental environments. In fact, because unit owners have an organization and share in the use, enjoyment and ownership of common areas, the amount of interaction between neighbors may, of necessity, be even greater in a condominium than in a rental community.

As titleholder to a unit, the unit owner has absolute freedom to decorate the interior of the unit, while a tenant who is bound by the terms of a lease does not. In addition, the owner knows that improvements to the unit should increase the value of his or her investment. Improvements made by a tenant increase the value of the property owned by someone else—the landlord.

In some respects, and for some people, renting does have advantages over buying a condominium unit. There are two financial drawbacks to condominium ownership. First, the purchase of a condominium unit usually requires a large commitment of cash. The tenant need not make a down payment, while in most cases the person buying a condominium must. Second, the monthly assessment payments for a condominium may exceed a month's rental payment for a similar residence because the unit owner directly shares in the cost of maintaining and repairing common areas and delivering common services, in addition to paying the mortgage, contents insurance, and real estate taxes.

There are other pros and cons. Condominium ownership may not be a good choice for the person who wishes to retain his or her mobility. The financially well off, however, may find that it provides a safe, secure home for them to visit as they travel, with no worry over maintenance or housing. Any kind of home ownership is likely to be incompatible with a mobile lifestyle, since a mortgage is far more permanent than a lease. Tenants may call on the management any time something goes wrong inside their apartments, whereas condominium unit owners are responsible for all unit interior maintenance unless the condominium association provides an in-unit services program.

It is important that a condominium association member be flexible, tolerant, and own a unit in an association where he or she will be content. The association is operated on the democratic principle of government. A majority approval of the owners is required to change certain bylaws and rules. Each unit owner should plan to accept some responsibility for serving the association at some time during his or her term of residence.

Condominium or cooperative?

Although condominium living requires a great deal of cooperation, a condominium is not synonymous with a cooperative. One of the disadvantages of being a shareholder in a cooperative relates to the way in which cooperatives are financed. Cooperatives usually are financed by a single mortgage on the entire property. No individual shareholder can personally negotiate better mortgage terms or obtain a personal loan. Instead, each shareholder is responsible for a proportionate share of the total mortgage. This usually presents no problem in sound economic times, but in more difficult times, some shareholders may be unable to meet their obligations, leaving defaults in payment to be made up by the other shareholders. In contrast, the condominium unit owner has no liability for the mortgage debts of other unit owners (although any unpaid assessments must be made up by the other unit owners).

However, the cooperative form of tenancy is not without benefits. The primary advantage of cooperative housing frequently is its cost—it generally is less expensive than a condominium unit of comparable size. In addition, many cooperatives are financed at lower rates of interest and their mortgages are payable over longer periods of time. Because a single mortgage is obtained to finance the purchase of the cooperative, the interest rate remains constant when a shareholder sells his or her stock in the corporation to a new shareholder. In contrast, a condominium unit must be refinanced whenever it is sold, and, as a result, the new owner is likely to pay a higher rate of interest on the mortgage.

Condominium association or traditional house?

The condominium unit owner and the owner of a traditional single-family home enjoy many of the same advantages. Each has certain income tax advantages, each can obtain a deed of ownership, each benefits from equity accrual, each can secure a separate mortgage, and each can treat the interior of his or her dwelling as taste and money allow. But condominium ownership and other types of community associations offer some benefits usually not found in single-family home ownership.

The condominium association ownership concept offers increased services and amenities through prorated costs. The unit owner may enjoy convenient and comparatively low-cost management and maintenance through collective bargaining of rates and prices by the unit owners' board of directors. The condominium association owner may also enjoy recreational amenities that are not available at a comparable cost to the average homeowner, such as a swimming pool. Similarly, the condominium association often provides a better security system than most single-family homeowners can afford to provide for themselves.

Condominium associations may be more conveniently located than single-family homes because many of them are located closer to downtown areas than most single-family home developments. Living in these urban or exurban communities is considered by many people to be a major advantage, as they provide better locations at less cost than would a similarly located detached house. Urban or near urban locations are important to persons who work in metropolitan areas and wish to be near their places of business. Of course, to some, convenient location means being on a beach and in a warm climate. Condominium associations more frequently offer an opportunity for this kind of lifestyle at less cost than can conventional houses in comparable settings.

The cost of housing is of major importance to the growth of the condominium association market. The price of an average condominium association unit is usually less than the price of a typical single-family dwelling, thereby bringing the association form of ownership within the range of a greater number of people.

When considering condominium association ownership, the prospective buyer should look at both sides of the picture. There are disadvantages to association ownership that should not be ignored. One major drawback is the very nature of high-density living. A person moving from a single-family, low-density community may encounter severe difficulties in adjusting to the condominium association's generally closer quarters. The high level of social interaction inherent in the condominium association lifestyle does not suit everyone, and the condominium association resident can expect to have greater difficulty in finding a place to be totally alone.

When buying a used dwelling, negotiation on the price between buyer and seller is quite common. This is rarely the case when buying a new unit in a newly developed condominium association. The documents (or book of laws for the association) are often prepared prior to construction or conversion of the development, and the prescribed price and conditions of sale are determined at that time, well in advance of initial sales. (However, the price and terms of sale may be negotiated when the unit is resold.) It should be pointed out that the stated percentage of ownership remains the same, as it is based on either the square footage of the unit or the original sales price, as each relates to the total development or the whole. "Merging" or "expanding" associations are treated somewhat differently.

Ownership in an association also implies certain social obligations and restrictions that are not necessarily required of owners of single-family homes. The condominium association unit owner must conform to a set of regulations that are not typically imposed on owners of conventional houses. Architectural limitations are almost universal as a measure to preserve the original facade and value of the other unit owners' investments. These may restrict one unit owner's ability to make structural or decorative additions and modifications or exterior changes, no matter how small. Although single-family homeowners also may be restricted by certain zoning regulations, these generally are not as stringent as a condominium association's architectural controls.

2
THE CONDOMINIUM ASSOCIATION AND ITS GOVERNING DOCUMENTS

Most condominiums are designed to make economical use of land. As a result, people who live in condominiums live in close quarters. Some condominiums tend to attract one type of owner. In fact, some have *occupancy restrictions* that define who may and may not buy units, such as condominium developments that accept only persons beyond a certain age or those that prohibit children. But such rigid owner restrictions are rare. Because condominium ownership appeals to people in a wide range of circumstances, condominium communities may be made up of residents of various ages and interests. In a condominium with no occupancy restrictions, older couples may live next door to young single people, animal haters may have neighbors who own a menagerie of pets, and childless couples may find themselves across the hall from families of four.

Despite the diversity of their lifestyles, interests, ages, and backgrounds, all of these condominium unit owners have at least one thing in common—membership in a private, involuntary, usually nonprofit organization. This organization is the *condominum association,* which is responsible for operation of the condominium community. Each unit owner becomes a member of the association when the papers are signed to complete the purchase of a unit. The association of unit owners is the condominium community's government and unites in a joint venture those who otherwise might have no common bond.

The Condominium Association

A condominium association may be comprised of individuals, corporations, partnerships, trusts, or any other entity capable of holding title to real property. In some states this group is collectively called a "condominium association." In other states it is referred to as a council of co-owners, a council of unit owners, or a unit owners association. Whatever its name, the purpose of every organization of condominium unit owners is the same: to encourage a form of ownership that reduces the cost of operations through the sharing of expenses with others, while realizing an appreciation of the investment that each unit owner has made in his or her home. The association acts as a minigovernment that operates the condominium, maintains the common areas, establishes procedures, collects assessments, and makes all the decisions that are vital to the operation of the association. Through the purchase of a condominium each owner joins the association. By such membership each owner becomes responsible for the economic and social success of the entire community. It is imperative that all people involved in a condominium association fully understand their responsibilities and duties.

A condominium association customarily holds title to no property but rather serves as the vehicle through which decisions affecting the property are made. Some of the more important responsibilities of an association include: (1) providing for the repair and maintenance of the common areas, (2) protecting the unit owners' investment, (3) establishing and collecting assessments to pay the common expenses, (4) ensuring that adequate reserves are collected annually for future replacement of major components of the property, (5) administering the rules and regulations of the association for the mutual benefit of all owners, and (6) creating a positive living environment for all residents. The manner in which these obligations are accomplished is usually set forth in a series of governing documents specifically designed for condominium ownership, as prescribed by law in the state in which the association is located.

The Governing Documents

Most people know that an individual, partnership, corporation, or other legal entity plans and finances the condominium. In this book, that legal entity will be referred to as the *developer*. Few may realize, however, that the condominium is actually created on paper. At the start, the developer holds the title to a parcel of land or a building that is recorded as an estate covered by only one deed, or a *single deed estate*. To form a condominium, the law requires that the developer subject the land or building to the condominium form of ownership. This is done by declaring the single deed estate to be numerous single deed estates (the individual condominium units) while also declaring the remaining portions of the property to be common areas or limited common areas. In effect the developer has declared the land or the building into defined salable space. A vehicle to operate the shared or common areas must then also be created. It is the developer who establishes the condominium association, not the future owners.

On the day when subdivision of the single deed estate into multiple single deed estates is recorded with the appropriate government office, the condominium is created. Although the number and types of documents required to prepare and record a condominium may vary from state to state, most states require that the developer file three basic documents: (1) the *declaration*, (2) the *bylaws*, and (3) the *individual unit deeds of ownership*. The declaration specifically defines who owns what and who is responsible for specific areas in the condominium. The bylaws dictate how the association shall operate. In addition to these documents most states require that the plats and the articles of incorporation of the association be recorded. Other documents traditionally created by the developer, but not always recorded, are the public offering statement and the house rules and regulations. Most states have legislation, often referred to as a Horizontal Property Act or a Condominium Act, that legally governs the creation of a condominium. This law specifically details which documents must be recorded and the form in which they must be done. Recently, three states have approved a Uniform Condominium Act that attempts to meet the needs of the developer, the local government, the lender, the unit owner, and the board of directors of the association through uniform laws.

The declaration

The declaration—known in some states as the enabling act; the master deed; the plan of condominium ownership; or the declaration of covenants, conditions, and restrictions—is the most important document related to a condominium. It subjects the land or the building to condominium use, thereby creating the condominium association. It describes all physical elements of the condominium and defines the method for determining each unit owner's share of common areas and a formula for assessing common charges. The declaration details what the unit owner specifically owns. It outlines both the owner's responsibilities to the association and the association's responsibilities to the owner. It is, in essence, the constitutional law of the condominium association and is considered the deed to the property—both individually-owned and commonly-owned areas.

Because of its importance, the conscientious developer may prepare the declaration with the aid of an architect, an insurance agent, a management agent, and an attorney. Since state laws governing condominium development vary, the content of a declaration written in one state may differ from the content of a declaration written in another state. In addition to state requirements, the declaration must also fit the specific needs of the respective condominium community. Since no two associations are identical, one set of documents may be brief while another may be quite lengthy.

Even a well-prepared declaration may require amendment. Therefore, procedures for amending a declaration are incorporated into the document itself. Amendment is a serious matter because, in effect, each unit owner's rights in the use of the owner's unit and the common areas is amended.

Thus, such amendment usually requires the approval of a majority of owners, often as great as 100 percent. In some instances amendment may require the approval of the mortgage lender holding first trust deeds. Because amendment of a declaration may be difficult, the developer should limit the document to those provisions that are absolutely required. A well-written declaration strengthens an association by adequately defining the unit, the common areas and the limited common areas, and their relationship to the association as a whole so that everyone knows their precise responsibility. Clearly written declarations limit restrictions to those which are necessary, making amendment a less likely occurrence. If the association feels that amendment is necessary, it should confer with its management agent, legal counsel, and any other appropriate professional before the declaration is amended. This will ensure consistency and conformance with both the statutes and the intent of the governing documents.

The condominium plat, a diagram of the total condominium area, is usually filed as an addendum to the declaration. It will include a survey map of the surface of the land, a metes and bounds description of the parcel of land, and floor plans of all buildings showing the common areas and the individual condominium units. The plat is especially useful to owners because it defines and separates the common areas from the privately owned units. The plat should also show utility easements, public rights of way, and other encumbrances on the property such as repair and safety easements, and easements for ingress and egress through common areas and limited common areas.

Other significant parts of the declaration are a statement that the declaration is in compliance with the statutes in existence at that time, and a summary of definitions of such things as common areas, limited common areas, lender or mortgagee, statutes, and unit boundaries. Requirements for exterior and interior maintenance of units and the delegation of the responsibility for maintenance may also be included in the declaration. Future easement rights, restoration of property in the event of major destruction, and priority of mortgage holders will be outlined. The proportional voting rights of each unit owner will be defined and the mechanism for decisions made by or on behalf of the association will be clearly detailed.

The bylaws

The declaration and, in cases where they are filed, the articles of incorporation create the condominium association and give it its legal authority. The bylaws dictate how this authority is to be exercised. If the declaration is thought of as the goal for a trip, the bylaws would be the road map for reaching that goal.

The declaration establishes an administrative framework for the association. The bylaws provide the general framework for governing the association. A cursory review may indicate that the declaration and the bylaws are similar. In fact, while the declaration creates a board of directors made up of a set number of members to govern the association, the bylaws spell out the officers' positions, the method of electing officers, their respective duties and functions, and the role of each director (officer and nonofficer) as it relates to the association. The requirements set by these bylaws may vary from state to state, depending on specific laws in each state.

Items that may be typically found in the bylaws are: (1) the name and location of the condominium along with a summary statement of those state laws to which the bylaws are subject; (2) definitions of terms, for example, "What is a unit?" "What is a unit owner?" "What are the common areas?" "What are the limited common areas?"; (3) a statement of who the members are, how they vote, and the lien rights for nonpayment of assessments; (4) the meeting requirements of the association, including the type of meeting (whether annual or special), its place, how the meeting will be conducted, and the type of notice required; (5) definition of a quorum, along with adjournment procedures; (6) an outline of rules for voting at meetings, voting by proxy, the order of business, and the keeping of records; (7) specifications of the number and qualifications of directors, their powers and duties (including hiring a management agent), terms of office, and removal from office; and (8) regulations on filling vacancies, amount of compensation of board members, minimum frequency of board meetings, and waiver of notice for regular meetings.

The bylaws will detail the method of management of the common areas, the responsibility of determining what the expenses of the common areas are, and notice of the expenses to each unit owner. As an example, the declaration may state that the association must hire a professional manager. The bylaws will outline the managing agent's responsibilities. Some items normal to most bylaws are the terms and conditions of payment, who provides the maintenance of the common areas and limited common areas, and the managing agent's right to gain access to units, under certain circumstances.

The manner of collection of assessments from unit owners, the creation of liens on units for unpaid assessments, and the method of assessment payment, whether monthly, quarterly, or yearly, may be addressed in the bylaws. Provisions for priority of liens on a unit, along with the rights of the mortgagees, are generally stated in the declaration rather than the bylaws.

The bylaws will usually have use restrictions indicating policy for residential versus nonresidential use, a method for leasing of a unit, nuisance controls, pet restrictions or guidelines, and procedures for recreational facilities. Easement rights of the residents of the association for use of the common areas and restrictions on who may use them will be described.

A section on insurance will clarify the requirements for and types of insurance necessary, including a provision for workers' compensation and public liability. The amounts to be maintained by the association, along with a requirement for an *insurance trustee* will be set.

The financial management of the association, including specification of its financial year (fiscal or calendar), how the books and records are to be kept, requirements for an annual audit, inspection of the books by owners, where the documents of the association are to be maintained, and who keeps the seal of the association are usually stipulated. Procedures for amending the bylaws and requirements for approval will be spelled out. Bylaws will further state whether mortgagees must be notified of such proposed changes and what must occur in the event of foreclosure on a unit. Miscellaneous items such as compliance, special notices, severability, waiver, captions, gender, and committee initiation, may also be covered.

The bylaws should be drafted not to just accommodate the present statutes and day-to-day needs of the association but also with an eye to possible problems and remedies in the future. Procedures for changing bylaws require the approval of anywhere from 33 to 75 percent of all unit owners. (See your set of bylaws and the state statutes to determine the correct percentage.) The fact that the bylaws are generally easier to amend than the declaration does not lessen the developer's responsibility to clearly establish how the property is to be run, giving proper authority to the board of directors to govern the association according to these bylaws. As with the declaration, amendments to the bylaws should be undertaken with the aid of the manager and an attorney both to establish sound association management and to ensure the association's compliance with state and local laws.

The unit deed

When the individual unit deed is recorded it legally transfers the title of a condominium unit from the seller to the purchaser, in the same manner as title to other property is transferred. The unit deed outlines the basic provisions of the contract of sale. These include the purchase price, a description of the unit, a declaration of easements, specific conditions of the sale, the percentage of the common area assigned to that unit, and other specifications that may be required by state law or the particular condominium association. In the deed, definitions of units and their share of common areas will be less detailed than in the declaration, or may simply refer to the declaration. The unit deed usually defines a unit by the unit numbers as assigned by the master deed or by a lot number as shown on the plat.

There is one key clause that distinguishes a unit deed from a conventional deed to a single-family home. It states that the purchaser has received copies of the declaration, the bylaws, the house rules and regulations, and any other pertinent documents by which the owner is bound or obligated.

The articles of incorporation

If articles of incorporation are filed, the articles "create" the condominium association as a corporation (usually a not-for-profit corporation) under the laws of that state. There are several reasons for incorporating a condominium: to ensure continuity, since the board members change; to limit liability of unit owners, since only corporation assets are attachable; and to hold title to real estate in the corporation's name, thereby making it easier to insure and to transact business. The articles of incorporation establish the general purpose and the type of business to be conducted by the corporation. They clarify the powers of the corporation and how and by whom they may be exercised. The articles define the composition of the directors and officers, their functions, powers, duties, tenure, and the method by which they are elected. Incorporation provides that the articles be administered and governed according to the declaration and bylaws. The articles provide for amending the articles of incorporation. Most important, the articles include a clause that indemnifies and holds harmless the officers and the directors of the corporation from actions taken on behalf of the association while in office and from personal liability for conduct of the officers so long as good faith and best interests of the association are in evidence. Finally, the articles provide for merger, dissolution, or consolidation.

In some instances a developer may create an incorporated condominium while also creating a second entity sometimes referred to as a master, or umbrella, association. This is done when two or more condominium associations are planned that will be separately incorporated but will share the use of certain amenities and facilities. For example, if a developer creates three separately incorporated associations that will share one swimming pool and several tennis courts, the developer would create a master association. The articles of incorporation for that master association would define the methods of use and management of the shared facilities. Customarily each of the three associations would be expected to provide a member to the master association board of directors. The master board would be responsible for establishing a budget and operational guidelines for the shared facilities. The expenses would be shared on a proportional basis by all three condominium associations in the same fashion that common area assessments are shared. A master association has no direct governing power over each independent condominium association except to the extent of the use of the shared facilities.

Public offering statement

Most states now require the developer to publish a summary of important considerations to be presented to all prospective buyers. Some states call this a disclosure statement; others call it a public offering statement. This document customarily includes an explanation of the condominium concept that includes references to a board's decision-making authority; the projected expenses of operating the association during its first year, including a current operating budget; an explanation of how assessments are calculated; and the developer's liability limits for assessments on unsold units (sometimes on a proportionate basis) from the date of declaration. The public offering statement may also contain copies of all contracts entered into by the developer's board of directors, including such contracts as a management agreement, laundry commission agreement, landscape contract, and utility agreements. The narrative should clearly explain the common areas and limited common areas, their respective uses and limitations. The creating of the condominium, the declaration, the appropriate plats and plans, the bylaws, and the articles of incorporation should also be explained. In addition, the developer's past development history, along with the developer's key people and principals should be discussed. Also the developer's team should be mentioned, such as the architect, planner, mechanical, electrical, and plumbing engineers, the general contractor, the construction lender, as well as permanent lenders if known.

The public offering statement will address the use of the property along with limitations on residential and commercial use. Terms of the offering will describe loans available for individual condominium units, unit selling prices, estimated settlement costs, initial contribution to working capital, and the estimated monthly assessment. Incumbrances or future easements to be exercised by the developer or entered into will be explained. The statement will contain a description of the surrounding area and explain financial matters of the association, including the budget and calculation of condominium assessments. It will describe the condominium insurances for fire, peril and protection, along with recommendations for individual property insurance. Real estate taxes, if any, will be estimated. Real estate taxes are normally assessed against the individual unit to include both the unit and the common and limited common areas in the same percentage of ownership used to establish assessments. Additionally, the condominium may pay real estate taxes if they own a staff unit or other facilities. Recording requirements to establish the condominium will be defined, as will the warranties provided by the developer on the common areas and on individual units.

If the condominium is a conversion, the public offering statement will include an engineering survey showing the condition of the building and any necessary or suggested repairs to be done by the developer. The developer's statement of agreement to undertake, or not to undertake, these repairs should be included. Along with this should be a statement of the condition in which the property will be finally turned over to the association.

The public offering statement serves as a prospectus of the condominium and should include samples of all documents related to the condominium. At the time the purchaser signs the contract to buy, a fully executed set of related documents should be given to him or to her for review.

Most public offering statements allow the purchaser a period of time (usually up to 15 days) during which he or she may withdraw from the purchase contract without penalty or loss of deposit. Some states have passed laws requiring these provisions to protect the consumer who may not understand what owning a condominium entails. If a public offering statement does not provide for this period of rescission, the purchaser should not sign the purchase contract until all documents have been carefully studied and all purchaser obligations are fully understood. If these documents appear complex, further review by one's personal attorney is recommended.

Items contained in the public offering statement that are particularly essential to the management agent include: the initial operating budget, the management agreement, recreational leases, maintenance of service contracts, and the duties of the agent that are delegated by the board of directors.

The Initial Operating Budget. The initial operating budget should clearly indicate the cost of operating the association, including maintenance of common areas and provisions for common services. The initial budget must be disclosed to prospective buyers to indicate the cost of operating the property. If the developer has underestimated the budget, projected maintenance costs may be much lower than they actually will be. A prudent developer will prepare the budget with the assistance of a property management firm, detailing both income and expenses with comprehensive explanations of major expense items. Effective budgeting will help avoid drastic budget increases in the first and second years of operation. One budget area that is usually difficult to forecast (especially in new buildings) is utilities—electric, oil, water and gas. Proper administration and monitoring of this budget is a direct responsibility of the management agent.

The Condominium Management Agreement. The condominium management agreement is a contract between a professional management firm and a condominium association executed by the association's board of directors. The contract will outline those functions for which the management firm will be responsible, the terms of the agreement, and the compensation to be paid to the management agent. In recent years, many states have enacted legislation limiting the term of the agreement to a maximum of two years. Where financing through Federal Home Loan Mortgage

Corporation (FHLMC), Federal National Mortgage Association (FNMA), and the Veterans Administration (VA) is available, the management agreement must have a provision that allows for termination of the management agreement without cause and without a termination fee on a 90 days' notice. Disclosure of service contracts made by the developer that will bind the association with outside contractors for the performance of maintenance services or for the delivery of common services should be made in the public offering statement. Such contracts are subject to the same cancellation terms as the management contract.

The Recreational Lease Agreement. Formerly, as an adjunct to the management agreement, a recreational lease agreement frequently was made with the person or persons who controlled and owned the condominium's swimming pool, tennis court, golf course, or other recreational facilities and leased them to the association owners. In essence, these leases were usually uncancellable and included automatic escalation clauses for costs of operations and were to be paid by the association. Recreational leases, historically the subject of abuse (especially in Florida during the early 1970s), have been virtually eliminated throughout the country. Currently, state laws now provide relief from these leases.

The house rules and regulations

The house rules and regulations are the guidelines that set personal behavior standards for each resident of the condominium community. All residents are expected to comply with these rules. The purpose of such rules and regulations is to outline proper conduct for all residents where their behavior may affect another resident or the use of common property. Problems among neighbors usually involve noise levels, parties, music, curfews, number of occupants residing in a unit, or pets. Ideally, house rules and regulations attempt to ensure that living in the condominium will be a pleasant experience for all without infringing on another resident's personal freedom or rights.

The house rules and regulations should be based upon

the provisions of the other governing documents, the specific requirements of each individual community, and sound judgment. The developer, with the assistance of a property management firm and possibly an attorney, usually provides the first set of rules and regulations. Each prospective purchaser is given a copy of these along with the other governing documents. However, after an association has had experience in operating the community on its own, it may wish to amend the rules by adding or deleting items. The board of directors is customarily empowered to change house rules and regulations, usually soliciting the help of various committees. This is a primary reason for house rules and regulations being an appendage to the governing documents. This arrangement allows amendment by the board of directors without the necessity of the entire community voting on the issue, the expense of recording the changes, or the expense of employing legal counsel. This gives even further importance to the use of a management firm and legal services when considering amendments to the rules and regulations.

What the Governing Documents Do

While the laws affecting condominium ownership vary from state to state, governing documents everywhere deal with similar subjects: (1) the definition of the individual unit, the common areas, and the limited common areas; (2) the method of determining percentages of ownership interest in the common areas and limited common areas; (3) the creation of the association and an outline of its purpose and administrative procedures; (4) maintenance and contractual responsibilities; (5) management agent requirements; (6) the initial operating budget and other fiscal policies; (7) insurance requirements both for common areas and for individual units regarding damage or destruction provisions; (8) rules, regulations, and other protective restrictions; and (9) the transfer of control from the developer to the association. A checklist noting which subjects are treated in which document is a valuable reference. *(See Appendix A for sample Governing Document Content Checklist.)*

Define ownership

The declaration is the descriptive document that defines the ownership of the unit. The declaration also defines the common areas—the buildings, grounds, the other facilities in which every unit owner has an undivided interest—and identifies, by means of the plat, the individual unit and the common/limited common areas. Older condominium documents may define the units simply as all of the property that is not owned in common with all other unit owners. More recent documents usually define the unit in very specific terms. The following is an example of the detail that can be used in defining a condominium unit:

---

6. **Dimensions of Units.** Each unit shall contain the space defined by the following boundaries:

A. One-Story Units. For each one-story unit, the vertical boundaries shall be the plane of the outermost (unexposed) surface of the drywall (or paneling) enclosing such unit. The horizontal boundaries shall be the plane of the unfinished (unexposed) surface of the wood, tile, or carpeted flooring of such unit and the plane of the bottom surface of the concrete ceiling slab, except where there is a dropped ceiling in which locations the upper boundary shall be the plane of the upper side (unexposed) surface of the drywall or tile ceiling of such unit.

B. Two-Story (Duplex) Units. For each two-story duplex unit, the vertical boundaries shall be the plane of the outermost (unexposed) surface of the drywall (or paneling) enclosing such unit. The horizontal boundaries of each two-story (duplex) unit shall be the plane of the unfinished (unexposed) surface of the wood, tile, or carpeted flooring of the floor of the lower story and the plane of the bottom surface of the concrete ceiling slab, except where there is a dropped ceiling in which locations the upper boundary shall be the plane of the upper side (unexposed) surface of the drywall or tile ceiling of the upper story of such unit.

C. Items Included in All Units. The following items shall be deemed part of a unit: (a) the door to the balcony adjacent to unit; (b) the front entrance door and any other entrance door to the unit; (c) all window screens and win-

---

dows opening into the unit; (d) the interior ceilings and floors within the unit; (e) the air-conditioning and heating components located within the boundaries of a unit or serving only one unit; (f) all but the unexposed surfaces of the firebrick and other apparatus constituting a fireplace within a unit; and (g) subject to the following sentence, all space, interior partitions and ceilings, and other fixtures and improvements (including without limitation sinks, bathtubs, other plumbing facilities, refrigerators, ovens, and other appliances) within the unit boundaries. In addition, if any chutes, pipes, flues, ducts, conduits, wires, bearing walls, bearing columns, or any other apparatus lies partially within and partially outside of the designated boundaries of a unit, portions thereof serving only that unit shall be deemed a part of that unit, while any portions thereof serving more than one unit or any portion of the common areas shall be deemed a part of the common areas.

Common areas are defined as all property other than an individual unit and are customarily defined in great detail. Typically, this detail includes the land upon which the condominium is or will be constructed; the foundations, load-bearing walls, columns, girders, beams, supports, and roofs; exterior surfaces; steps, lobbies, halls, stairways, entrances, fire escapes, exits, and communication ways; yards, streets, parking areas, garages, and open space gardens; the clubhouse, pool, and other recreational facilities; central utility services that are used by the common areas or that serve more than one unit; elevators, trash containers, trash chutes and compactors; and any enclosed air spaces in the building that are not included within a unit.

Limited common areas are defined and described in the declaration. Limited common areas are those which are a physical part of the common areas but are reserved for exclusive use of a specific unit owner or a group of owners. Limited common areas may include a patio, a balcony, a storage locker, a parking space, an exterior front door, or stairs leading to a single unit. If the condominium owns any dwelling units for resident staff personnel, these are also classified as limited common areas.

Units and their proportionate share of common areas may also be described in the unit deed. But since the declaration contains a more detailed explanation, a careful reading of the declaration is required to understand not only who owns, but also who maintains limited common areas.

Determine percentage of ownership interest

Determination of a unit owner's percentage of ownership in the common area is described in the declaration. The unit deed stipulates the percentage of common area ownership as set forth by the declaration. This section is one of the more important sections because it determines each unit owner's share of the *common expenses,* or the share in the cost of operating, managing, and maintaining the common areas and administering the affairs of the association.

Although the method of assigning percentages of ownership may be determined solely by the developer, a number of states now have guidelines that must be followed. The percentage of ownership is usually determined by the ratio of the square-foot area of a unit to the total square footage of the entire condominium. Another method is the ratio of the unit sale price to the total of all sales prices. The square-foot method is the most accepted, because value is relative to time and could change even during the initial sale. Therefore, the sales price method is not a recommended way to determine percentage of ownership. However, if the value basis of ownership interest is used, fees would be determined by the following formula:

$$\frac{\text{Original sales price of unit 1}}{\text{Original sales price of total units}} = \text{Percentage of ownership interest}$$

If the percentage of ownership interest is based on the square-foot area of a unit, the formula is:

$$\frac{\text{Square-foot area of the unit}}{\text{Total square-foot area of all units}} = \text{Percentage of ownership interest}$$

A *one-unit/one-share* concept may be applied in townhouse condominiums where units are equal in both size or value. The one-unit/one-vote concept is used in a number of associations for voting purposes, and simplifies the voting process significantly.

When reconciling the percentages of ownership in the declaration, the sum of the percentages of all units must equal 1, or 100 percent. If not, then the computation of proportional shares of ownership is incorrect in one or more of the unit percentage assignments.

Both the declaration and the unit deed will clearly indicate that the percentage of interest in the common areas is undivided and that individual shares in the common area or common expense cannot be severed. The unit itself and its respective percentage of ownership are conveyed together. They are inseparable.

Although the percentages of ownership usually remain constant, a declaration may provide for changes in these percentages. This will occur in an expandable, or add on, condominium. An expandable condominium is one which is designed to add units as new sections or phases of the condominium are completed. This is sometimes referred to as a merging condominium. The developer is usually left the option as to whether or not full or partial expansion will be completed, logically assuming that the developer would not wish to expand in a declining market while certainly wanting to do so in a good market. Regardless, the percentages of ownership must always add to 1, or 100 percent.

Establish administrative procedures

Few communities, if any, can run efficiently and successfully without an orderly governmental process. The condominium community is no exception. A condominium association is created and based on the government structure of the declaration and the bylaws. The bylaws of an association establish most of the administrative procedures, although the declaration may also contain administrative provisions. Since most states now require that the bylaws be submitted and recorded with the declaration, the declaration will usually discuss association issues in general terms, referring unit owners to the bylaws for specific operations. The articles of incorporation may also provide certain administrative guidelines.

The declaration usually establishes two distinct administrative procedures. First, it usually recognizes the board of directors, sometimes referred to as a board of trustees or simply the board, as the official governing body of the association. Second, the declaration indicates how many votes each unit owner has. An owner may be entitled to a vote equal to his or her percentage of ownership interest, or a one-unit/one-vote rule may be applied.

The governing documents will outline the method of election of the board of directors, the number of board members and their qualifications and terms of office, and the powers and duties of the board. The officer positions—usually a president, vice president, secretary, and treasurer—will be defined, along with the method of election. The documents also will establish the association rules for calling meetings, requirements for notifying members of meetings, voting procedures, and a model agenda for the annual membership meeting. They will also discuss provisions for matters such as filling board vacancies, removing directors or officers, calling and conducting board meetings, and creating a committee system.

As a result of differences in state laws, some provisions found in the bylaws in one state will be found in the declaration in another state. Therefore, a careful review of all governing documents is critical to fully understanding how the association operates. An information sheet that lists administrative requirements is a useful reference item for most associations. *(See Appendix A for sample Condominium Association Record of Administrative Requirements.)*

Determine maintenance responsibilities

The documents should specify which maintenance responsibilities are the unit owner's and which are the association's. This is done to ensure a clear delineation between common expenses and individual expenses. The documents will define unit-owner liability for maintenance and repair costs inside the unit, including redecorating, upkeep of interior surfaces, repairs to all appliances, utilities (if individually metered), and similar singular owner items. They will require that the condominium association operate and maintain the common areas properly and provide for certain (or all) utilities, trash collection, all insurance, and certain services.

Delegate management authority

Although the board of directors has ultimate, or fiduciary, responsibility for managing the condominium, most bylaws allow the association to hire (and some bylaws require) a professional management agent to assist the board in fulfilling its duties and obligations. Some documents authorize a board to delegate any or all of its duties to the agent. Others may list which duties the board may or may not delegate to the management agent. In most cases the responsibilities that cannot be delegated or decided unilaterally are (1) the filing of a lawsuit without the approval of the board of directors, (2) establishment of the common expenses, and (3) changes to either the declaration or the bylaws. Some bylaws include provisions for contract cancellation, contract approval and acceptance, notice requirements to all first mortgagees when a management firm changes, and the length of an agent's contract.

Establish fiscal policies and procedures

Since the operation of a condominium association can be a very expensive undertaking, the documents provide the mechanism for adequately funding the operation. Procedures are outlined for assessing each unit owner his or her proportionate share of the common expenses, along with the requirement that a yearly budget be adopted. The budget is based upon the estimated cost of operating the association during the coming fiscal or calendar year. Each unit owner is assessed a share of this cost based upon the unit percentage of ownership interest. The bylaws will generally outline assessment collection procedures as well as the procedures to be taken against delinquent owners.

The documents specify that assessments are an annual amount. However, collection may be in 12 equal monthly installments or in quarterly installments.

A unit owner's assessment is determined by the following formula:

$$\text{Percent of ownership interest} \times \text{Yearly estimated common expenses} = \text{Unit owner's annual assessment}$$

If, for example, a unit owner's percentage of ownership interest is .0048 percent, and the total annual estimated common expenses is $250,000, then the following calculation determines the owner's share of common expenses:

$$.0048 \text{ percent interest} \times \$250,000 = \$1,200 \text{ per year}$$

If the assessment is paid monthly, it would be $100 ($1,200 ÷ 12) each month.

An important fiscal responsibility of an association is the establishment of adequate reserves. Most bylaws specifically require reserve funds. Generally two types of reserves may be found: *replacement reserves* (sometimes referred to as capital reserves), or those monies set aside for the repair or replacement of major common area components at some future time; and *contingency reserves*, or funds to cover unanticipated emergencies or major expenditures that may unexpectedly arise and that cannot, therefore, be included in the budget as a specific expense. Bylaws also give a board of directors (in some cases, only with the approval of a majority of all unit owners) the right to make special assessments when monies are needed due to a shortfall in the budget or for major repair or replacement of an item not contemplated when the budget was drafted. Whichever funding mechanism is used, it requires forethought, so that a board is not tempted to use reserve funds as a means to compensate for poor budgeting. Other types of reserves that also may be funded are *operating reserves* and *working capital reserves*.

Operating reserves are monies set aside in an interest-bearing account specifically designated for the payment of an annual expense. Operating reserves may include monies accumulated for the yearly insurance premium and those accumulated for the yearly auditor fee. Monies for the operating reserves are accumulated monthly from all assessments (just as with replacement reserves). The reserves are drawn from when the bill or premium comes due.

Working capital reserves may be of two types. The first involves funds set aside each month to pay bills in months where there is a negative cash flow. For example, during a summer month the bill for filtering the swimming pool may surpass that month's assessment potential. Funds must be set aside during the excess collection months (in this case, winter) to pay the bills in months when costs exceed collection. This points out why cash flow projections and proper budgeting techniques and forecasting of working capital reserves are critical to an association. *(See Chapter 10 for a discussion of establishing sound fiscal policies.)*

The second type of working capital reserve involves those funds paid by each *initial* purchaser of a unit. It is commonly referred to as *initial working capital*. These funds are usually collected at the time of settlement at the rate of two times the current monthly budget assessment for a period of three months. The funds are used to establish working capital for the association and are nonrefundable. The initial working capital fund may be used as the board of directors chooses. When a condominium is developed, the developer has the responsibility to finish and complete the building and amenities as stated in the public offering statement. However, the association must purchase the tools and other equipment to maintain what has been built or developed. During the early stages of the association, funds to purchase items not in the operating budget are generally not available. For example, an association may have halls with both carpet and tile floors to maintain but have no equipment. The working capital paid by each first purchaser at settlement may be used to purchase this equipment for the association.

Once the community is sold out and all first owners have contributed their portion of the working capital reserves, any unspent funds remaining in this account should either be converted to the first type of working capital reserve account or spread over all other reserves as determined by the board of directors.

The governing documents may also contain guidelines for internal financial controls, such as yearly audits of the financial records by an accounting firm or a certified public accountant, signing of checks by two persons designated by the board of directors (countersignature), and annual audit reports to be given to each unit owner.

Outline insurance requirements

Individual unit owners are responsible for their own personal property located within the confines of their unit. However, insurance responsibility for protecting the common areas rests with the board of directors. Adequately determining the insurance requirements for the common areas is a comprehensive task. In most cases the documents require certain minimum coverages and set guidelines for the association.

Basic insurance requirements are generally detailed in the bylaws in accordance with certain state stipulations. Some fundamental insurance issues that are addressed in most associations are the requirements to hold adequate replacement cost coverage against fire and other hazards, to carry adequate liability insurance, to appoint an insurance trustee, and to secure liability coverage for directors and officers.

The documents should outline steps for repairing or replacing common area items in the event of a major casualty. They may also prescribe how to obtain bids for repair or reconstruction, and how to levy special assessments if insurance reimbursement is insufficient. Where unit owners choose not to rebuild the community because of excessive destruction, procedures will be outlined for dissolution of the condominium. Often, when more than 50 percent of the condominium is destroyed, the association is not required to rebuild, but such a decision requires agreement of first trust holders as well as unit owners. In the event of total dissolution, distribution and disbursement of funds should also be prescribed. *(See Chapter 11 for a complete discussion of insurance.)*

Establish rules, regulations, and restrictions

The total success of a condominium association, along with appreciation in value of property, relies heavily upon the rules, regulations, and restrictions that govern resident conduct. Typically, the declaration cites general covenants, while the bylaws and the house rules and regulations provide specific, basic living guidelines. Without these restrictions, and their enforcement, community living would become chaotic. The condominium community should have two categories of restrictions: *use restrictions* and *architectural restrictions*. Use restrictions attempt to regulate resident behavior, while architectural restrictions set the guidelines that the unit owner must follow when changing the exterior of his or her unit or structurally altering the unit. These restrictions are vital to proper use of the common areas and to enhancing and preserving the design or character of a condominium community.

Use restrictions may appear in the declaration, bylaws, or house rules and regulations, or in all three. The declaration often states that common areas should be used for the purpose for which they were intended, as long as that use does not hinder or encroach upon the lawful right of the other owners, leaving further detail to either the bylaws or to the board of directors through the house rules. Use restrictions are usually purposely prohibitive in tone. They may prohibit certain kinds of pets, subdivision of the common areas, storage of trash or flammable materials, or construction of outdoor structures in the common areas. Occupancy restrictions may prohibit children under a certain age, or limit the number of persons living in one unit. Restrictions of this type are essential to protecting a community's character and should rightfully be a part of the principal association documents.

House rules and regulations that relate to day-to-day living, on the other hand, may be subject to more frequent change. Since rules and regulations are designed to serve a specific purpose at a specific time, they must change as time and situations change. The board is, therefore, authorized to modify, delete, or adopt new rules and regulations as the need arises. House rules and regulations usually cover matters such as parking, the conduct of children and pets, noise levels, guest provisions, and use of recreational facilities.

Architectural controls are designed to protect the integrity of the condominium's original architecture, hopefully enhancing its value. The standards that are set for design, material, color, use, and replacement are intended to preserve rather than stifle creativity. To adequately protect the property, architectural regulations should be extremely detailed. Here is an example of one set of restrictions:

Additions, Alterations or Improvements by Unit Owners. No unit owner shall make any structural addition, alteration or improvement in or to a unit without the prior written consent of the board of directors. No unit owner shall paint or alter the exterior of a unit, including the doors and windows of the latter, nor shall any unit owner paint or alter the exterior of the building, without the prior written consent of the board of directors. The board of directors shall be obligated to answer any written request by a unit owner for approval of a proposed structural addition, alteration or improvement (by painting or otherwise) to or in such unit owner's unit within 45 days after such request and failure to do so within the stipulated time shall constitute a consent by the board of directors to the proposed structural addition, alteration or improvement. If any application to any governmental authority for a permit to make any such structural addition, alteration or improvement in or to any unit requires execution by the council of unit owners and provided consent has been given by the board of directors, then the application shall be executed on behalf of the council of unit owners by the board of directors only, without, however, incurring any liability on the part of the board of directors or any of them to any contractor, subcontractor or vendor on account of such addition, alteration or improvement, or to any person having claim for injury to person or damage to property arising therefrom. Subject to the approval of any mortgagee of such affected units, the board of directors and any unit owner affected, any unit may be subdivided or may be altered so as to relocate the boundaries between such unit and

---

any adjoining units. The provisions of this Section 6.08 shall not apply to units owned by the developer until deeds of conveyance of such units shall have been recorded. The developer shall have the right to make such alterations or subdivisions, including the reapportionment of percentage interests, without the consent of the board of directors and the board of directors shall execute any such application required. All such alterations and subdivisions shall be evidenced by an amendment to the declaration as required by Section 11-107 of the Condominium Act.

Almost without exception condominium documents require that an architectural control committee be created. A primary function of this committee is to review applications for architectural change and recommend approval or rejection to the board of directors. The key here is *recommend* to the board of directors, since only the board has the authority to make such decisions. The committee is not empowered to approve or reject proposed changes.

Define how control is transferred

The bylaws serve one additional important function. They state the way in which control of an association will be transferred from the developer to the association of unit owners. This transfer usually occurs at the first annual meeting of the association, when representatives from unit owners at large are elected to the first owners' (official) board of directors. The time at which the first annual meeting is to be held is usually specified in the documents.

Proper Chain of Authority

The board of directors and its on-site manager or management agent must understand and follow the proper sequence of documents when searching for guidelines in making a decision. If, for example, the board is asked a question on how something should be done, the first place to look would be in the house rules. If the house rules do not address the issue, they should refer to the use restrictions in the bylaws. If guidance is not provided in the use restrictions then they should look to the bylaws as a whole. Following this, the next step is to look at the declaration, the articles of incorporation, and then the state statutes in that order for guidance. The chain of authority of the governing documents is crucial to settling questions of precedence. The final authority for settling any question is the courts. Many of the statutes which affect condominiums have evolved from the judicial process.

3

TRANSFERRING CONTROL

*M*any *people* purchase a condominium unit expecting to settle into a carefree life. They soon discover that the protection of their investment depends on their willingness to become involved in the operation of the condominium association. A unit owner automatically becomes a member of the association at the time of purchase. At first the new owner may be totally unaware of the existence of the condominium association or of how to participate in it. But later the owner realizes that he or she must participate actively. Most first-time condominium unit owners know little about the operation of an association, and therefore they must prepare themselves to assume new responsibilities. They must learn the fundamentals of both the financial and physical operation of the condominium, along with methods of properly enforcing the community's rules and regulations.

Condominium associations go through three stages of development. The first is the *interim period*, the time during which unit owners have begun to live in the condominium while the developer continues to retain control of the association. The real responsibilities for an association—and sometimes the real difficulties—begin in the second stage, which occurs as the developer transfers control of the association to the unit owners. This is the *period of transfer,* when the resident board of directors become accountable for all the problems previously handled by the developer. The third stage, the *period of ongoing governance*, usually occurs after the first year of self-government, when the association has grown into its responsibilities and has developed the process for handling them. The transfer of responsibility from the developer to the owners should begin well before the required legal transfer of control, continuing until the owner-controlled association is firmly established.

Some condominium projects sell out almost immediately, seriously limiting the interim period. In such cases, the unit owners assume control without an initial period of reliance on the developer. In other cases, the interim period may take one, two, or even three years or longer. Whatever its duration, this phase is crucial to the association as it begins to make decisions and set precedents that will influence its operation for the many years to come.

The transfer of control of the association to the unit owners presents them with a new and complex enterprise, and developers should assist new unit owners in assuming these new responsibilities. Unfortunately, some developers do not or cannot, resulting in inadequate preparation of the owners for a very important role. Ideally, the developer should inform, train, and assist the owners in procedures for running their organization. The developer should explain the governing documents that provide the guidelines for condominium management and decision making necessary to association success. As the popularity of condominium living increases, more and more developers are realizing the importance of adequately preparing owners for the new demands that will be placed on them. In many cases this is accomplished through a property manager selected by the developer, who works with the association to avoid an all too typical atmosphere of developer versus owner animosity. With the increase in consumer protection and awareness, many more developers have acknowledged and accepted their responsibility for a constructive educational program during the interim period. Those developers who ignore their responsibilities place unit owners in the very vulnerable position of having to learn association responsibilities on their own.

The Interim Period

Whether the transfer of control is smooth or rocky depends in large part on the way in which the developer treats the association during the interim period. To understand the developer's critical role, the unit owner should first know how the developer establishes and controls the association.

The governing documents authorize the board of directors to govern the association. The first board of directors is formed at the beginning of the condominium's creation, and is appointed by the developer. This first board of directors, also called the declarant's board, is usually composed of persons employed by or representing the developer, such as financial partners in the project. This board governs the association under the developer's control. The developer initially controls the association both to protect the firm's financial interests and to effectively promote the sale of the condominiums in this project. The fiduciary responsibility to the unit owners may result in some conflicts, since the developer, whose interest in the condominium project is short-term, must make decisions which will affect the association for many years to come. One of three approaches may be used by developers, the last of which is considered the most positive.

Some developers may run the associations as dictatorships, either failing to organize them or dominating them so completely that the residents play no important roles. When all of the units in a project have been sold, the developers operating this way may leave the residents to fend for themselves. These developers may do a good job of protecting the initial value of the condominium developments with high rates of sales, but they fail in their obligations to prepare the unit owners for association responsibilities after their departure.

A second approach that may be used by some developers is to transfer control of the association too soon—that is, before leaders have been adequately trained or organized. These unit owners, forced to manage by trial and error without effective guidance, make decisions without considering their long-term effects. This is a frequent problem in condominium projects that sell too quickly.

The third—and model—developer controls the early stages of the association through an effective management agent who has the proven skills to train the future association leaders. Unit owners will experience a smoother transition if they are fortunate enough to purchase their condominium units from a developer who educates the owners in this manner. The management agent, as the guiding hand, prepares the association for its future responsibilities while also looking out for the best interests of the condominium. The management agent, then, becomes both educator and protector, providing the necessary liaison between owners and developer.

Orientation needs

Unfortunately, studies indicate that few developers provide association members with the counseling that is needed. Some developers are either unable to provide this invaluable service or do not fully understand how a condominium association functions. It is for these and many other important reasons that the management agent should help fill that role. Those developers who initially hire management agents usually experience both smoother transitions and better reputations.

Since residents new to the condominium usually are eager to get involved, they should be brought into the operation as soon as possible. This is the critical time to tell them about the association, the role it will play in their lives, and the role they should play in it. This orientation program should begin in the sales office, with the developer's sales representative explaining to the purchaser exactly what the community association is and how it operates.

The initial education process is often accomplished through the formation of ad hoc committees by the management agent. These committees encourage the participation of the unit owners and serve as educational vehicles for informing new members of the responsibilities of the association. These committees also provide an effective mechanism for communication between the association and the developer via the management agent.

During the early- to mid-1970s, developers saw the conversion of apartment developments to condominiums as a road to quick profits in real estate. Little responsibility was shown to the purchaser who was seeking the "romantic, carefree lifestyle" that was being promoted as condominium living. Since that time, legislation such as Uniform Condominium Act and state condominium acts, together with consumer pressure, have now forced the proper definition of these responsibilities. As a result, today's developers generally provide much more information and counseling to owners through their sales and professional management programs. In addition, management agents have acquired much greater experience and exposure to condominium environments during the past decade. They have become more competent in orienting both developers and owners to the educational process that is necessary during the interim period so that the association can be successful in its long-term operation.

Interim assessment practices

The developer is responsible for all operations and management of the condominium while in control of the association. Money to meet the operating responsibility is usually collected through assessments. The method of handling assessments during the interim period may create some problems.

Once the condominium association has been established, the developer, as one of the unit owners, and by law, is required to pay monthly assessments on all unsold units. Some developers, rather than pay a monthly assessment on each unsold unit, pay only the difference between operating expenses and the assessments paid by the other unit owners, in other words, they only absorb the deficit. This practice is legal when the documents and state statute so provide. In other cases the unit owners each may pay a low flat rate to cover expenses until an owner-controlled board of directors is elected; the developer makes up the difference.

Regardless of the method used, the problems arise when assessments have been understated or when developers have subsidized common expenses to suppress assessment costs without the knowledge of the owners. Assessments are underestimated because low assessment rates help promote sales. However, this practice—now illegal in many states—results in excessive special assessments to restore financial stability after transition. Assessments may be low in part because the developer does not establish adequate operating and replacement reserve budgets. In this case, an association may find itself with inadequate operating revenue and reserves when developer control ends. This may be a major problem where sales have been slow and the developer has been in control for an extended period of time. When control is transferred to the association certain major repairs may be needed without the funds available to make them.

It is extremely important that an ad hoc committee work with the developer and management agent in creating sound fiscal policies for the association through involvement in the annual operating budget process. The importance of establishing and maintaining adequate operating and reserve revenues cannot be stressed too much. In particular, the accrual of reserve funds, which should be placed in interest-bearing investments, may prevent the future need for a special assessment due to a major repair.

The transition board of directors

In the interim period, the developer can do a great service to the unit owners by appointing one or more of them to a transition board of directors. Some states require such a board by law. Since many developers offer no more orientation than is required by state law, the association members may wish to form an ad hoc committee to determine whether a transition board is desirable. If the committee identifies a need for a transition board, it may ask the developer to relinquish some seats on the board to unit owner representatives.

Ad hoc interim committees

Ad hoc committees should be established once a reasonable number of owners have moved into the association. The term *ad hoc* means "interim," which allows the first elected board of directors to restructure the committee makeup if they so choose. Ad hoc committees, as interim committees, are essential to the involvement of unit owners in the activities of the association during the early stage. Once control of the association has been transferred to the elected board of directors, the ad hoc committees may be replaced by standing, or permanent, committees. Management agents, from the first occupancy, should begin to identify those individuals with leadership potential or experience who demonstrate an active interest in the association.

The Ad Hoc Physical Plant Committee. One of the most important committees to be established during this early phase of a condominium's life is the *ad hoc physical plant committee.* The purpose of this committee is to work with the management agent and developer to resolve any construction or landscape problems in the common area for which the developer is responsible. Owners with expertise in landscaping, engineering, construction, plumbing, or electrical contracting make ideal members for this committee.

Unlike the transfer of control of the association, which occurs on a specific date, ownership of the common areas and facilities gradually transfers from the developer to each unit owner. At the time of purchase each unit owner acquires his or her share of ownership in the common areas. Although ownership shifts gradually, the common areas must be delivered in complete and acceptable form with all special facilities as promised by the developer.

Final acceptance of the entire common area usually occurs through the first elected board of directors, at which time the physical plant committee becomes a standing committee. The completed project should be compared to the original plans and specifications, and compliance with building codes should be verified. After a comprehensive inspection of the condominium project, the committee should list all problem areas and present this list to the board of directors, who then refers it to the developer. The developer should prepare a schedule for completion of any incomplete or unacceptable items, submitting copies to the board and committee. This committee usually remains intact, with a new assignment which most often includes periodic review and inspection of all common areas to determine general physical conditions and standards of maintenance.

Other Ad Hoc Interim Committees. The establishment of ad hoc committees eases the transfer of responsibility from developers to owners. Committees which are social in nature should be established during the early stages of occupancy to encourage resident interest and participation. For example, an *ad hoc welcoming committee* can help residents adjust to their new homes and inform them about their association. An *ad hoc social and recreation committee* should plan programs which encourage resident interaction and active use of the recreational facilities. An *ad hoc communications committee* may keep residents informed of association events and news through the publication of a monthly or bimonthly newsletter. Other ad hoc committees which are desirable in the beginning stages are: *architectural review and control committee, budget and finance committee,* and *covenants and rules enforcement committee.* The size and structure of each condominium project usually determine what committees are needed.

These committees customarily elect chairs. Each committee chair then becomes a member of the *ad hoc advisory committee,* which discusses its findings and concerns with the interim board of directors.

The success of ad hoc committees depends in large measure on the attitudes of their members and on the nature of their specific goals and functions. In some cases, the formation of certain committees is for a specific project only, and the committee is disbanded at the attainment of its assigned goal. The committee may be reactivated as the need arises. The formation of any committee which has no essential function is a waste of time, and should be avoided so as not to discourage otherwise productive owners.

The Transfer of Control

Ideally, the developer gradually hands over responsibility for operating the condominium association to its members. However, the legal transfer of control occurs at a specific time—when the association members elect their first board of directors composed of unit owners. The real life of a condominium association begins after this owner-controlled board is elected. The election takes place at the first annual membership meeting, the date of which is usually prescribed by the condominium's governing documents.

The date of the first election is customarily decided upon by the percentage of units sold and closed. As an alternative, some governing documents require that the first annual meeting be held after a certain period of time following the first sale if the percentage requirement is taking too long to meet. Most state laws require the first annual meeting to be held either after 75 percent of the units have been closed or within three years after the first closing, whichever comes first. Other states, or other documents in the absence of a state requirement, have different percentage rules. The condominium's governing documents must specify the meeting. A review of them prior to purchase gives the prospective unit owner this information.

The transfer of control from developer board to owner board is markedly different between a converted property and one that is developed new as a condominium. Generally, in a conversion a certain percentage (anywhere from 25 to 75 percent) of unit owners have resided in the property previously as renters. They have greater familiarity with the property, including its past methods of operation and maintenance, and have a sense of continuity with their neighbors. Their decision to make an investment in unit ownership is an indication that they were pleased with the past maintenance and operating standards of the property. It is essential that the developer and the management agent educate these owners as to their new role in the continuing upkeep and maintenance of their investment. Since a conversion usually occurs in an older property, it is critical to stress that adequate reserve funds must be maintained at all times.

The time immediately following the legal transfer of control and the following year or two are the most critical in the life of the association, as it is the period during which an association adjusts to self-government. During this time, unit owners must learn to make important decisions that will have a major impact on the future value of the property as well as on the owners' level of satisfaction in living in the condominium.

If construction of the project is incomplete, the developer may continue to remain involved after control has been transferred. A management agent should continue to work with the association, since newly elected boards of directors usually include very competent people, but rarely include anyone versed in condominium property management.

The First Elected Board of Directors

In its first year, the board of directors can expect to have to deal with a number of problems. In the interest of a smooth-running and relatively peaceful operation, the management agent must be available for counseling and guidance. Many developers view the first annual membership meeting as their signal to withdraw completely from a project. However, the developer has an ongoing responsibility at least until all warranty and construction matters are properly resolved.

The developer must furnish the new board of directors with all records of the association, including a detailed account of all assessments and fees collected, delinquencies, and expenses incurred by the association while under the developer's control. The developer also should, when possible, supply a comprehensive record of contract and bidding activities, copies of all pertinent documents and architectural plans, copies of warranties on all common area equipment, and files of all correspondence related to the association.

The newly elected board of directors should obtain a certified audit of the financial condition of the association so that it may be aware of any inconsistencies or problems. The audit will indicate the costs of managing, operating, and maintaining the condominium. From this background information budgets can be prepared, assessments set, and contingency or replacement reserves established.

Since developers seldom set aside the reserves necessary for future major expenditures, the new board of directors may have the immediate task of setting up a progressive reserve based on a replacement schedule in order to avoid unpopular special assessments. The new board may also find itself with a large sum of uncollected assessments which the management agent can help to collect.

The board of directors should obtain all original copies of the association insurance policies from the developer. The aid of a qualified insurance agent can be enlisted to review the adequacy of the condominium's insurance coverage.

The board should seek, at an early date, a competent attorney who is recognized as a specialist in condominium law and operations. This attorney should become acquainted with the condominium's documents, bylaws, rules, and regulations. The services of the attorney should be utilized by the board whenever it is unsure of the potential legal ramifications and liabilities of its actions. It is much more cost-effective to use an attorney's services to avoid making an erroneous decision than to risk litigation.

The biggest task of the new board of directors is to review all these records, to create an operating budget, and to take action where necessary. A myriad of questions must be answered, and important decisions made regarding contractors, insurance coverage, maintenance, and common area services. Most—perhaps all—of these problems may be resolved if a management agent has been involved from the beginning of the development. Proper orientation and education by the developer, through the management agent, makes any transition process much smoother.

All owner-controlled boards of directors will be faced with problems relating to financial management, legal matters, and the inevitable disputes among neighbors. The ultimate responsibility for all decisions rests with the board of directors. Even with the help of an able management agent, the operation of a condominium can be a very time-consuming business. The board members must help the owners realize that they are neither tenants in an apartment building nor residents of detached houses, but members of an association whose success depends on them collectively. A task that is equally important is to clearly define the condominium board's role as one that relates to common areas only. Individual unit problems are strictly the problem of that unit owner.

4

THE BOARD OF DIRECTORS

The real work of the condominium association begins after the developer transfers control to the unit owners. While certain matters that affect the condominium must be put before the entire membership, most decisions are made by the board of directors, the official policy-making body of the association. (The board of directors is referred to in some states as a board of managers.)

Although it is unlikely that anyone in the community will have had experience managing a multifamily housing development, there probably will be individual unit owners who possess basic leadership qualities. A successful board is composed of individuals who work together toward the best interests of the association. Those who serve should be free from disruptive political motives. The position of board member carries with it various significant responsibilities. Members who assume a position on any board must be willing to be objective on all issues and to remove themselves from voting on issues in which they may benefit personally. They must try to remain congenial even among disparate personalities. A member of the board must be a negotiator and a communicator, a leader and a partner, a supervisor and an organizer. Although a strong vocational background can be an asset, leaders should be judged principally on the time they have to invest in association activities and the sincerity of their interest in the future of the association. He or she may be a lawyer, an insurance agent, an architect, an accountant, an electrician, a gardener, or a retiree, or other individual who is familiar with the community's everyday problems.

Smoothly operating associations are a direct result of boards that are prepared and well organized, conduct business in a professional manner, and respect the talent and expertise of each other, their management agents, and other advisors. A board that shares in its commitment will seek management, legal, and accounting advice from professionals.

The Responsibilities of the Board

"The board of directors shall have all of the powers and duties necessary for the administration of the affairs of the unit owners association and may do all such acts and things as are by the Condominium Act, the declaration, or by these bylaws required to be exercised and done by the unit owners association. The board of directors shall have the power from time to time to adopt any rules and regulations deemed necessary for the benefit and enjoyment of the condominium; . . . shall delegate to one of its members or to a person employed for such purpose the authority to act on behalf of the board of directors on such matters relating to the duties of the management agent. . . ."

The preceding typical paragraph extracted from the bylaws of a community association shows that the authority and responsibility for the operation of a community association rest solely with the board of directors. The board has numerous means to accomplish these responsibilities, including delegating some duties to others while maintaining final approval. The board of directors may hire a property management firm or a full-time on-site manager, engage various consultants or part-time staff, or do all the work themselves. The specific duties of the board depend upon the size and the complexity of the association. The most typical responsibilities of a board include:

1. Preparing and adopting an annual budget; establishing reserve funds.
2. Levying assessments against unit owners.
3. Opening association bank accounts and designating signatories.
4. Collecting the assessments, depositing them in the proper accounts.
5. Providing for the operation and upkeep of the property.
6. Designating, hiring, and dismissing personnel.
7. Making and amending the rules and regulations.
8. Letting contracts for repairs.
9. Enforcing provisions of the declaration, bylaws, and rules and regulations.
10. Obtaining and renewing insurance.
11. Paying for all authorized services.
12. Keeping books with detailed accounts in accordance with accepted accounting practices.
13. Borrowing money on behalf of the condominium.
14. Acquiring, holding, and disposing of condominium units in the event of foreclosure.
15. Doing such other things as specified in the condominium act, the declaration, the bylaws, or as passed by resolution of the unit owners association.

The board, then, is responsible for all operations, policies, procedures, and enforcement and delegation of duties and responsibilities that are not specifically stated as nontransferable to others.

Policies and resolutions

For the board of directors to make consistent and methodical decisions, it must establish administrative policies for handling specific needs or problems through resolutions. A *policy resolution* is a formal statement that is adopted by the board of directors to chart its plan of action.

As a first step in adopting policy, the board should provide all residents with an opportunity to voice their opinions regarding policy resolutions that it is considering. This is especially important in the case of resolutions that relate to the residents' rights and obligations, such as resolutions to establish guest parking guidelines or to set rules governing the use of common areas. Copies of such resolutions should be made available to all members of the association, either by mail or through the association newsletter, together with a notice of a public hearing at which they will be discussed. Although the board must make all final decisions adopting or defeating resolutions, these hearings (which may coincide with a regular or special meeting of the board of directors) give the members an opportunity to participate in the policy-making process.

A public policy hearing should not be mistaken for a special membership meeting and therefore need not comply with the membership meeting requirements set forth in the governing documents. By properly advertising the hearing as a special meeting of the board, the board can expect only those persons who are genuinely interested in the resolution at issue to attend and state their views, thereby giving the board background for making a reasonable decision.

When a policy resolution is adopted, the original copy should be filed in a book of resolutions and copies should be sent to each unit owner and/or published in the condominium newsletter. Some associations have found it convenient to adopt a standard form for use in stating policy adopted by resolution. *(See Appendix A for sample Policy Resolution.)*

Some associations have encountered difficulty enforcing resolutions that have not been recorded and made a matter of public record. As a result, some states are considering legislation that would allow policy resolutions to be recorded with the condominium governing documents, giving the association greater power to enforce them.

Delegation of duties

The most common and cost-effective method of delegating a board's duties is to engage a property management firm.

The firm should have a CERTIFIED PROPERTY MANA-GER® (CPM®), designated by the Institute of Real Estate Management (IREM), or a Professional Community Association Manager (PCAM), designated by the Community Associations Institute (CAI).

A property manager of community associations acts as both an agent and an executive director of the association, much as in a trade association. Just as an executive director has a full-time staff to carry on the function of that trade association the management firm has staff at the property, or staff in another office to carry out the functions and the duties of the board. The management agent and the management firm act as an extension of the board.

The management agreement (or contract) will specify the duties that the board of directors has delegated to the management agent. Although the board will assign additional tasks to committees, only the board of directors has the authority to set policy.

Elections

To be a member of the board a unit owner must be elected by the members of the association. In some associations this electoral process is extremely competitive and political, while in others just finding enough individuals to fill the seats on a board may seem nearly impossible. The governing documents usually require the association to elect an uneven number of unit owners to serve on the board of directors. The declaration and the bylaws prescribe methods of election, terms of office, and methods of removing directors and filling vacancies.

Notifications and nominations

The primary purpose of an annual membership meeting is to elect the board of directors. All of the seats on a board are filled at the first annual meeting, with staggered positions being filled in all subsequent elections. Prior to the annual meeting, all unit owners should be notified of the upcoming election according to procedures outlined in the governing documents. A general invitation to run for the board should be distributed to all members.

The invitation can take the form of a nomination application or questionnaire, which can be answered and returned by anyone interested in serving on the board. *(See Appendix A for sample Nomination Application.)* The application, a copy of which should be sent to each unit, might ask potential candidates for general personal information, business and educational data, and any other information that may be necessary or helpful. Potential candidates also may be asked to state why they believe they could serve the association well and why they want to be seated on the board of directors. Many associations also require an owner's candidacy to be endorsed by a certain number of other unit owners.

An ad hoc nominating committee often is appointed to review the questionnaires objectively. The committee should be composed of persons representing various interests of the association, including a cross-section of ages and occupations of members. After studying the questionnaires and evaluating the respondents' qualifications, the committee should nominate those who appear to be most capable of serving the association. An information sheet about each of the nominees (perhaps a copy of the application) should be sent to each unit owner with the official meeting notice. This provides residents with adequate time and information to make their voting decisions.

In addition to candidates nominated by the ad hoc nominating committee, nominations may be accepted from the floor during the meeting, in accordance with *Robert's Rules of Order* or such other parliamentary procedures manual that has been designated. Traditionally, all nominees are introduced at the meeting and given a few minutes to tell the association members why they believe they should be elected.

Balloting

Balloting, or secret voting, can be a complicated process. Certain voting procedures should be outlined in the governing documents and explained to all association members prior to the actual balloting. Some documents allocate one vote to each unit. Others state that an owner of each unit may cast a vote equal to his or her percentage of ownership interest. Only one vote may be cast per unit even though the unit may be owned by more than one person.

A sufficient number of ballots should be prepared in advance of the meeting. Ballots should list in alphabetical order those persons nominated by the ad hoc nominating committee and provide blank spaces in which to add floor nominations and write-in candidates. *(See Appendix A for sample Ballot.)* Ballots may be distributed at the door of the meeting room. As members enter, they may be handed their ballots as their names are crossed off a membership roster.

Very small associations may be able to conduct elections less formally with all nominations being made from the floor. Blank sheets of paper on which each unit owner can cast his or her vote may serve as ballots.

Percentage of interest voting. Elections that permit each unit owner to cast a vote equal to a percentage of ownership interest in the common areas present special problems. The vote is cast collectively for the owners and weighted by the percentage of ownership allotted that unit. For example, a unit owner who has a share in the common area equal to 1.27 percent can cast 1.27 votes for the nominee of his or her choice, but the 1.27 percent cannot be split between two owners of an individual unit. Because some unit owners may not remember their percentage of interest, the percentages should be shown on the roster and written on the ballots as they are handed to members.

Cumulative voting. Some documents call for cumulative voting. When cumulative voting is required, each unit owner is allowed a total vote equal to his or her regular vote multiplied by the number of directors to be elected. If the one-unit/one-vote rule is applied, an owner has as many votes as there are seats to be filled. For example, if three directors are to be elected, the unit owner will have three votes. If the percentage of interest rule is applied, the owner's percentage of interest is multiplied by the number of vacant seats. For example, if three directors are to be elected, the unit owner with a 1.27 percent ownership interest can cast 3.81 votes (1.27 × 3). Subject to the provisions of the governing documents, the owner may be able to distribute votes. For example, the unit owner with 1.27 percent ownership interest may be permitted to cast 1.27 votes for each of three nominees, 3.81 votes for one candidate, or to divide the votes in other ways.

Tabulating votes. After the balloting, the votes should be tallied and the results announced immediately. Tabulation of an election conducted according to cumulative voting requirements may be a time-consuming and difficult task, especially in larger associations. One solution is to create an ad hoc elections committee which serves somewhat as an adjunct to the ad hoc nominating committee. The elections committee administers the mechanics of the election itself. In addition, the management agent usually assumes some responsibility for preparation for the annual membership meeting and for tabulating votes.

The terms of office

The terms of office of the board members are delineated in the bylaws. Generally, each term is for three years. Customarily, the terms of the directors are staggered to avoid the complete turnover of the board in an election and to facilitate the ongoing operations of the association. At the first annual meeting staggered terms are established by varying the terms for the members of the first elected board. Thus, in the first election, a five-member board will have two members elected for three years, two for two years, and one for one year. In each succeeding election, the newly elected director serves a full term of three years.

Removing directors and filling vacancies

The documents usually provide for the removal of directors from a board as well as a method for filling vacancies. Typical language in condominium documents states, "Any one of the members of the board of directors may be removed with or without cause by an affirmative vote of a majority of the unit owners." Prior to a vote to remove a director, a public hearing should be held to permit that director to present his or her side of the issue to all the unit owners. Most documents require that these procedures be followed for the removal of a director, whereas vacancies created in other ways are filled by appointment by the board. The bylaws should be consulted in all cases to ascertain the appropriate procedures to be followed.

The Association Officers

Soon after its election the board of directors will meet to select its officers in an organizational board meeting. The governing documents specify when this will take place— usually no more than 10 days after the election.

The bylaws of the association will designate the titles and duties of officers and directors. Generally the officers are the *president, vice president, secretary,* and *treasurer.* Unless otherwise stated in the bylaws, the general membership elects a board of directors at the annual meeting of each association, then the board selects the officers from the elected directors.

The president

The president of the condominium association acts as the chief executive officer, or chair of the board of directors. The president's ability, judgment, and enthusiasm are important in determining the level of success of the association. The president is charged with numerous duties normally associated with this title. The president controls and operates all meetings of both the board and the association at large, and serves as liaison to the management agent. In some associations the president refrains from voting except to break ties. The president customarily signs all contracts on behalf of the association. It is safe to say that a good, strong president who is effective in controlling meetings will have an effective condominium association.

As the most visible representative of the condominium association, the president probably will become a sounding board for many of the unit owners. Ideally, the president will be an impartial and diplomatic mediator for complaining residents, with time to listen to all grievances. The president must follow the will of the majority and serve the best interests of the association. Many controversial issues may arise during the president's term of office. He or she must take a statesmanlike attitude and not abuse the power of the office by attempting to influence the other board members.

The documents probably will authorize the president to appoint committee members. Therefore, it is important that the holder of this office know the other unit owners and their strengths and weaknesses in order to make intelligent appointments.

The vice president

The vice president presides in the absence of the president. The vice president may also have other designated responsibilities, such as coordinating all standing committees and meeting with the various committee chairs and cochairs to assure the board that the committees are functioning as the board desires.

The bylaws of some associations may specify the election of three, four, or five vice presidents, each of whom is in charge of a major function within the association. For example, there may be a vice president for building and grounds; another vice president for finance; and a third vice president of communications. These vice presidents meet with their respective committees to ascertain that they are functioning as directed by the board. Another approach is to retain the four designated officer positions, while assigning each officer and director a liaison position to a specific committee. The president or vice president serves as ex officio member of all committees.

The secretary

Many bylaws define the secretary's role in far greater detail than the roles of president and vice president. The secretary is the official record keeper of the association and, as such, is responsible for keeping accurate minutes of all meetings and filing them in a minutes ledger. The management agent, an administrative assistant, or a recording secretary, will perform the actual taking of the minutes of meetings. The secretary, then, is charged with reviewing and editing draft minutes of meetings, keeping the corporate seal, and reviewing final minutes for approval. The secretary keeps all official files of the association, copies of governing documents of the association, and a file of association history. Additionally, books of resolutions and copies of board and management-related correspondence are maintained by the secretary.

The person who accepts the position of secretary should realize fully the importance of accurate records since they may at some time be needed to support legal commitments.

The treasurer

The treasurer is responsible for overseeing the association's financial affairs. The treasurer ensures that all transactions, unit owner rosters with assigned assessments, collections, and actions on collecting delinquent accounts are properly completed. The treasurer assists in the selection of an auditor for the annual financial report to unit owners. As the logical liaison to the budget and finance committee, the treasurer meets with the committee regularly and takes an active role with the committee and the management agent in preparing the annual budget proposal.

5
CONDUCTING
EFFECTIVE
MEETINGS

Meetings can be either the lifeblood or the death of a condominium association. Properly conducted meetings provide a forum for reasonably discussing differing viewpoints while adequately dealing with administrative needs. Meetings must be conducted in a businesslike manner to encourage unit owners' interest and contributions, thereby creating an effective owners' association.

The governing documents establish requirements for scheduling and conducting meetings. These must be complied with. However, the ultimate effectiveness of both board meetings and general membership meetings depends heavily upon the creation of, and the adherence to, sensible, pertinent, and equitable guidelines.

Membership Meetings

While a board of directors has the authority to make many of the decisions affecting the condominium, certain important matters, including the election of directors, must be decided by all members of the association. Therefore, it is essential to have the majority of residents attend annual membership meetings. Every board of directors should share the goal of persuading as many members of the condominium community as possible to attend these meetings.

Notification procedures

To encourage attendance at membership meetings, every unit owner must be given proper notification. The requirements for notification are clearly outlined in most governing documents. Preparing and mailing the official meeting notice may be done by the board secretary or the management agent, or they may do it together. The governing documents usually also prescribe how far in advance of the meeting the notice must be sent. *(See Appendix A for sample Notice of Annual Membership Meeting.)*

The board of directors should take steps in addition to the documents' requirements. For example, an announcement of the meeting should be placed in the association newsletter, with a proposed agenda. A personal letter from the board, stressing the importance of the meeting, may also be incorporated into the newsletter. Election committee or board members may contact owners by telephone to encourage attendance, and other "personalized" efforts may be used.

Time and location

The annual membership meeting is the one session that the entire membership should attend. Although the date of the first annual meeting is usually determined by the date on which a set number or percentage of units have been sold, or within a certain period from the date of the first settlement, some documents prescribe a certain day of a certain month as the date for all subsequent annual meetings. In other cases the documents simply state that the day and month of the first meeting shall become the day and month for all subsequent annual meetings. For example, "The annual meeting of the council of co-owners shall be held at 8:00 P.M. on the third Thursday in the month of October of each succeeding year." If the documents do not specify the time of the meeting, the association should schedule it when more residents are free to attend.

In providing guidelines for the location of the annual meeting, most documents simply state that meetings "shall be held at such place as may be designated by the board of directors." The meeting room should be large enough to accommodate all who may attend, so a condominium clubhouse is often an ideal meeting place. Very small condominium associations may meet in a variety of places, including one member's unit or the lobby. Large associations may meet in facilities such as school classrooms or other local civic facilities provided for a nominal charge.

Meetings which must be held away from the association complex should be held as nearby as possible, since the farther away the meeting is, the fewer will attend. When the meeting is held away from the condominium, the board must be sure that adequate parking is available and that there is good access for handicapped members.

Special membership meetings of an association may be called either by the board of directors or by a group of unit owners representing a certain percentage of votes as stipulated in the governing documents. Again, proper notice must be given. The nature of the business to be discussed should be stated in the notice of the meeting.

Most governing documents require one annual meeting. Many associations hold second general membership meetings approximately midway between elections as a mechanism for direct communication between the board and its members. These meetings are frequently referred to as "town hall meetings" after similar such meetings historically held in various small towns throughout the United States.

Quorum requirements and voting rules

A quorum is the minimum number of votes held by unit owners which must be represented, in person or by proxy, in order for the meeting to be legally conducted. Unless otherwise stated in the documents, a simple majority (51 percent of all owners of record) constitutes a quorum. This quorum requirement helps to ensure the democratic process, thereby avoiding the potential for a small number of residents to unduly influence the outcomes.

The documents usually outline voting procedures. They prescribe the number of votes assigned to each unit owner in one of two ways. Each unit owner may be assigned one vote per unit owned or a percentage vote based upon their unit's percentage ownership of common area. Usually all assessments and liens on a unit must be paid in order for the owner to exercise the right to vote.

The vote of a majority of the unit owners present at a meeting is usually sufficient for action on most issues brought before the membership. However, issues such as amendments to the declaration may require a percentage of the total vote greater than the simple majority.

Most governing documents permit *proxy* voting. A proxy authorizes one unit owner to vote for another who is absent from the meeting. The proxy is usually in writing. It must be filed with the association secretary within a certain number of days prior to the meeting or presented to an inspector of election at the time of voting. Some documents may limit the number of proxy votes each unit owner can cast. *(See Appendix A for sample Proxy.)*

The agenda format

To assure that membership meetings run smoothly, the agenda, or order of business, for the meeting should be planned and followed. The agenda is often prescribed in the documents. If it is not, the board should then develop one for use at membership meetings. The following is a sample format:

Agenda: Annual Membership Meetings of the XYZ Condominium Association
Call to order by the president
Certification of proper notification of meeting
Roll call
Certification of quorum
Reading and approval of minutes of last meeting
Reading and acceptance of treasurer's report
Report of the board of directors
Report of committees:
   Standing (itemize)
   Special (itemize)
Report of the management agent (optional)
Election of officers (if applicable)
Approval of budget for the next fiscal year (if applicable)

Old business
New business
Open discussion
Announcements
Adjournment

A well-organized order of business facilitates the democratic process and stimulates ideas and opinions.

Board Meetings

With the exception of those matters requiring a vote of the membership, most responsibilities for administration of the affairs of the condominium association are discharged by the board of directors. Thus, a great deal of business is transacted and many important decisions are made at board meetings.

Notification procedures

The governing documents usually require the board secretary to notify the other directors of scheduled board meetings and often indicate the amount of advance notification needed. Even if it is not required by the documents, it is wise that the board give open announcement of board meetings so that owners may attend.

Holding open meetings fairly assures the integrity of the board. It is also a mechanism by which owners may communicate directly with their board. However, if owner discussion is part of the regular board meeting, owners who wish to speak should inform the board secretary that they request to speak and state the subject they wish to discuss. This assures the board of control. Any such request should also have a deadline for submission (at least two, preferably seven days before the regular meeting), thereby affording the board an opportunity to know what they may be required to respond to.

Time and location

The requirements for convening regular meetings of the board of directors should be specified in the governing documents. Documents often specify that "regular meetings of the board of directors may be held at such time and place as shall be determined, from time to time, by a majority of the directors." It is to the advantage of both the board of directors and the owners if meetings are held at the same place each month. Monthly meetings are usually sufficient to handle most administrative matters, but the frequency of meetings will vary from association to association and from topic to topic. Some documents require that a minimum number of regular board meetings be held each fiscal year, usually two to four. The documents also should provide guidance for calling special meetings to handle urgent business.

To encourage homeowner participation, regular board meetings should be held on the same day each month at the same time—for example, 8:00 P.M. on the third Thursday of each month. Many board meetings are held in the evening to allow more residents to attend. It should be kept in mind, however, that board meetings are essentially for business purposes. Wherever possible, they should be held during business hours.

As with membership meetings, these meetings should be held at a consistent location and, if possible, on the association's premises. The meeting place should be large enough to comfortably accommodate at least 10 percent of the membership.

Quorum requirements and voting rules

A quorum—a majority of the directors—usually must be present at a board meeting in order to transact business. This protects the association from domination by one or two board members, and assures that all motions which carry represent the majority of the directors.

The agenda format

Board meetings, like membership meetings, should follow a standard order of business. Where the governing documents do not specify an agenda format, the following may be used:

Agenda: Regular Meeting of the Board of Directors of the XYZ Condominium Association

Call to order by the president
Approval of minutes as submitted (reading is optional)
Review and acceptance of treasurer's report
Report of management agent
Reports of committees:
    Standing (itemize)
    Special (or ad hoc)
Old business
New business
Public discussion
Adjournment

Parliamentary Guidelines

Following parliamentary procedure is essential to a successful meeting. Therefore, it is critical that every association follow *Robert's Rules of Order* or other specified parliamentary procedure when conducting business meetings. Most governing documents require that basic parliamentary procedures be followed. Since these rules assist in smoothing the flow of a meeting and in providing a procedural structure, their importance cannot be overemphasized. They are especially important at large meetings where formality enhances the control necessary to transact business and to protect each member's rights.

Making and acting on motions

Parliamentary procedure requires that each item of business be brought before the board in the form of a *motion*. A motion is a formal proposal by a member on which the membership (or, at a board meeting, the board) must act.

Making a motion and acting on it requires seven steps:

(1) The member wishing to make a motion *obtains the floor* when formally recognized by the chair, thus gaining exclusive right to speak.

(2) The member *makes a motion* or proposal that is introduced by, "I move that . . ." and then the motion follows. A

long or complex motion should be submitted in writing to the secretary prior to the meeting. Upon making the motion, and completing it, the speaker sits.

(3) The motion is then *seconded* by another member. The second to the motion indicates that at least one other member believes the subject to be important enough to be brought to discussion before the membership. If there is no second to the motion, it fails and cannot be discussed.

(4) The chair *states the question*, that is, he or she restates the motion, opening it to discussion. If a motion is not clear in its intent, the chair should put it in language that clarifies that intent. Before the question is stated, the maker of the motion may reword it or withdraw it entirely. Once the question has been stated, no changes may be made.

(5) The motion is open to *debate* (discussion). The maker of the motion should be the first person to be called on. Each person wishing to speak should be given one opportunity to do so. A second opportunity to speak may be awarded after everyone has had an opportunity to speak once. All discussions must be limited to the motion before the membership (or board).

(6) The chair *puts the question* to a vote by repeating the motion and calling for the vote on it. Most motions are passed by a simple majority of those votes present.

(7) The chair then *announces the results* of the vote, stating whether the motion has passed or failed.

Kinds of motions

Most motions can be classified under four categories—main motions, subsidiary motions, privileged motions, and incidental motions. A main motion brings before the association members or board business that must be acted upon. The other types of motions, collectively called *secondary motions*, may relate to the main motion or to emergency or procedural questions.

Subsidiary Motions. A subsidiary motion changes or affects the way the main motion is handled, and must be voted on before the main motion is put to a vote. For example, a subsidiary motion to *postpone indefinitely* may occur when the main motion requires further study or more information, or is of questionable merit. When a motion is postponed indefinitely, the main motion is killed for the present and may not be given further consideration until the next meeting or a future meeting.

A member who wishes to modify a main motion in either its wording or by adding to it makes a motion to *amend*. An amendment to a motion only changes the wording of the original motion; it does not mean that the original motion is approved.

When a motion is felt to have inadequate information, preventing reasonable debate or consideration, a motion is made to *commit* or *refer* it to a committee for study and resubmission at a later date. A motion to *postpone definitely* a decision on a pending question until a definite time serves to delay action on the pending questions until that time. This motion may also specify that date on which the question is to be recalled.

A problem common to many association meetings is debate that goes on indefinitely. To avoid this situation, a member may make a *motion to limit debate*. Such a motion may state a time limit for debate, or that it should end at a set time. It may also limit each speaker to a set amount of time for the debate. A motion may also be made to *extend the limits of debate* if the limits are too constrictive for an important topic. Another method of controlling time is to *call* the question—that is, bring it to an immediate vote.

The motion to *lay on the table* is one that is often abused or misused, as it permits temporarily setting aside a pending question in order to address more important matters. No specific time is set for readdressing the question. A motion to table, although a necessary tool to enable the membership to deal with perhaps more important issues as they arise, should only be used to delay consideration of other questions, not to kill the pending question.

Privileged Motions. A privileged motion relates to urgent or special matters and allows the interruption of other matters. As an example, a *motion to call for the orders of the day* requires conformance to the prescribed order of business and is made when the chair does not adhere to the agenda. A member also may make a *motion to raise a question of privi-*

lege. This permits a member to interrupt pending business to state an urgent request or make a motion on an immediate problem, such as its being too noisy to hear the business being conducted.

A *motion to recess* proposes that a short intermission be called. It does not end the meeting and business is resumed after a recess at that point at which it was interrupted. A recess might be called to permit members time to count ballots, gather necessary information, hold informal consultations, or to recall a meeting due to failure to meet quorum requirements.

A *motion to adjourn,* which can be made and passed even while business is pending, proposes to end the meeting. The next meeting is scheduled before such adjournment, which may be done by a motion or a simple administrative solution. Under certain conditions, the members may wish to set a time at which to hold another meeting prior to the next regularly scheduled meeting. In such cases, a *motion to fix the time to which to adjourn* can be made.

Incidental Motions. An incidental motion may involve a question of procedure that arises from another motion and must be considered before the motion in question is voted on. Most incidental motions are undebatable and must be acted on immediately before business can proceed. Although numerous kinds of incidental motions may be made, there are five basic incidental motions.

A member who believes that the chair is not following parliamentary order may call attention to the fact by calling a *point of order.* The chair then rules on the point of order. If a point of order, or parliamentary rule, is to be intentionally violated, *a motion to suspend the rules* may be made. Where a member wishes that a main motion not be discussed, an *objection to the consideration of the question* is offered to prevent discussion of the motion. Such a motion may only be made before debate on the main motion has commenced and before any subsidiary motion has been stated.

If a pending main motion, or an amendment to it consists of two or more parts that may stand as individual questions, it can be moved to treat each part separately. This is a *motion for division of the question.*

Discussion on a motion may be made either by voice vote or by a show of hands and the results are announced by the chair. If there is a question as to the chair's announcement of the vote, a member can demand a *division of the assembly* or a count.

Motions to Renew a Motion. Robert's Rules of Order also provides a method by which motions that failed earlier may be brought up a second time. One such motion is a *motion to take from the table,* which reopens a motion tabled in a previous session. A *motion to rescind* cancels a previous action, while a *motion to amend something previously adopted* may be made to change the text or wording of a motion that already has been passed. This motion may be used only so long as the intent of the original motion is not changed.

While a question referred to committee is under study or review by the committee, no further motions to the question may be made. A *motion to discharge a committee* removes the question from the committee, returning it for vote. This parliamentary measure prevents unfair or unnecessary delay of a question by a committee.

When a motion already adopted is substantially reconsidered at the same meeting, a *motion to reconsider* must be made by a member who voted for the motion the first time. This action brings the question before the members or the board as though it had not been previously considered.

Parliamentary procedure also prescribes that certain motions take precedence over certain other motions; that some motions need not be seconded; that some motions may not be amended, debated, or reconsidered; and that some motions require more than a simple majority vote. *(See Appendix A for Parliamentary Rules Governing Motions.)*

Facilitating business meetings

Although parliamentary procedure facilitates the functioning of both board and membership meetings, associations should consider adopting additional guidelines which will make meetings more effective. One of the first requirements for an effective meeting is advance preparation. The agenda (order of business) should be prepared before each meeting and sent to each participant. Thus, an agenda should be provided each unit owner prior to a membership meeting, and to each director before a board meeting. The agenda must be carefully adhered to during the meeting. To encourage resident participation at meetings a limited time for resident discussion should be set on every agenda. Any time allocated for debate must be totally controlled to promote proper order.

It is essential that the beginning and ending times for meetings be announced before the meetings and be placed on the agendas. It is equally important to start meetings promptly and to adjourn them at the scheduled time.

Parliamentary procedure serves to streamline meetings, and the appropriate motions facilitate the decision-making process. The efficiency of the meeting is greatly enhanced if debate on a motion is limited, while planning motions carefully will help to avoid unnecessary amendments and discussions. Motions which are presented to the chair in writing are often helpful. There should be proper control of the speakers to a motion, including limiting each speaker to one opportunity to speak until all others have had an opportunity. It is especially important to have a competent recording secretary to ensure efficient operation of the meeting. The board secretary must work closely with both the recording secretary (who takes minutes) and the board president. The appointment of a *parliamentarian* is often a very worthwhile consideration.

6

THE COMMITTEE STRUCTURE

Once a board of directors has been elected and its officers chosen, the next step is to appoint committees. The committee system can relieve the board of some of its work load and facilitate the business of the association by researching issues prior to their debate at meetings. Committees should be assigned specific tasks and encouraged to take minutes of their meetings and make brief but complete reports and recommendations at board and membership meetings. No board of directors can function adequately without the assistance of others, and every association is composed of members with a broad range of talents. A committee structure of *standing committees* and *special committees* will, therefore, enable the board to draw upon this expertise. Committees will help both to run the association and serve as an excellent way to train future association leaders.

The Standing Committees

Standing committees are created to recommend changes in and implementation of policies. They do not establish policy —that is the responsibility of the board. Standing committees are created by the board of directors to take care of each recurring need of the association. An average-sized condominium—from 150 to 300 units—with some recreational amenities may have as many as 10 basic areas of responsibility that can be overseen by committees. These areas include architectural control, landscaping and grounds, budget and finance, insurance, maintenance, rules and regulations, social/recreational communication, and legal concerns. As the board of directors gains experience, it may wish to change its committee structure by combining some, adding some, and discontinuing others. The number and types of committees in a condominium association depend on its size, its complexity, and its specific needs.

The president of the board usually makes committee appointments, seeking advice from other board members. The process should begin with a careful survey of all unit owners to determine who has specific attributes or talents that will help ensure the association's success. One method is to send a questionnaire to all residents. This questionnaire should be designed to determine who is interested in serving on a committee, what their talents are, and what their specific interests are. The questionnaire should ask respondents how much of their time they can give to committee work. *(See Appendix A for sample Committee Interest Questionnaire.)*

The board should establish the size of each committee, based on the committee's function and work load. For example, three members may be adequate for a social committee, while seven may be needed for the more detailed work of the architectural control committee. A management agent or a board officer should be an ex-officio member of each committee. These ex-officio members will attend meetings to advise and counsel committee members but will have no vote in actual committee decision. A balance must be reached in both number and types of persons appointed to committees. Members must interact with each other; therefore, it is imperative that they be able to work together and to debate issues intelligently with consideration for each member's viewpoint. Only in this way can committees reach a meaningful consensus.

The architectural control committee

Each association should have an architectural control committee to preserve the architectural integrity of the community. In fact, the governing documents of a number of condominium associations require architectural control and may require such a committee.

The committee goal should be to maintain the appearance and value of the property. Its primary functions are to recommend architectural standards, and to review all the proposed changes that would affect the appearance of the condominium in relation to those standards.

The architectural control committee is usually assigned the task of establishing a procedure for reviewing and acting on all proposed architectural changes. Most governing documents offer guidelines for developing a procedure, often a four-step process: formal application, review by the committee, recommendation to the board, and approval or rejection by the board. If an association's documents require only committee approval or rejection, the third step is omitted.

Architectural standards must be adopted so that the review can be accelerated and fair and consistent decisions ensured. Architectural standards may deal with such items as fences, patios, exterior paint colors, and porch railings. In fact, any change to a unit by a unit owner or the association or any change to the common areas may be subject to architectural control. Initially the developer may guide the committee in adopting standards. In most cases, however, the committee develops its own specifications consistent with the governing documents and state and local law.

Even when a management agent is employed by the association, membership on an architectural control committee may be the most demanding assignment in the entire association. This is especially true of garden and townhouse communities, where most units have outdoor areas that owners wish to modify. In many associations the architectural control committee meets as frequently as the board of directors, if not more frequently. For this reason committee members should be available for regular meetings and for inspection of proposed changes.

The landscape and grounds committee

Many associations have large outdoor areas for playgrounds, parks, parking lots, and driveways. Consequently, a considerable portion of their budget is often earmarked for landscaping and grounds care. In such an association, the landscape and grounds committee (sometimes called the outdoor maintenance committee) serves a vital function.

Although few residents wish to do the actual maintenance of the grounds, many take an interest in the outdoor environment. These people are quick to comment on landscape maintenance that does not meet their personal standards. Because the exterior of any residential development creates the first impression for visitors, much time and effort should be invested in proper care of the grounds.

This committee should work with their management agent to write specifications for landscape and gardening contracts, prepare bid packages, evaluate formal bids, and make appropriate recommendations to the board of directors. Once the board has negotiated a contract for outdoor maintenance, the committee will wish to monitor the contractor's performance. The committee should work with their management agent to ascertain that contracts are properly prepared and fulfilled. All evaluative comments and suggestions should be channeled through the management agent to enhance contractor performance.

The landscape and grounds committee should make expense recommendations for landscape maintenance and improvements to the board of directors when the annual budget is prepared. In addition to maintenance required on a regular basis, the committee should work with the management agent to develop comprehensive, long-range embellishment plans. Many condominium owners who formerly lived in single-family homes retain an interest in grounds and gardens. Their experience can be most helpful.

The landscape and grounds committee is frequently asked to review individual owners' applications for permission to plant shrubs and flowers or make other changes to the grounds. The committee must review all requests for change, since it has set landscaping and grounds maintenance standards. It then makes recommendations that the board approve or reject these applications.

The budget and finance committee

The budget and finance committee, one of the most important advisory bodies of any condominium association, works with the board of directors, the treasurer, and the management agent on all financial matters. The committee, in which the treasurer is usually a member, assists in preparing the preliminary annual budget for submission to the board of directors. This responsibility requires that the committee meet with chairs of other committees to determine their funding needs for the coming year. The budget and finance committee may recommend maximum limits for expenditures in all operating categories. It should then advise other committees of these limits.

The budget and finance committee should review the monthly operating costs of the association and inform the board of areas that require special attention. When a management firm services the association, the monthly financial summary should originate from the management agent, with copies to the budget and finance committee.

If actual expenses seriously exceed budget projections, the committee (with the help of the management agent) can recommend ways to resolve the funding deficiencies. A special assessment may be recommended; this requires a detailed explanation to all unit owners to justify it. If available funds are insufficient because current assessments are too low, the budget and finance committee may recommend an in-term increase. Similarly, if efficient operation factors have resulted in lower costs, a reduction in assessments or an end-of-financial-period refund may be suggested.

Another function of the budget and finance committee may be to recommend an auditor to perform the annual review of the association's financial operation. This often requires that the committee obtain bids from accounting firms and make recommendations to the board of directors. Most bylaws specify that an audit be performed annually. The auditing firm will usually perform the audit along with filing the tax returns of the association.

In addition, this committee may recommend other accounting functions, such as reviewing tax laws, monitoring reserve funds, and suggesting reporting techniques (cash accounting or accrual accounting basis). The committee may be asked to propose guidelines for collecting delinquent assessments. These guidelines are usually set forth in the governing documents. When a management firm is involved, these activities should always be coordinated through the management agent.

The insurance committee

Most governing documents establish the initial insurance needs of the condominium association. Since these requirements tend to be complex, the association may consider appointing an insurance committee to review the association's insurance policies annually (or 60 days before expiration). Bids should be obtained from qualified insurers to compare rates and coverage. Again a management agent may be responsible for assisting the committee in handling this along with the submitting of claims.

The insurance committee should see that the values of the insurance policies are upgraded annually to reflect increasing or appreciating property value. Directors' and officers' liability insurance must be a part of any insurance package. Board members should be bonded if their signatures are on reserve or operating accounts.

The maintenance committee

The maintenance committee's function is similar to that of the landscape and grounds committee but usually includes responsibility for the interior and structural portions of the common areas. Some of its responsibilities are to periodically inspect the interior common areas, review work specifications and contracts, inspect work in progress, and work closely with the management agent. All instructions and suggestions should be channeled through the management agent.

The maintenance committee should meet regularly—monthly or bimonthly, depending on the size of the development—to inspect the common areas, noting any defects. It should then make recommendations to the board of directors for the appropriate repairs, improvements, or replacement. A major portion of the committee's time will probably be devoted to preparing bid specifications for contracts and recommending selection of contractors to the board after consulting the management agent.

Many associations will have members with experience in construction or home improvement, such as plumbers, electricians, and carpenters. These people are excellent candidates for the maintenance committee. Daily housekeeping, essential to the preservation of the condominium's assets, may be monitored by the maintenance committee or a subcommittee. A subcommittee can play an important role in a self-managed condominium by making regular inspections of the interior common areas, reporting its findings, and suggesting solutions to the board of directors. A subcommittee may review work schedules of employees with the management agent. Review of employees' salaries and benefits is usually the province of the budget and finance committee.

The rules and regulations committee

It is periodically necessary for an association to change its rules and regulations. The bylaws may need updating to meet changing attitudes or to comply with new state laws. House rules and regulations may require review and modification. Thus, a committee to review the governing documents in response to the changing needs of condominium living and suggest necessary changes is valuable to any association.

Many state regulations require a two-thirds or three-fourths vote of all owners—not just those present—to approve changes in the bylaws. The requirements for house rules and regulations are less strict. Most documents allow a board of directors to adopt and modify house rules and regulations. However, for these rules and regulations to be effective they must be reasonable, and the committee—together with the board—has a duty to ensure this reasonableness.

Recent court decisions have struck down house rules and regulations that were too stringent—that did not permit free expression or allow full use of the common areas—or that were not enforced uniformly. Therefore, both the rules and regulations committee, sometimes called the bylaws committee, and the board must be reasonable when making decisions that will affect the entire association. Action on the issues must be considered objectively, in light of the interests of all association members, not be too subjective or self-serving.

The social/recreation committee

One of the best ways to bring unit owners together is through a social/recreation committee. The social/recreation committee may plan parties, cookouts, swimming parties, tours, bridge clubs, etc., to generate a friendly atmosphere and a true sense of community. Easter-egg hunts, Christmas caroling, and similar festivities or events around holidays of other religions are desirable seasonal social activities. The committee can usually support a number of activities by charging fees to attend specific events.

Although small associations may have little need for this committee other than to plan activities, larger associations use it to evaluate supervision and operation of their recreational facilities. These facilities may include a swimming pool, tennis courts, a community clubhouse, a health club, or Jacuzzi rooms. Therefore, in larger associations the functions of the social/recreation committee are sometimes divided into three categories: facilities, pool, and activities.

Facilities' expenses should be planned with the annual budget. Plans for seasonal facilities and their related services—for example, lifeguards, pool chemicals, tennis court maintenance—must be open to competitive bidding. Once the season begins, the committee should monitor the operation of all recreational facilities, making recommendations for change when and where necessary. An amenity rental fee structure, vending machine revenue control, annual swim meets, tennis tournaments, bicycle field trips, and similar functions are clearly part of this committee's interest area.

The newsletter committee

The associaton newsletter is a vital link in the network of communications within an association. It should be prepared and published on a regular basis by a newsletter committee. Newsletter content may be supplied by the board of directors, committees, the management agent, or by other contributors. The newsletter should report decisions, made by the board or by committees, that affect the membership. Residents can be kept abreast of social functions and other functions that are scheduled. The newsletter may be fully funded by the association, or it may support itself in full or in part by selling advertising space.

The newsletter should bring the association together. It should not be a vehicle for debating issues, creating divisiveness, or provoking issues that are negative in nature. The newsletter can be a source of valuable information for all unit owners, and serve as a sunshine committee by acknowledging all types of noteworthy occasions. Obviously, anyone with experience as a journalist would be ideally suited to serve on this committee.

The welcoming committee

Moving can be a traumatic experience, and a welcoming committee can help to make the transition from one home to another a pleasant experience. This committee functions like the social committee. It plans activities to bring new owners into the mainstream of the community and informs new residents about the association and its form of governance. A member of the welcoming committee should visit all new residents and provide them with information on the local area; a map of neighborhood schools and churches; a list of residents; and information on association committees, rules, board meetings, names of committee chairs, board members, and the management agent. This committee should submit the names and addresses of new owners for publication in an association directory and include a note of welcome to them in the newsletter.

The covenants committee

The covenants committee may assist outside counsel in preliminary work on such items as nonpayment of assessments, violation of association rules and regulations, and foreclosures. More important, however, is the fact that the convenants committee is a judiciary for hearing cases involving violations or infractions of rules and reporting its recommendations to the board. The importance of a covenants committee cannot be overemphasized. In many cases it carries great weight where legal enforcement and judgments of a punitive nature are to be made. Often the rules and regulations committee referred to earlier is an adjunct to, and under the control of, the covenants committee.

Ad Hoc Committees

The board of directors may have special needs that require ad hoc committees. These committees are appointed to carry out specific nonrecurring or cyclical tasks. They are disbanded as soon as these tasks are completed. A special comittee usually ceases to exist after it makes its final report to the board of directors. Ad hoc committees, like standing committees, should represent diverse viewpoints. This representation will help assure that their decisions will be acceptable to a majority of unit owners.

Special committees should not be established to perform functions that are part of the responsibilities of existing standing committees because this disrupts the normal flow and can be demoralizing to the standing committees.

Guidance of Association Committees

If committees are given proper guidance by the board of directors, they can be of great value in the efficient functioning of an association. Appointing committees is only half of the board's job. Guidelines for each committee should be drafted to indicate its purposes and explain its exact role in the overall administration of the association. The tasks of all committees should be carefully delineated, and lists of these tasks should be given to all committee members to avoid misunderstanding about their roles. Since the role of one committee may overlap that of another, the importance of cooperation must be stressed. To further enhance committee functions, the board should establish administrative guidelines and policies for all committees.

Guidelines for commitee chairs

A committee chair acts as liaison between the board of directors and the committee as a whole. Ideally, the chair is able to work with various groups. The overall effectiveness of a chair is determined by this ability, which will greatly assist him or her to guide the committee toward clearly defined goals. The following guidelines for committee chairs are suggested to help them carry out their responsibilities effectively, and to enable them to play appropriate roles in the overall administrative effort:

(1) Begin meetings on time and announce the time at which they will be adjourned. When members are aware that a meeting will end at a specific time, business should move more quickly.

(2) Have a written agenda and follow it precisely. Give a copy of the agenda to each committee member before the meeting.

(3) Assign a secretary to keep minutes of each meeting and see that all committee members, as well as the board of directors, receive copies of them.

(4) Control general discussions so that extraneous conversations do not disrupt the business at hand.

(5) After each speaker finishes the discussion of an issue, summarize briefly what was said.

(6) Encourage reasonable debate and constructive disagreement. Halt rambling discussion that is obviously inconclusive. Appoint subcommittees to research major issues.

(7) Avoid hasty actions if time for consideration is inadequate. Unless the issue is of urgent importance, table discussion until the next meeting.

(8) At the end of the meeting, ask committee members if they are satisfied that each subject has been given adequate attention.

(9) Use appropriate parliamentary procedures to facilitate the flow of the meeting. (Small committees, however, can use less formal, modified procedures.)

(10) Be prepared to present complete, brief, formal committee reports to the board of directors. Each report should be submitted in writing. It should present the results of any research and, where applicable, recommend actions to be taken.

Guidelines for committee members

While the committee chair is instrumental in making decisions on issues within the committee itself, each committee member must recognize an obligation to contribute to overall group effectiveness. The rules that follow should enable the committee members to work together toward meeting committee goals.

(1) Prepare adequately for each meeting. Complete any required research or reading. Study the agenda prior to the meeting. If reports have been assigned, prepare them in writing and distribute copies to all committee members before the meeting.

(2) Ask for the floor when you wish to contribute to the discussion. Speak clearly and loudly enough to be heard by everyone present.

(3) Keep your remarks brief, and do not stray from the subject being debated. If a speech must be long, conclude with summary remarks.

(4) Avoid issues which are not on the agenda. Refrain from extraneous conversations.

Unit owners may be unfamiliar with committee operation. Therefore, the board of directors of each condominium association should adopt its own guidelines for committee chairs and members. Lacking such guidelines, committee meetings could dissolve into gripe sessions with the purpose of the meetings forgotten, and the objectives of the meeting not achieved.

7

MANAGEMENT ALTERNATIVES

Whether or not living in a condominium community is a profitable and pleasurable experience for each unit owner depends considerably on the association's management plan. A well-planned, well-managed condominium will provide residents with full enjoyment of all benefits of condominium ownership. In contrast, ownership can become a nightmare in a poorly-operated condominium.

The term management, as it applies to a condominium and its unit owners, relates broadly to all of the community's activities. Condominium management encompasses far more than just the management of the physical structure. It is a mixture of many disciplines, including law, engineering, accounting, business management, insurance, communications, maintenance, and psychology. It is a unique function that requires special training and a multitude of skills.

Each condominium unit owner should understand that the association is a self-governing organization that elects a board of directors to make the decisions that affect the operation of the community. One of the board's most important decisions is in the selection of a *management plan*. There are four recognized types of association management: *self-management; on-site management,* provided by an employee of the association; *financial management,* provided by an outside source under contract to the association; and *full agency management,* provided by a property management company under contract to the association. No matter which plan is chosen, the board retains the responsibility for adopting comprehensive operating procedures and administrative policies. The management plan is the way by which these procedures and policies are implemented.

The best management plan is the one that meets the specific needs of the specific condominium community for which it has been designed. A management plan for a 12-unit condominium will not necessarily work for a 60-unit condominium. It is even less likely to work for a 250-unit condominium. The small condominium may operate effectively with volunteers performing most management tasks. The larger condominium may require only financial management. The very large condominium may require a management agent plus on-site staff. The size, financial capability, and objectives of each condominium dictate which management format is most appropriate and effective.

Self-Management

Self-management is a do-it-yourself form of administration. This plan places the association in the position of both deciding the policies and carrying them out. The board of directors assumes the role of supervisor and coordinator of all activities on behalf of the community.

Self-management does not normally require self-maintenance, as some condominium unit owners suspect it does. Choosing to self-manage does not place the burden upon unit owners to cut the grass or haul away the garbage. It does, however, make the directors responsible for fulfilling administrative, operational, and fiscal obligations. One facet of this responsibility is properly allocating the time necessary to perform these functions and duties. To this end, the self-managed association may contract for certain services, hire full- or part-time employees for other services, and also use volunteers from within the condominium to complete other services. The most viable self-management plan combines all three approaches.

Employing staff

Although a full-time staff may be too costly for small associations, one or two part-time employees may be hired to perform certain tasks. These may include mowing the lawn, typing minutes of meetings, cleaning common areas, or keeping financial records.

Employees who are hired to carry out various association duties are directly accountable to the board of directors. The responsibility for monitoring their performance is usually delegated to an appropriate committee. Employing staff allows the board to delegate certain responsibilities while retaining control over the operation of the condominium. However, the board's job then becomes very demanding because the directors must be involved in hiring, paying, and firing personnel, complying with federal and local labor laws, providing for hospitalization, and supervising workers.

Dealing with contractors

Even if it has a support staff, the self-managed association will undoubtedly have to retain contractors to provide certain services. These may include landscaping, special maintenance, janitorial, and trash removal services, and contracts for such jobs as exterior painting or common area plumbing. Many contracts are for services performed on a regular basis at a fixed annual fee, which is payable in monthly installments.

Although hiring a contractor may relieve the board of dealing with some personnel, it places the board in another position of responsibility—contract negotiation. Preparing contract specifications that will lead to a satisfactory performance on any job is quite a task for anyone. Therefore, the board should have all contracts reviewed by both a professional property manager and legal counsel before they are finalized. In addition to negotiating a contract, the board will also have to oversee the performance of the contract to ensure that the contractor is fulfilling his or her obligations.

Using volunteers

A self-managed association will probably discover that few, if any, of its members will be willing to perform maintenance, repair, and management jobs on a long-term basis. Although members may volunteer to mow the lawn or oversee weekly custodial duties, finding a permanent replacement if the volunteer leaves or becomes disinterested, or a temporary replacement in the event of illness, absence, or vacation, can be a serious problem. Where there are not enough active volunteers in a condominium community, the board members end up doing chores as volunteers. This places too heavy a load on any board, and will result in failure of the volunteer program concept.

The volunteer approach works as long as the volunteers continue to enjoy their jobs and do not neglect their responsibilities. Unit owners who once were very maintenance-conscious as owners of single-family homes may feel less of a commitment to a condominium association, since many purchasers of condominiums seek to escape the work and responsibility associated with single-family ownership. Volunteerism, then, may become a short-lived novelty. When it does work, the condominium association will be certain to enjoy a successful self-help/self-management program.

Choosing self-management

For self-management to be successful, unit owners must have plenty of time and experience, and a professional attitude toward their work for the association. For example, the treasurer must understand accounting, bookkeeping, and investment requirements and be willing to devote a significant amount of time to the maintenance of proper financial records and timely collection of assessments. The chair of the grounds committee should have both landscaping and gardening experience so that either a landscape contractor or a gardener can be properly supervised. If the association is fortunate enough to have members who have the three main attributes—talent, time, and concern—self-management may be the best choice for an association.

Size of the development is an important factor. Although it should not be the ultimate factor in deciding to self-manage, a sound case can be made for limiting self-management to condominiums of fewer than 100 units with limited common area space and no recreational facilities.

The main advantage of self-management, especially for very small associations, is cost. Self-management is inexpensive. However, if the motivation for adopting self-management is purely economic, the board should scrutinize that decision closely. It makes little sense to save each unit owner a few dollars a month by avoiding management fees when the value of their property may decrease by thousands of dollars as a result of that decision.

Equally important is the question of who directs contractors, employees, and volunteers. Supervision cannot come from a unit owner who wants to boss. Supervision should come only from one person, and that person must have adequate authority to oversee and control work performance.

The board must consider the legal implications of self-management, since the board itself is liable for its decision or indecision. The board's responsibility is to both fellow unit owners and the general public. Although many governing documents contain a *hold harmless clause* that seeks to protect board members from legal repercussions for their actions, this does not prevent their being sued for mismanagement. The board must decide if it has the experience to run the association without possibility of mismanagement. Premiums paid for directors' and officers' *liability* coverage as well as for *blanket fidelity bonds* may be higher for an association that does not employ an on-site manager or a management agent, thereby raising the cost of self-management.

If condominium residents consider the self-management of their community to be an adventure, their level of enthusiasm may be high enough to make self-management workable. However, that initial enthusiasm may decrease as the demands on volunteers increase. Before selecting self-management, a board should consider how it will operate when the volunteers begin to ignore their duties, a situation that can spell disaster for the entire condominium.

Self-management need not end in failure. The success stories of associations for which it has worked well are numerous, but it demands that everyone take ownership responsibilities seriously. Taking a professional approach in executing these responsibilities and sharing a positive and cooperative attitude will result in a rewarding, successful association.

On-Site Management

In this context, the on-site manager is one who is hired by and works exclusively for the association and is not the employee of a property management company. If a condominium is large enough to support the salary and amenities of an on-site manager, it is a good management alternative. Whether the on-site manager lives on or off the property depends on the availability of an on-site unit, along with all other associated costs.

When a board employs an on-site manager to oversee all operations of the community, the board establishes administrative policies and the manager carries out these policies as established. An on-site manager's role varies, depending on the size of the condominium. The extent of authority an on-site manager is given and how closely the board oversees the manager's work determine the level of control or autonomy the manager will experience.

The on-site manager usually hires additional staff (maintenance, bookkeeping, and secretarial personnel) on a full- or part-time basis. Major services are generally contracted. An on-site manager relieves the board of the day-to-day administration and operation of the community, enabling the board to spend time on long-range planning and policy making. Although the manager works directly with and reports to the board, committees may also have very important and visible functions in an association.

The on-site management plan permits the association to retain control over the operation of the community while relieving its members of routine, time-consuming daily tasks. In addition, on-site management provides continuity to the association despite changes in the board that may result from annual elections. If the on-site manager leaves the association, continuity is lost, especially if the board has become dependent on the manager. The greatest loss is the loss of knowledge and experience of the association that the departing manager has gained over the years. Problems may arise, too, in training a new manager or if the on-site manager is absent for illness or vacation.

To prepare for occasional absences and possible turn-overs in on-site managers, the board should appoint a liaison who regularly communicates with the manager. It should also set up a system of regular checks to maintain the balance of responsibility between board and manager. This system should include periodic reviews of the manager's work by the association secretary. Items such as financial reports, organization of contracts, board and committee minutes, and other documents kept by the manager should be reviewed.

Selection of an on-site manager

One of the more difficult jobs of the board that elects to use the on-site management concept will be finding a person who is both experienced and qualified to manage the condominium. The process must be a careful one if this management plan is to meet the needs of the association.

The board's first step should be to list all responsibilities to be assigned to the on-site manager. These may include maintaining correspondence, handling all maintenance functions, and working with unit owners to resolve disputes. In addition, all responsibilities to be fulfilled by others should be listed. Creation of such lists will help the board to clearly define the responsibilities it wishes to assign a manager, provide a better basis for estimating appropriate compensation for the manager, and will help the board and the manager better understand each other's roles and responsibilities.

A job description can be prepared from the list to help evaluate candidates realistically. The job description will tell the board exactly what it is looking for in an on-site manager. The job requirements can then be effectively communicated to employment agencies, to management organizations, and through want ads. One mistake sometimes made by boards is that of setting the ideals and goals so high that the people interviewed will be overqualified for the amount of compensation the board is offering. Job descriptions should be clear and concise and within the compensation level the association can afford.

The selection process should include a careful study of each candidate's resumé and a check of references. If the board remains interested in the candidate, an interview can be arranged. The professional qualifications of candidates are not the sole measure of their worth to an association. Personality, appearance, the ability to communicate, and an interest in people are equally essential.

Financial Management

Financial management services are accounting and bookkeeping services provided to an association by a professional in that field. When an association contracts for financial management it usually includes the collection and recording of assessment and other income, and the recording and disbursement of all payables. Investment counseling is generally not a part of this service but may be available for an additional fee.

Full Agency Management

A plan of full agency management relieves the board of directors of much of the need to devote personal attention to operating and maintaining an association. A board of directors considering different management plans should remain aware that some boardships may change yearly as a result of the election process outlined in the governing documents. The character of a board will change somewhat from one year to the next because of this cyclical turnover.

A full agency condominium management plan utilizing a property management company provides continuity in the operation of the association. A trained management agent from the property management firm serves as a stabilizing force in a community that might otherwise be in a constant state of change. The management agent brings new board members up to date on the activities of the association, thus serving as a link between one board and the next. On-site management, by itself, cannot offer the kind of long-term continuity that a management agent can. The loss of an agent through vacation, illness, or termination does not affect the management of the association in the manner that loss of an on-site manager may because management firms have additional personnel to support the activities of the assigned property management agent.

Condominiums of 100 or more units can usually support a management fee that will cover most management functions and still be acceptable to unit owners. Full agency service for smaller condominiums may present a challenge. Condominiums of 50 or fewer units may have to have full agency management plans tailored to their needs. Smaller condominium associations must realize that the full agency's management fee, regardless of condominium size, includes certain irreducible costs that have no direct relationship to the size or operation of the condominium.

A full agency management plan need not be all-inclusive. The services of the agent can range from consultation, financial and accounting services, to full management services. Full agency management and association self-help are not mutually exclusive, as the two operate hand in hand. The board, by law, retains ultimate responsibility for the operation of the association. Full agency management enhances the quality and accuracy of planning necessary to the association's operations.

The role of a management agent

The board is charged through its bylaws with delegating association management needs. A 12-unit condominium may need only consulting services. A 25-unit condominium may require consulting and accounting services. A 70-unit condominium may need a management agent to handle all tasks, including supervision of maintenance contracts. To determine the role of a management agent, the board should list all management functions with which the association is charged, following the guidelines provided in the documents. Although the documents may limit the duties that the agent may perform on behalf of the board, the primary assignable management responsibilities usually fall within one, two, or all three of these categories: fiscal, physical, and administrative. The board members, working with the various committees, should list all management functions within these three categories and then check off those it wishes to assign to a management agent.

The board should tell the management agent only what it wants done, not how to do it. Sometimes an inexperienced board will not know what services it wants a management agent to perform. It may, therefore, be advisable for the board to hold organizational meetings with the agent to outline the board's needs and the agent's understanding of those needs. If meetings seem inappropriate, outlining these needs in writing for the agent is recommended. A review should then follow.

Fiscal Responsibilities. One of the management agent's more important responsibilities may include preparing and recommending an operating budget to the board of directors, usually through a budget/finance committee. Although in most cases the board retains ultimate responsibility for adopting an association's budget, the management agent's experience in estimating operating expenses is extremely valuable. The management agent's experience in collecting data, analyzing details, and considering various alternatives is probably much more extensive than that of a board of directors. However, both the board and the management agent should remember that the agent acts only in an advisory capacity and that the agent should not be allowed to dictate how the unit owners are to live or make decisions about how large their assessments will be.

The budget establishes all assessments. In most condominiums the collection of these assessments and other income is done by the management agent. This requires that the management agent bill, receive, record, and deposit all revenue, as well as follow up on delinquent payments. The extent of the management agent's authority to act in collecting late assessments may be set by the board as a matter of policy, or it may already be prescribed in the documents. The management agent's responsibilities may be limited to sending out second notices to overdue assessments, or may be broad enough to file liens and suits against delinquent accounts. In all cases the management agent should be authorized to pursue an aggressive collection procedure with immediate right to turn unresolvable delinquencies over to the association's attorney for legal action.

To carry out these responsibilities the management agent will have to spend association money. Thus, the board must determine how disbursements are to be treated. A management agent is usually authorized to make expenditures within the budget without obtaining formal approval from the board of directors. A limit, often $500 to $2,000, may be placed on the amount the management agent is authorized to spend for any single nonrecurring budgeted expense. Any disbursements exceeding this limit would require board authorization.

Emergency situations are sure to occur, and this must be considered when preparing the full agency management plan. A management agent should have the authority to make emergency expenditures when major safety or equipment problems arise, with a requirement that the board liaison be notified shortly after such occurrence.

The board must decide how its management agent is to handle the association's money. A management agent's fiscal responsibilities, therefore, will include establishing accounting procedures and banking accounts. The board will typically require the management agent to deposit association money into accounts that are separate from the management agent's other accounts. A checking account is used primarily for the day-to-day operations of the association, while escrow or savings accounts are created for replacement reserves and working capital funds. The association should consult periodically with investment advisors to ensure maximum yields on all savings, at the same time making sure that accounts have varying maturity dates.

The difficult job of preparing financial statements is greatly facilitated by a management agent. Monthly statements of income and expense, accompanied by a financial summary, will show the cash flow position of the association, the delinquency status of unit owners, and the balance in reserve accounts. A comparative statement showing the variance of expenses to budget should also be prepared. A professional auditor should prepare an annual financial report at the association's expense and complete the association's tax return. Federal government and state agency tax reports regarding association employees are generally filed by the management agent. *(See Chapter 10 for a complete discussion of the financial reporting needs of an association.)*

Physical Responsibilities. The management agent may also be delegated responsibility for maintaining and repairing the condominium physical plant. The board is responsible for setting maintenance standards. It then must authorize the management agent to assure that these standards are met. Adequate funding must be provided so that the management agent can carry out this responsibility. Therefore, an immediate priority for the agent is to develop an annual operating plan for maintenance and repair to be scheduled on a weekly, monthly or other basis and include provisions to meet nonscheduled and emergency needs. This annual plan of operation should also include a schedule for staff work and contractor evaluations.

To implement this operating plan, the management agent may require additional staff to be hired on-site. This creates the need for the management agent to write job descriptions, hire, supervise, and dismiss staff in the name of the association. The agent will pay the salaries out of association funds, negotiate collective bargaining agreements, and determine tax withholding and other employee-related expenses. Some management firms will insist that certain of the condominium staff be employees of their firm for reasons of control, training, promotional opportunities, and company morale. In other cases management agent will want the association to be the employer. In all cases, the management agent is the personnel administrator. The costs of employees who work specifically on behalf of the condominium are association operating costs and are paid by the condominium.

The agent may also assist in preparing maintenance service contracts and supervising the work of contractors. As dealing with contractors is a routine management function, an experienced management agent will be an asset to the board in this area of operations.

Regularly scheduled inspections of the property should be made by the management agent as a means of monitoring the operation of the project as well as of evaluating on-site staff performance. Property inspections are also useful in preparing for short- and long-term site improvements, ensuring architectural control, and evaluating major maintenance needs. A report of monthly or quarterly findings should be sent to the board liaison for transmittal to the board.

Administrative Responsibilities. A management agent may be given certain responsibilities on behalf of and at the expense of the association. One very important assignment is that of preparing a report for and attending regular association meetings. Although attendance at all meetings is not normally required, the management agent should attend regular board meetings and the annual membership meeting. It is also advisable for the management agent to attend certain committee meetings periodically.

Many management agents are assigned duties in preparation of meetings. Examples are preparing and sending meeting notices; planning the agenda; preparing ballots, proxies, and other annual membership meeting forms; researching specific subjects to be discussed at a meeting; and handling various correspondence. Minutes of the meetings are generally taken by a recording secretary who is usually paid by the condominium association. Other administrative record keeping, such as unit resident lists, additional copies of minutes, duplicate contract files, and tenant leases, should be kept by the management agent. Financial records; transfers of title; pet and automobile registrations; committee and officer reports; equipment manufacturers' data; legal documents, including the governing documents; copies of insurance policies; and other material of administrative importance should be kept in current or in historical files under the supervision of the management agent.

Communications are critical to any association's success. The management agent can be most helpful in guiding a committee that is learning to publish a regular newsletter. In addition to the newsletter, other forms of communications, such as periodic letters from the board, letters of special information from the property management firm, and other forms of media, are vital to keeping a community "alive." Correspondence directed to a specific resident should always be courteous, concise, and clear in intent or purpose. In many cases letters will be written by the management agent for the board president's or other officer's signature.

Exclusions. Certain administrative functions are clearly beyond the professional scope of a management agent, and should therefore be handled by experts. Such things as architectural, legal, tax and audit, and engineering functions are specialized areas of expertise. Management agents should be able to recommend experts in those specific areas. When these experts are to be hired to settle questions or disputes between the association and the developers or individual unit owners, management agents should keep their distance. They should neither act as negotiators nor as arbitrators.

Selecting a management firm

Like many decisions that a board of directors is required to make, selecting a management firm requires intuition, knowledge of the management experience, and an understanding of the manager's and board's duties. Selecting a management firm involves more than guesswork or falling for the slick sales pitch. The decision must be based on a complete knowledge of the qualifications of the management firm and the management firm's agent to meet the needs and requirements of the association.

One of the most important qualifications is that the management firm have experience in condominium association management, which may be difficult since condominium management in the United States has become prominent only in recent years. The dissimilarity between rental management and condominium management adds to this difficulty. The nucleus of this dissimilarity is that rental managers seek the highest dollar yield while keeping the property in the best possible condition, whereas the condominium association is solely nonprofit and seeks to control costs within a fixed assessment budget and not necessarily make a profit. Both types of property, however, usually have the goal of keeping a community in excellent condition.

Condominium owners exercise control over the management agent, while a rental property agent is employed by and reports to one person. A condominium management agent must deal with a board of directors, which may have as many as 11 members. The level of service expected by condominium owners is often higher than that of tenants who have no ownership interest.

A board of directors, then, should seek a management firm that both understands the concept of condominium ownership and has exceptional skills to work with people and effectively manage the physical plant. The management firm must be familiar with the legal documents of condominium, be aware of applicable state laws, and clearly understand the differences between what is unit owner responsibility and what is association responsibility. Therefore, management firms that have operated solely rental properties may not necessarily possess the expertise required to manage a condominium association.

After the board of directors has decided which responsibilities it wishes to assign to the management firm, it should prepare a complete and consistent package of information for each firm from which it is seeking a management proposal. This package, often called a request for proposal (RFP), should include a complete list of the services the association requires, the governing documents, an information sheet showing the number and types of units within the property, a list of contracts, financial summaries including the current year's budget, and any other information about the community association. After receiving these specifications, many management firms may require additional information before they can establish a fee for their services to the association.

The specifications should be submitted to four or five management firms that have good reputations and the expertise, integrity, and ability necessary to manage the association. When selecting the firms to whom requests for bids will be sent, the board should ask the following questions: Is the prospective agent a CERTIFIED PROPERTY MANAGER® (CPM®) through the Institute of Real Estate Management (IREM) or a Professional Community Association Manager (PCAM) through the Community Associations Institute (CAI)? Is he or she a licensed real estate broker, a Graduate, REALTOR® Institute (GRI), or a member of the Urban Land Institute (ULI)? Is the agency firm designated by IREM as an ACCREDITED MANAGEMENT ORGANIZATION® (AMO®)? Such designations and memberships will give the board an indication of the abilities of the management firm it is considering.

After the bids have been received, the board should interview each of the prospective management agents. Standard questions should be asked of each agent at the interview, and interviews should be limited to one management firm per day, with none scheduled on weekends or holidays. Scheduling one interview per day allows enough time for spontaneous discussion, which will give more insight into the prospective agent's capabilities.

Predetermined questions, by themselves, may be too formal and may somewhat dehumanize the selection process. Some suggested topics are: What bookkeeping method is used? How will it affect the association? Is it cash or accrual? How many employees will work for the condominium? How will they be supervised? Where is the agent's office located? Are the fidelity bonds, errors and omissions, and liability insurance adequate? Does the management firm provide emergency service?

References should be provided by the prospective management companies, and these should be checked by a board member. These references may include a board member at a condominium the agent formerly managed. Questions should come from a prepared list that focuses on the management agent's overall effectiveness. A member of the interviewing board should visit condominium properties currently or formerly managed by the prospect. Such an inspection may reveal the effectiveness of the physical plant management, assuming, however, that the former association adopted the prospective agent's recommendations.

Cost considerations always play a major role in the selection process, but the board's selection of a management firm must also evaluate management systems and performance, often more important than a low fee. Once the selection process has narrowed the choice to two or three firms, the price factor may be considered more seriously. Automatically selecting the least expensive bid without first gauging a firm's ability to perform may prove to be a very costly mistake in the long run.

The condominium management agreement

After the board of directors has selected the management firm, a management agreement, or contract, must be signed to formalize the arrangement. This contract may have many stipulations, including detailed performance requirements and fees for services rendered. Well-composed management agreements are the foundation for pleasant and lasting relationships. On the other hand, an inadequate, poorly drafted agreement will only result in complications and bitterness. The benefit to and protection of both parties—association and management firm—are critical considerations. A clear statement of the responsibilities and authority of the management agent will significantly reduce opportunities for misunderstanding.

Although the management firm usually drafts the management agreement, the board of directors should know what an agreement must include. Many firms use a standard contract for the basic negotiations. However, additional provisions must be made for requirements that pertain specifically to the client condominium. Tailoring the agreement to fit the particular needs of a condominium association is very important. All responsibilities, as stipulated in the governing documents of the association, should be specifically delegated to the board or the management agent and must be clearly stated. Guidelines for general administration should also be incorporated into the agreement.

The management agreement should not be a complex document, but rather one that is easy to understand and is written in clear language. This will help avoid misunderstandings at some later time, especially as board members change. Both parties should have the contract reviewed by their respective legal counsels to ensure that the intent of the agreement is in accord with the needs of both parties.

The Contracting Parties. Most management agreements begin with a preamble that identifies the two parties to the contract. Although it may appear very legalistic, this opening paragraph initiates the legality of the agreement. It verifies the authority of the board of directors to hire a management agent and confirms the agent's willingness to assume the agency responsibilities.

The preamble further states that the association and the management firm mutually wish to enter into the contract, with both parties benefiting from its terms. In simplest terms it states that the management firm expects to receive just compensation for performance and that the association expects to derive the benefit of a well-run, enjoyable community from the management firm's expertise.

Property Covered. A major difference between rental management and condominium management is that, unlike condominium management, rental management is responsible for the entire property, including the interior of individual residential units. Therefore, the condominium management agreement must clearly distinguish the common property—the common and limited common areas—whose care and responsibility is delegated to both parties. The management agent customarily has no authority or responsibility for maintenance or repair of the interior of the individual dwelling units, a fact that is usually stipulated in the legal documents. A clause clearly outlining the parameters of responsibility sets the legal basis for deciding against correcting nonemergency repair problems within a unit, to cite an example.

Although the condominium, through its management agent, is not responsible for individual condominium units, some contracts may authorize the management agent to arrange for repairs and provide certain maintenance to the units, for example, changing filters and cleaning an air conditioning condenser unit. Such a provision requires that the cost of this work be paid for by the individual unit owner. Frequently such in-unit service allows for more efficient operation of mechanical systems, saving both money and aggravation over the long term. Economies of scale are also created, so that ultimate costs to the residents become commensurately lower.

Lines of Authority. The most significant difference between condominium management and rental management is the presence of resident owners in condominiums. To streamline the operation of the community and keep lines of authority well defined, the management agreement should clarify to whom the management agent reports. This should be one individual (often the president of the board) and one alternate. The management agent will routinely discuss the day-to-day operations of the association with that liaison. This will help prevent a management agent from spending excessive amounts of time on individual matters. It will also emphasize that the management agent acts as the agent for the entire association and answers to the board of directors who are liable for the operation of the association.

Terms of Contract. The management agreement specifies how long it is to be in effect, typically covering one-, two-, and three-year terms. Two- or three-year terms are most beneficial to both the management firm and the association. This time frame affords the management firm sufficient time to establish systems, achieve operation at full potential, and identify how to effectively work with the various personalities of the community leaders. Many documents preclude the board from signing a contract for a term longer than one year. In this case, the contract can be made an automatically renewing contract, wherein the board signs the new contract at each anniversary.

An escape provision is also very important. It provides that under certain circumstances either party may cancel the contract prior to its expiration date. Such a provision allows the association to terminate an agreement when a management agent does not perform in accordance with standards or criteria set in the contract. This provision also gives the management agent a right to cancel for cause. Most cancellations require that a minimum 30 days' notice be given prior to cancellation. A 30-day clause (for cause) is typical for a breach of contract. A 90-day clause is typical where either party simply wishes not to continue with the other and no breach exists. Another clause for canceling the agreement without prior notice by one party should the other party do something illegal may appear in some agreements. Automatic renewal clauses and proper notification of intent by either party prior to expiration are also typical.

Responsibilities of the Management Firm. The sections of a management agreement that list the responsibilities of the management firm are of great importance. These responsibilities must be spelled out in detail and address the specific needs of the association, as itemized in the original request for proposal. When a board of directors has made a comprehensive list of responsibilities to be delegated to the management firm, as well as what will not be delegated, fewer problems result in finalizing this portion of the agreement. This list should include all fiscal, physical, and administrative responsibilities relegated to the management firm by the board. This part of the negotiation process is critical to a successful relationship between the two parties to the contract because the agent's fee is predicated on the amount of work to be done.

Compensation to the Management Firm. In addition to listing all of the things the management firm is to do for the association, the agreement also must specify what the association is to do for the management firm—or, more simply, terms of compensation.

The cost of full agency management is based on the amount of time and the kinds of services to be rendered. The size of the property, number of employees, number of service contracts, and a multitude of other factors each play an important part in contract fee formulation. An annual fee paid in 12 equal installments is customary. The level of services required usually sets the fee, which should cover the costs of all administrative, physical, and financial management. Some contracts are for full management services, others are for financial services only. Cost-plus clauses will also appear when a specific service is provided as an extra to contract. Consideration must also be given to the cost of on-site personnel—usually employees of the association—and related administrative expenses. These then become local management costs and may become a time-consuming part of the management agent's responsibilities.

Since different management firms use different methods to determine the cost of their services, boards of directors should be aware that there are ways to increase and decrease the cost of full agency management. For example, many management agreements require the management agent or a representative to attend all board meetings, which is a direct cost to the management agent. Many board meetings do not require this attendance. This is usually known in advance, and the board should notify the management agent when attendance is unnecessary. It will help keep fees down and improve management effectiveness if a board determines approximately how many meetings a year a management agent must attend. It also will facilitate writing a defined contract.

Another approach is to hold board meetings during normal business hours, thereby reducing management costs. Parallel to this is requesting only reports—management, financial, etc.—that are necessary to the association. Otherwise management costs may increase significantly to cover the expense of volumes of extraneous reports.

The management agreement must state what services not expressly listed in the management agreement will be provided and at what additional expense. Examples of such additional expenses are having a secretary of the management agent take board minutes, having the management agent prepare the newsletter, having special printing done for the association, and having a management agent attend all meetings. Some of these costs, however will be incurred whether the management agent or volunteers perform the tasks. The basic costs of running a multi-million dollar business—which a condominium is—such as postage, photocopying, and printing, are management-related expenses that must be provided for in the association budget. The method for additional compensation to the management agent should be clearly listed in the contract to avoid disputes or confusion.

Agent Indemnification. Management agents will insist on *indemnification* or *hold harmless* clauses, which are designed to protect both the management agent and the association. In their absence the management agent may be held fully accountable for all acts of negligence, even though the board of directors is legally responsible for the operation of the property. Indemnification clauses acknowledge the board as having full responsibility for the association's operations, including those tasks delegated to the management agent. Logically, the board is not responsible for the gross negligence or willful misconduct of the management agent, and the board should request certificates of liability insurance, blanket fidelity bonds, and other forms of insurance that protect both personnel and funds. A hold harmless clause should stipulate that the board pay all legal and court costs incurred if the management agent is sued in relation to the operation of the association; that adequate public liability insurance and workers' compensation be provided; and that the board pay all fees for violation of any laws covering employment or fair housing, or similar statutes.

8
BUILDING OPERATIONS: MAINTENANCE, SECURITY, LIFE SAFETY

The condominium represents a long-term investment for all the unit owners. It is also their home. Thus, maintenance and repair, security, and life safety must figure largely in the association's long-term plan.

In a condominium, adequate maintenance is essential to preserving and increasing the value of the individual units and common property owned by association members. Therefore, much of the attention of the board of directors—and much of the assessment revenue of the association—must be allocated to maintenance, or the upkeep, repair, care, and cleaning of the common areas, along with the related utilities and services.

Maintenance may be the most subjective matter with which the organization must deal. Each unit owner has his or her own priorities. The owner who enjoys the outdoors and the exterior common areas may be adamant about a meticulously manicured lawn. Another owner may be indifferent to the care of the lawns, yet become upset when a building is not repainted at the first sign of chipped paint, or when carpeting is not immediately shampooed when it becomes soiled.

For the board to meet its obligations and appease all the unit owners, it must plan a total maintenance program of inspection, repair, replacement, and cleaning, and establish the quality standards. Although outside service contractors, a management agent, or an on-site manager may be responsible for actually supervising and/or maintaining the common areas, the board and its appropriate committees must have a general knowledge of what they have been hired to do. Job descriptions and work schedules should be available to all the respective committees so they know what to expect of the maintenance staff. Knowing how things operate and which maintenance procedures are effective will help the board deal intelligently with contractors and the management agent in overseeing the work to satisfactory completion.

Physical Maintenance

The first impression of a community is based on the way it is maintained physically—inside and out. The landscaped grounds and paved areas form a backdrop for the property and should serve as an outward reflection of the interior of the building. Grounds that are well cared for and litter-free usually indicate that the inside is also clean and well maintained, making the project a pleasant place in which to live.

A developer usually plans a condominium project to include attractive interior and landscaping features. The unit owners will want to keep it that way. This requires maintenance of the physical elements of the condominium, that is, the grounds, paved areas, and exterior and interior common areas.

Grounds maintenance

Most landscape plans include grass, shrubs, trees, and flowering plants. Although the board of directors may contract with a professional landscape specialist to maintain the grounds, the landscape and grounds committee should know something about the contractor's work in order to deal with him or her effectively. Maintenance of community grounds usually requires seven tasks: mowing and trimming grass, pruning and trimming trees and shrubs, controlling weeds and pests, fertilizing, mulching, watering, and policing the outdoors. The amount of outside service for each task depends on the level of service the unit owners desire and how much they are willing to pay for it.

Mowing. In planning a program for lawn mowing, two questions must be answered: How often should it be cut? How short should it be cut? Although most lawns need to be cut about once a week or when grass is about three inches tall, the answer depends on climatic conditions and the grass growth rate. Grass should be cut short enough to present a neat appearance but not so short that its root system is damaged. Cutting grass to a height of two inches should achieve this balance. During dry periods and extremely hot weather, a one-inch height is suggested even with frequent watering to sustain the roots. Grass clippings should be raked and carried away off site before they turn brown and unsightly. Short clippings which do not lie in clumps may be left on the lawn, but periodical dethatching is necessary to avoid dead spots in the turf and to encourage root growth. The edges of the lawn along driveways, sidewalks, and planted areas should be trimmed and edged about every third week to give it a finished appearance.

Pruning and Trimming. All trees and shrubs need occasional pruning and trimming to shape them and to remove excess growth. Trees should be pruned as closely as possible to their natural shapes, or pruned to avoid electrical wires or other obstructions. Although rules for trimming shrubbery vary according to the kinds of shrub and their location, there is one general guideline: early-blossoming shrubs usually should be pruned just after they bloom, and late-blossoming shrubs usually should be pruned in late winter or early spring. No shrubs should be trimmed in late summer, since the new growth will not be mature enough to endure severe winter weather. New growth on trees below the first main branches, called suckers, should be pinched off at any time as they rob the upper branches and other new growth of valuable water and nutrition.

Weed and Pest Control. Weed control is easier and more economical when done before weeds have a chance to grow. Tiny sprouts that begin to emerge in the spring and early summer can be eliminated much more efficiently than can mature weeds. Weeding should be done at least monthly during the entire growing season, more frequently in hot, humid areas. Chemical weed control by trained specialists is highly recommended.

Trees and shrubs are vulnerable to attack by aphids, borers, mites, and numerous other kinds of pests and insects. Plants should be sprayed to prevent attacks of these pests. Tent worms are particularly damaging to trees and must be treated when observed. Herbicides and pesticides for killing weeds and insects are toxic and, if not handled properly, can damage other plants, pets, and beneficial insects. Therefore, the board should consider obtaining professional services to handle weed and pest control.

Fertilizing. Few soils will remain rich enough to support a good cover of grass, healthy trees, and shrubs for an indefinite length of time. A soil sample should be taken every three years to determine what nutrients may be lacking, and the soil should be revitalized with an appropriate fertilizer. Most state universities or state or county agricultural agencies will test soils free of charge if the sample is sent directly to them. The landscape contract should also include soil testing. There are many brands of fertilizers from which to choose. Instructions come with them and indicate how much should be applied based on the soil analysis. Usually, fertilizer application requirements are based on the number of pounds per 1,000 square feet for every month of the growing season. Depending on geographic location, fertilizing may be done from two to four times a year.

Mulching. A mulch is a protective covering, usually organic, that is placed around trees and shrubs to reduce weed growth and to help the soil retain moisture. Straw, pine bark, tan root, dried leaves, and peat moss make good mulches. The depth of mulch each year should be no more than one to two inches. Also, care must be taken near building foundations to prevent moisture retention or run-off restriction that could lead to interior leaks.

Watering. The secret of a good watering program is to soak the lawn thoroughly at regular intervals, providing only enough water to keep the grass alive. A soaking to a depth of about six inches a week may be preferable to numerous light sprinklings. Timing and amounts of water must be determined by weather and soil conditions. Avoid sprinkling during the high-sun periods of the day. The hours of 4:00 A.M. to 11:00 A.M. are best, as late or evening watering promotes growth of fungus.

Policing. The appearance of lawns and well-maintained trees and shrubs can be ruined by trash, litter, and other debris. Daily checks must be made in all outdoor areas to ensure prompt removal of wastepaper, animal droppings, piles of dirt and leaves, and any other material that clutters the landscape. Every unit owner should be encouraged to participate in keeping the areas litter-free.

Paved-area maintenance

Walks, driveways, and parking lots can either complement or detract from the landscaping plan. Paved areas should be kept clean and free of ice and snow, faults, potholes, and litter.

Snow and Ice Removal. Snow and ice removal is a major consideration in many parts of the country. If the condominium has large open areas, such as parking lots and sidewalks, the board should consider hiring a snow removal service. Snow and ice can be cleared from smaller areas with snow-melting chemicals or sand, or by shoveling. Rock salt, the least expensive of these methods, damages pavements, plants, and carpeting, and is not effective when temperatures are extremely low, generally below 18° F. Snow-melting chemicals may be more expensive but cause less damage, and work at all temperatures. Sand is good for traction but can also harm finished floors and carpets. Shoveling snow is the least harmful of any method, but is costly in personnel time. A combination of shoveling, sanding, and chemical treatment provides traction for pedestrians and reduces liability. The size of the budget for this work obviously depends on a forecast of the severity of the winter. One year may be very mild, but the next severe. A check with the weather bureau in each locale may give some guidance, but even this is not a guarantee.

Repairing. All paved areas require maintenance from time to time. Changes in temperature and in the level of moisture in the air, as well as normal traffic, will cause cracks, holes, and damage to the pavement The most efficient approach to pavement maintenance is to detect minor defects early and repair them immediately. Cracks that may be barely visible in their early stages can develop quickly into serious, costly repair problems.

Pavement repairs should be made when the air is dry and warm, but not hot. Inspection of all paved areas should occur in early spring, and potholes or cracks should be repaired at that time. The most common method of repair is cold patching which involves cleaning or cutting out the damaged area, applying the patch and packing it down, then tamping or rolling it to form a smooth surface. The use of paving contractors is wise where large jobs must be done.

Resurfacing. Paved areas cannot be patched repeatedly. Asphalt surfaces should be resealed every several years to increase their total life. An emulsion coating of coal tar placed over the surface will help to prevent cracking and drying. Resurfaced paved areas present a very attractive appearance. Each reserve budget should include the cost of periodically resealing and resurfacing paved areas and re-striping parking areas. It is rare, however, that the entire pavement has to be replaced unless the original installation was inferior.

Policing. Keeping paved areas clean is an important part of a total maintenance program. Loose paper and rubbish can be blown into the parking lots, oil can drip onto paved surfaces from cars, and careless residents can leave trash in the parking lots. Therefore, daily policing is a necessity. Sidewalks and driveways should be swept and hosed with water; grease spots and oil stains should be removed; and all paved areas should be kept in a clean and presentable condition. Occasional cleaning of privately owned streets, driveways, and parking lots of a project may be included in a landscaping contract. Blown debris and grass clippings that accumulate in the gutters or along curbs should be cleared at regular intervals.

Sidewalks, Stairs, and Curbs. The cost of repairing sidewalks can be very expensive. Some associations include it in the annual operating budget, while others include it in the reserve funds. Obviously all the sidewalks will not completely deteriorate simultaneously, but necessary repair or replacement should be done each year. Damage occurs through cracking or spawling, the erosion or wearing of the surface. While the affected areas can be patched or skim-coated once or twice, the only real cure is to replace the block. An annual inspection by the management agent, board, or maintenance committee should be made each spring. Each block to be removed or repaired can be marked with paint so a contractor bidding on the work knows the extent of repair. Work specifications should include the thickness of concrete and a warranty on the work.

Concrete stairs should be inspected to ensure that the slabs have not pulled away thus allowing water to infiltrate or rodents and vermin to infest the area. Such areas should be sealed quickly to prevent further damage, and slabs removed and reinstalled to the proper grade.

Concrete, asphalt, or railroad-tie curbing should be checked for damage and replaced as needed. Superficial repair is usually ineffective.

Drainage. Storm drains and inlets should be periodically checked and cleaned of debris and trash that accumulates. Although storm drains and inlets may be maintained by the local government authority, the trend is to dedicate these facilities to the local governments while maintained by the association (except for major repairs). Entrance grates should be checked for safety, to protect small children and prevent vehicles or bicycles from an accident due to improper maintenance. Sewer covers should also be inspected regularly for the same reason, and repairs undertaken immediately to avoid any liability on the part of the condominium.

Exterior building maintenance

In addition to the grounds and paved areas of a condominium community, the exterior of the building itself must be carefully maintained. Areas not commonly noticed by owners, such as roofs, and gutters and downspouts, will become major sources of complaint if they are not properly cared for and functioning. Other exterior elements that must be inspected and maintained include eaves, soffits, shutters, and miscellaneous outside items.

Roofs. It is vital that roofs receive regular care, as sun, wind, water, changing temperatures, and settlement of the building can cause major problems. Unfortunately many associations overlook the roof until the rainy day when water begins pouring into the building. The best way to adequately and economically care for a roof is to inspect it at least twice a year. One inspection should be made in the autumn, prior to approaching winter weather, and another should be made in the spring before the hot summer. Special inspections should be made after violent rain or windstorms. If routine inspections are ignored, small holes may become large holes and the condominium may suffer extensive— and expensive—water damage.

Anyone can find the big holes that result in leaks; but only a qualified individual can be counted on to find the small holes that may grow into big ones. Problems usually develop at those points where the surface of the roof joins something else, such as a stack, chimney, or roof drain. A competent roofer will know which areas require attention. If a roof receives proper inspection and maintenance, it should last as long as the building itself. Regularly coating the surface with a roof preservative can extend the life of a roof designed for such coating. New technology dictates that various alternatives be explored before deciding on the specific repair method.

Roof maintenance is a job for skilled persons who know what they are doing and who know the kind of repair and materials needed for each kind of roof. Roofing is not only dangerous work, but unskilled workers can cause additional damage. Thus, a qualified roofer should write the specifications and supervise the installation.

Gutters and Downspouts. Most construction includes prefinished gutters and downspouts which will require some maintenance in the future. The annual inspection of the property should include a review of all gutters, to assure that they are properly pitched to remove water, and that all downspout joints and elbows are connected properly. Extensions of any downspouts to underground systems should be cleared annually to remove the buildup of leaves and other debris. The installation of metal gutter guards or other types of screening may help to prevent tree debris from accumulating in these critical areas. This can be done by a contractor or by on-site staff. The life of most gutter systems should exceed 20 years, and will probably require minimal painting. Newly installed galvanized gutters and downspouts should be thoroughly washed down with a vinegar solution, so that any future paint will adhere properly and will not peel off.

Eaves, Soffits, and Shutters. Buildings with peaked roofs will probably have areas with wooden or textured soffits and eaves. It is also very common in garden and townhouse communities to install decorative shutters. All such areas will need painting periodically, every four years to eight years depending on the quality of material originally used, the level of maintenance, and the weather. Before any of these surfaces are painted, specifications should be written to include repairs where necessary, scraping and sanding of peeled areas, priming and at least two finish coats of quality exterior paint. Although paint is decorative, its primary purpose is to be a preservative of the surface or material that it covers. Careful consideration must be given to the specifications of a painting contract, and it is often wise to specify the grade and brand of paint to be used.

Miscellaneous Exterior Areas. There are numerous areas of an association which should be inspected at least semiannually, probably in the spring and fall of each year. Repair needs should be noted and instructions given to staff or contractors to correct the deficient areas promptly to prevent further deterioration. Areas that should be considered include:

(1) Fencing, including the underground portions of posts which must be treated with creosote or other preservative to avoid rotting.

(2) Light poles and underground wiring.

(3) Electrical timers, to assure proper operation and maximum energy conservation.

(4) Public doorways, including the closers, hinges, locks, and other hardware.

(5) Patios (even when this is the responsibility of a unit owner) for general appearance; unit owners should be notified of needed corrections.

(6) Balconies; particularly those with wooden cantilevers and decks, since these are subject to deterioration due to weathering.

(7) Trash enclosures, to assure that shelving and cans are clean, neat, and sanitary.

(8) Public area lighting fixtures.

(9) All glass in common areas; glass that is cracked or chipped should be replaced immediately due to safety precautions and appearance.

The overall maintenance of the buildings adds to the general appeal of the condominium. Associations that are maintained properly will usually sell for higher amounts.

Interior custodial maintenance

All of the common areas inside the condominium—the lobby, guest and community rooms, elevators, laundry rooms, stairways, hallways and corridors, windows, and floor coverings—must be kept sparkling clean at all times. Walls should be free of fingerprints and smudges, floors should be clean and free of dirt, wood and metal surfaces should be polished, loose debris should be picked up, and any defects, such as inoperable lighting, should be corrected promptly. This is not always easy to accomplish, but the board can help to achieve these goals by seeing to it that basic housekeeping chores are both scheduled and completed. A regular program of policing and cleaning must be planned, job descriptions formulated, frequency of work determined, and the work properly supervised. The frequency of interior cleaning depends largely on weather conditions, the type of building and its location, the characteristics of the residents, and the amount of traffic through common areas. The quality and types of materials used for wall and floor coverings (such as tiles versus carpeting) and the cleaning methods and materials used are major considerations.

The Lobby. Most condominiums, other than townhouses, have some form of lobby, foyer, or entrance that is used by residents and guests. Since this is the first interior area that people may see when they enter the building, it is essential that it present a pleasing appearance. Cleaning should be performed daily, with special care being given during rainy and snowy weather. The amount of work to be done will depend on the size and level of furnishing.

Guest Rooms and Community Rooms. Some associations have rooms available for overnight guests or for social occasions. These areas must be cleaned immediately after each use. A reasonable charge should be made to pay for private functions to offset cleaning costs and to assure care of the area used. Security deposits should be considered. Extra attention will always be necessary due to the use of these areas and their visibility in the condominium. Special care must be taken to control utility use and to provide security to prevent vandalism. Alarm systems and special lighting should be considered.

Elevators. Elevators make a strong visual impact on the residents of high-rise properties. Cleaning the flooring of the elevator, polishing the metal, and removing dirt and fingerprints from walls, doors, control panels, ceiling grates, entry thresholds, and fans must be included in the daily housekeeping program in order to maintain its overall attractiveness. Carpet or tile should be replaced when necessary in order to provide strong eye appeal. Emergency systems and lighting must be checked regularly to assure proper operation.

Laundry Rooms. Keeping a laundry facility clean is a very important maintenance function. Floors should be cleaned regularly, and the washers and dryers wiped down daily. If the association owns the washers and dryers, the maintenance schedule should include daily cleaning of lint filters, cleaning the laundry tubs, and any other maintenance tasks associated with the operation of the machines. If the machines are operated by an outside contractor who is responsible for their upkeep, the contractor should be given specific, written performance requirements.

Stairways. A large number of the condominiums in this country are of the low-rise and garden style. Few of these buildings have elevators; most have stairways that must be cared for. The frequency of stairway cleaning depends in part on the amount of traffic they receive. A flight of stairs between the first and second floors, for example, would require more frequent cleaning than a flight of stairs between the third and top floors, presumably serving less traffic. The maintenance schedule should reflect these variances.

While stairways are cleaned and waxed, signs should be posted to warn the residents that such work is being done. This will help to avoid the danger of accidents caused by wet and slippery landings or stairs.

Corridors and Hallways. As in most interior housecleaning, the best time to clean hallways and corridors is during the time they are least used by residents. This usually is right after most people have gone to work in the morning. The cleaning should start while many unit owners can see the staff busy at work. This helps them appreciate the services they pay for in their monthly fees and avoids criticism that workers are not doing the assigned jobs.

Windows. Unit owners usually are responsible for cleaning the interior glass of their windows, but the association is responsible for cleaning common-area glass and the exterior glass of the units, especially in high-rise buildings. All glass should be kept clean and free of fingerprints, and windows should be washed on a regular schedule. The frequency of cleaning will be based in large part on environmental conditions of the area, the amount of use the glass receives, and the ease with which the work can be done. The windows in especially tall buildings should be serviced by outside contractors, generally in late spring and early fall.

Window washing should include more than just washing and drying of windows. It also should include washing window sills and frames, dusting the outside of frames and sills, and checking safety catches and frames. Provision may be made for cleaning storm windows and screens. In buildings with door attendants, they should clean the entrance door glass several times during each shift.

Floor Coverings. Carpets and rugs should receive regular care. Those that are in areas of frequent use should be vacuumed each day and professionally cleaned at least once a year. Professional carpet-cleaning services or contractors are recommended. These professionals can get rugs cleaner, provide a service warranty, and usually prolong the life of the carpet. The early spring, after the snow season, is a suggested carpet-cleaning time.

Other kinds of floor coverings also must receive routine care. A well-planned daily maintenance schedule should take into consideration the type, amount, and kind of flooring, and the level of cleanliness that is desired. Each type of floor covering requires a certain manner of attention. Asphalt tile, for example, can be permanently damaged by varnish, and wood floors should never be scrubbed with harsh cleansers or allowed to remain wet. The special needs of the flooring should be determined before any maintenance work begins. Manufacturers usually recommend the proper materials and care.

Mechanical and Building Systems Maintenance

The maintenance program in any association must include care of mechanical equipment and other building systems. It is important that the board of directors and the maintenance committee know the location and repair requirements of all mechanical and building systems. Instruction manuals usually are prepared by equipment manufacturers. These should offer guidelines to repairing and maintaining most equipment. These, together with plumbing and wiring schematics, should be turned over by the developer to the association.

Guarantees on mechanical equipment may be printed somewhere on the equipment, included in an instruction pamphlet, or printed on a certificate. The guarantee will state what services are covered if the equipment needs repair or replacement. Guarantees printed on pamphlets or certificates should be kept in the association's files. Needless to say, the association should not pay for any maintenance that is covered by a warranty.

A condominium may have a variety of mechanical equipment, including heating, ventilation, and air conditioning (HVAC) systems, boilers, electric motors and pumps, elevators, fans, tanks, and possibly other items. The board, the maintenance committee, and, most important the management agent, should become familiar with the basic operations and maintenance requirements of each piece of equipment. Although contracts for professional maintenance service are common, knowing something about the mechanical equipment will allow the board to work more effectively with the management agent and contractors.

Heating, ventilation, and air conditioning maintenance

In many condominiums the HVAC equipment for individual units is individually owned and controlled. However, a central system that supplies heating or cooling to the units or systems that service the common areas will be the responsibility of the association. It is essential that a routine maintenance program be planned throughout the year, so that this equipment will provide many years of good service.

The HVAC system usually requires at least two complete changeovers each year. One occurs in the spring when the system is changed from heating to cooling; the other is in the autumn, when it is changed from cooling to heating. Depending on the policy of the board, large fluctuations in day-to-day temperatures may also require changeovers. Although major maintenance work can be done at these times, the equipment needs regular maintenance throughout the year. For example, air filters should be changed, ducts should be cleaned, cooling towers and condensers should be checked regularly, and condenser and chiller tubes inspected for wear and to improve operating efficiency. A reliable air conditioning service contractor should make regular inspections of the heating-cooling units and outline the maintenance plan for the year. Equipment over 10 tons should be placed on a regular service and repair contract to preserve the life of the machinery.

Boiler maintenance

A boiler is a pressure tank in which water is heated and then circulated in the form of either steam or water, depending on the design of the system. The maintenance committee should have a basic understanding of the function and care of this equipment. Even a minor part of a boiler's failing may rupture the tank, causing the boiler to explode. For this reason, the equipment should be inspected and the operation of all components should be checked regularly. Many insurance companies and municipal, state, or county governments require such inspections. The frequency of boiler cleaning depends in part on the hardness of the water, and a chemical treatment should be considered. A knowledgeable person should be contracted with to inspect the boilers and clean the equipment.

Even with a careful program of inspection and cleaning, repairs to the boiler will be necessary. The system must be shut down, causing inconvenience to residents. In order to speed the repair process, a supply of principal parts should be kept on hand if possible. Repairs that can be planned should be performed during periods of minimal use or out of season. Annual inspections of the fire box, tubes, and flues must be made, with needed repairs scheduled at the end of the heating season.

Electric motor maintenance

Electric motors are used to drive fans, air conditioners, swimming pool pumps, and for many other purposes. These motors need to be inspected, cleaned, and lubricated. Regular inspection of all motors will keep minor problems from becoming major breakdowns. Inspections should be performed by persons who know electric motors and are able to locate early signs of possible malfunctions. Electric motors get dirty, so dust is a major reason behind many motor problems. Therefore, all motors should be cleaned regularly.

The third maintenance requirement of electric motors is lubrication. A bearing lasts far longer when the surfaces are smooth and properly lubricated. Although it is possible to apply too much oil, a light layer will separate bearings, reducing friction. The manufacturer's instructions on the amount and type of oil to use should be followed closely. Older buildings may consider replacing older motors in excess of 5 horsepower with new, more efficient ones to reduce energy costs. A 10-horsepower motor running 24 hours a day can cost an association over $1,000 per year; newer motors may cut that cost by as much as 50 percent.

Elevator maintenance

Elevator maintenance requires highly technical expertise and demands the services of a trained specialist. Although elevator maintenance is usually performed under a service contract, understanding the important points of its operation and maintenance will help the association assure that the elevator is receiving proper service.

Before the inspection begins, the main electric power switch to the elevator should be turned off. The inspection should include a thorough examination of the elevator car for structural defects, such as loose bolts or other fastenings. The car switch should be tested and the cables checked. Regular care of an elevator includes lubrication, which is determined by its operating conditions. The elevator manufacturer or the local elevator inspector may provide assistance in developing a regular maintenance schedule. Local laws in most areas require periodic safety tests, which should be included in the terms of the service contract.

Water line maintenance

One of the primary building systems which most condominiums must maintain is the plumbing serving the individual units with central water, and possibly hot water, heating, and air conditioning.

For the most part such systems only need periodic, corrective maintenance. The maintenance committee and the management agent should occasionally inspect main plumbing in such critical areas as the boiler or mechanical room. Special attention should be paid to areas where water is condensing on pipes due to improper insulation. These areas should be dried, sanded, painted, and re-insulated as necessary to prevent continued corrosion leading to eventual deterioration and leakage.

Heating and air conditioning lines must be well insulated to avoid energy loss and improve building efficiency of operation. No matter how insignificant a leak may appear, it must be repaired promptly to avoid potential damage to other areas of the building, including the individual condominium units. It may sometimes be difficult to determine the responsibility for a leak. Most condominium documents require that the maintenance and repair of piping serving only a single unit be maintained by that unit owner, while those serving two or more units are maintained by the association. This responsibility should be clearly delineated in the documents and also through reminders to the unit owners. Ambiguities should be qualified to the satisfactory understanding of everyone.

Where air conditioning condensation lines are within the individual units, it may be necessary to periodically check these to prevent unfortunate backups and damage to floors or ceilings of apartments. Many boards assume that it is the responsibility of the association to prevent damage and answer to claims against the insurance policy. An interpretation of this should be obtained from the association's attorney.

Wiring maintenance

As with plumbing facilities, the association may be responsible for electricity risers, particularly in high-rise or garden communities. Generally, what occurs beyond the breaker panel or meters is the responsibility of the individual unit owner. The association should ensure that all main breaker lines supplying more than one unit are functioning properly, are the correct size, and that all connections are properly tightened. Aluminum wiring requires particular attention to tightening. A qualified electrical contractor should be employed to inspect an aluminum wiring system. The wiring should be inspected to determine that it is installed properly and that it complies with current building codes and fire codes. If fuses or circuit breakers are installed in central areas, the association should maintain a replacement supply at all times.

Recreational-Amenity Maintenance

The recreational areas of a condominium will probably be used frequently by many people. Maintaining these amenities requires special consideration. The areas around swimming pools, tennis courts, and other outdoor amenities should be routinely policed for litter. In addition, each facility will present its own unique maintenance and security requirements which must be recognized by the board.

Swimming pools

Swimming pools need expert care to prepare them for use at the beginning of the season and to close them properly at the end of the season. If they do not receive this care, costly repairs may occur during the season, causing the pool to be closed. Swimming pools need regular chemical water treatment in accordance with manufacturers' suggestions and local health codes. Treatment may be done by a lifeguard, a professional pool service, or through automatic chemical feeders. The total cost of pool services will depend on the size of the pool, days and hours of operation, local laws, staffing, chemicals, extent of use, and special programs offered.

Tennis courts

In addition to regular sweeping and cleaning, tennis courts need periodic resurfacing. Depending on the original surface, resurfacing may be required every 6 to 10 years. Replacement reserves should include this cost. The nets will require periodic inspection and replacement. Specific guidelines should be developed to coordinate the use of courts with the routine maintenance schedule.

The Maintenance Program

Understanding all of the maintenance functions that must be performed is only half the maintenance job. The other half is developing a program to perform these functions. This program should include daily housekeeping and routine maintenance chores, along with the regular inspections essential to the successful, continuing operation of the association. A management agent or an on-site manager, if employed, will handle this scheduling task. If the association is self-managed, the board of directors and the maintenance committee should prepare the schedule and oversee completion of each scheduled task. An architect, civil engineer, the developer of the project, or a management agent acting as a maintenance consultant should be able to provide assistance in setting up the maintenance programs for a self-managed association. If maintenance jobs are contracted out, the board or committee will have to work with the vendor to schedule the work and to specify the standard operating procedures.

Several kinds of maintenance should be considered when a schedule is developed: *deferred maintenance, preventive maintenance, custodial maintenance,* and *emergency maintenance.*

Deferred maintenance

Deferring maintenance does not imply that repairs are to be put off forever. Deferred maintenance refers to work which can be scheduled at a future date without permitting a minor problem to become a major disaster. Repair of a hole in a roof, for example, cannot be deferred because the hole will get bigger and the problem will get worse. On the other hand, painting the woodwork in a lobby usually may be deferred for a period of time without harm.

Deferred maintenance is anticipated and planned for through repair and replacment reserve funds for those maintenance tasks not requiring immediate attention. The deferred maintenance schedule is based on the capital improvements reserve schedule, and money should be set aside for these maintenance functions through regular assessments. *(See Chapter 10 for a discussion of establishing repair and replacement reserves.)*

Preventive maintenance

Preventive maintenance is of primary importance. By providing regular care and making scheduled inspections of mechanical equipment and structural elements, potentially serious problems can be detected early and perhaps prevented altogether. Preventive maintenance must be scheduled on a regular basis. A good program will keep the project's equipment in working order and all of its components functional. Typically, associations with progressive preventive maintenance programs enjoy lower operating costs than those that make repairs only when needed.

Setting up a preventive maintenance program involves three steps. The first step is to examine the common areas and to inventory all mechanical equipment which requires service, and all structural elements. Anything that can break down or seriously disrupt the lifestyles of the unit owners should be listed. This list should include boilers, electrical motors, HVAC systems, pool filters and pumps, driveways, circulating pumps, automatic doors, hot water tanks, alarm systems, storm drains, and roofs. The second step is to note all routine work that is required by each item, including inspection, cleaning, and lubrication. The third step is to determine how often each maintenance function should be performed. Manufacturers' handbooks normally provide guidelines for frequency of maintenance. *(See Appendix A for sample Preventive Maintenance Schedule.)*

The association may want to contract for the services of a professional engineer to develop a preventive maintenance schedule. A visit to the site annually to determine if all work is being performed in accordance with the listed instructions should be part of that service.

These preventive maintenance lists should be reviewed at least annually to ensure that they are adequately serving the needs of the association. If new equipment is purchased, its maintenance needs must be reflected in the lists.

Custodial maintenance

Custodial maintenance refers to all policing and housekeeping functions within the common areas. Preparing a maintenance schedule for routine custodial duties is less difficult, but no less important, than drafting a preventive maintenance schedule. Although neglecting a preventive maintenance plan can be financially disastrous to an association, the unit owners will probably be more aware of custodial performance than they will be of a preventive maintenance schedule being performed.

Preparation of a custodial maintenance schedule requires the same procedures as preparation of the preventive maintenance schedule. The first step is to make an inspection of all physical areas that will need regular attention, including the lobby, hallways, elevator cars, laundry rooms, grounds, and any other public areas. The second step is to note the housekeeping chores associated with each area, and the third is to determine how often each chore should be performed. For example, hallways need vacuuming daily, while elevator cars may need vacuuming several times a day. The equipment and tools required must also be determined.

A custodial maintenance schedule serves as a reminder of the work to be done and provides a guideline for staff levels needed to perform routine housekeeping tasks. Typically, custodial schedules are put in the form of daily, weekly, and monthly checklists. These list all routine custodial duties and provide spaces for indicating what has been done and when. Occasionally, a time study should be made to determine if additional staff is needed. *(See Appendix A for sample Custodial Maintenance Schedule.)*

Emergency maintenance

Even with far-sighted deferred, preventive, and custodial maintenance programs, unexpected repairs are certain to be needed. For that reason, emergency maintenance must be planned for as practically as possible. One way to prepare for emergencies is to make a list of important telephone numbers, such as those of utility companies, electricians, plumbers, general contractors, and police and fire departments. *(See Appendix A for sample Emergency Telephone Number Checklist.)* In addition, the association should maintain a small inventory of parts and equipment with which to make emergency repairs. Where it is necessary to make an emergency repair within a unit to avoid potential damage to the common areas or other units, the cost must be assessed against the respective unit owner.

Maintenance Service Contracts and the Decision Process

Preventive and custodial maintenance schedules are meaningless unless the assigned tasks are completed. If the association is self-managed and utilizes a self-help maintenance program, many of the maintenance functions may be assigned to volunteer members or a staff hired by the board. If a management firm is employed, the firm should establish the maintenance schedules and provide the necessary personnel to perform the various tasks. If an on-site manager is hired to run the project, he or she may be responsible for doing much of the work alone or for hiring personnel to complete the work.

But no matter what management arrangements the association operates under, there are certain services that must be contracted to the outside. As a general rule outside service is needed when complex machinery is involved or whenever special equipment or skills are required. For example, air conditioning and elevator maintenance demand very technical skills, and the complicated and expensive machinery they involve requires professional service. Washing windows in a high-rise condominium requires special equipment and should be contracted to an experienced service company. In addition to technical and special skill functions, other services may be performed more efficiently or more effectively by contractors. For example, an association may find it appropriate to contract for janitorial services or grounds care services. Regulations may stipulate that only licensed individuals may perform certain services such as exterminating, trash removal, and fire extinguisher service. *(See Appendix A for sample Service Contract Record.)*

If the association recognizes a need for service contractors, it must be prepared to become involved in contract negotiations. First, a bid proposal accompanied by a statement of specifications must be prepared in writing, stating the exact services required. *(See Appendix A for sample Grounds Care Program Specifications for Bid.)* Bid proposals should be submitted to three reputable contractors, with a deadline set for submission of bids. The board should accept only those bids that are presented in writing. In some cases it may not be practical to always solicit three bids. Each association will develop certain close relationships with various service companies, and a mutual respect and trust will evolve. When a board is comfortable that a particular contractor is remaining competitive and performing to standard, they may not wish to re-bid to the outside at renewal time.

In evaluating bids the board should select the contractor who offers the best service for the most reasonable cost (not necessarily the cheapest), taking into consideration the contractor's reputation by checking with previous clients, credit bureaus, and lending institutions. The vendor selected should demonstrate a desire to cooperate with the condominium association, proving that there will be adequate personnel to perform the functions within the contract.

To formalize the agreement between the contractor and the association, a contract must be prepared. It should include a detailed statement as to when and how the services are to be performed. Lacking such specific instructions, the board will have no way to evaluate the services that the contractor performs. The contract should also specify the terms of compensation to the contractor, and contain a cancellation clause indicating under what circumstances either party may be released from the agreement. The contract also should contain a statement on the lines of authority, that is, who will be the liaison on the project. The liaison so designated may be a committee chair, a member of the board, the management agent, or some other individual.

All contracts should be reviewed by the association's attorney or management agent before they are signed. This will help to ensure that the association is protected under workers' compensation, liability insurance, bonding, and any other potential exposure areas. The board should require the contractor to present, at the time each contract is awarded, certificates of four types of insurance: (1) if a vehicle is to be used on the condominium premises, insurance to protect the association against vehicle-related injury and property damage claims; (2) comprehensive general liability to cover their employees against bodily injury or property damage while on the condominium premises; (3) blanket fidelity bonds to protect the association if the contractor's employees divert funds illegally, or to protect against theft of materials designed for use on the condominium premises; and (4) workers' compensation, to provide for the payment of benefits determined according to the law for covered occupational injuries or disease incurred regardless of fault of the employer. In the event the employees are not covered, the association may be required to pay for injuries or damages.

The board may also require contractors to show proof of *completed operations and products liability* coverage, a type of liability insurance intended to cover accidents that occur while the contracted services are being performed. For example, this type of insurance could cover claims that might result if a hot water heater burst while being installed by a plumber.

After the various committees and the board of directors have considered the various maintenance responsibilities outlined in this chapter, general procedures should be developed and time frames established for getting the work completed. In many cases the association will perform all that is necessary to obtain the contracts, but will delay the awarding of contracts. This delay is costly in many areas. There may be loss of value due to unattractive appearance resulting from continued deterioration of those areas in need of repair. The potential for damage to other areas because of delay may increase, as with roof leaks. Too long a delay may lose a good-faith position with a reputable contractor, who cannot wait unnecessarily long. The board should set a date by which they will announce the contract award, and then send letters to the contractors who did not get the award, thanking them for their time and effort.

Once the work has been awarded, it is the responsibility of the management agent or the appropriate liaison to have periodic follow-up meetings with the contractor to determine that the work is being completed satisfactorily and invoices are being paid on time. Many contractors become very upset with associations that unfairly delay paying bills, even though work has been satisfactory. Although the association should not authorize payment for unsatisfactory work, it cannot hold up payment without cause. Even when withholding a payment is justified, it should be adequately communicated to the contractor.

Contracts for services that are performed from year to year should be reviewed annually by the board. A brief discussion of the performance of the contractors and the status of the equipment and areas they maintain should be taken into account. If a particular contractor is rendering proper services, strong consideration should be given to continuing the contract for another year, even when prices escalate. Many associations make the mistake of changing contractors every year for the sake of change. A particular service industry that becomes aware of these constant changes may simply add an extra charge to the contract or decline to bid altogether. During the annual contract review, changes to the contract should be discussed along with any modifications involving types or levels of performance.

Finally, the board should establish a very firm policy with respect to resident involvement with the contractors. All residents must be advised that there is one liaison responsible for coordinating the work with any contractor or staff. At no time should an owner be allowed to interrupt the contractors' work or give directions. Such interference may aggravate contractors, and may cause them to quit the job before its completion or to refuse to bid on future work. Thus, it is essential that a professional working relationship be maintained at all times.

Security and Life-Safety Systems

The advent of large multifamily community associations has increased the requirement to prepare and maintain sophisticated security and life-safety systems. Townhouse and garden projects are lower in density and height than mid- or high-rise developments and do not usually maintain high levels of security and surveillance programs. Therefore, the focus of the security measures covered here will center on mid- and high-rise buildings. Life-safety measures, although more complex in a high-density building, are essential for all communities.

Security systems

Although it is usually much more economical to install an electronic security system while the building is under construction, the cost of installation in a completed building will have to be weighed against the other means available and the benefits to be derived. Most high-rise buildings constructed since 1965 contain somewhat elaborate limited-access systems and alert devices. The board of directors and all residents should be informed of the proper use of these systems through an ongoing education process. In many associations these systems are routinely upgraded to match advancing technology in crime prevention, therefore such awareness programs are critical.

Lighting, intercom systems, elevator lockouts, alarms, closed-circuit television, and guards may be employed to increase the security of an association.

Lighting. One of the least expensive methods of improving security is to increase the amount and intensity of lighting. Mercury, sodium-vapor, or quartz lighting help create a more intense lighting effect. A lighting consultant can assist in determining the proper placement of and types of lighting.

Intercom. Many newer buildings have intercom systems between the entrance and the individual units. Some systems use separate on-site telephone lines and require the installation of an electronic door strike.

Intercom systems may also be used by residents to contact on-site staff for emergency services or requests for maintenance. Some more sophisticated systems may provide direct access to police or fire departments.

Elevator Lockouts. Most buildings are very accessible from the elevators. A security system using key or card switches to operate the elevators restricts their use to key or card holders. Although keys and cards are difficult to duplicate, they should be changed periodically for security reasons.

Where round-the-clock personnel are employed, a remote control may be installed which allows the employee to call the elevator to a specific floor, thereby limiting access into the building to authorized personnel or residents.

Alarms. In buildings that are staffed at all hours, an alarm button similar to that used by bank tellers may be installed. This can be monitored by the police, who are automatically summoned when the button is activated.

Closed-Circuit Television. Many mid-rise and high-rise buildings have additional channel capacity on their master television systems. When combined with the installation of camera monitors at various locations they can provide residents with visual control of visitor access. A resident who wishes to deny access can refuse to depress the electronic door release located in the unit.

Additional closed-circuit television monitors may be installed at locations where full-time reception or door personnel are employed. Selected exterior entrances and exits may be monitored by either fixed or automatically scanning cameras. Signal devices indicating that a specific door is open will direct an employee's attention to that particular monitor.

Monitor systems are only as effective as the people who operate them. Careful background checks on all security personnel are necessary.

Guards. In some communities a contract guard service may be used as an auxiliary to electronic surveillance systems. However, the cost of such a service must be carefully evaluated against the total cost of all security. Most professional guard services charge an hourly rate that can be quite expensive when all the hours are totalled.

Life-safety systems

Each community should have plans for emergencies and disasters. These plans should be publicized and posted in appropriate places within the community. The community that is aware of the plans and prepared to follow them will react in a more sensible and predictable manner if an emergency arises. Knowledge of fire alarm systems, the use of emergency generators, availability of lifesaving techniques, and plans for evacuation and storm warnings will facilitate their ability to handle a serious situation properly.

Fire Alarms. Most local building codes now require some type of fire alarm system within a residential dwelling, regardless of the architectural design of the property. These systems may require direct monitoring by a service company on-site, or by the fire department. They may be activated either manually or automatically, and are often connected to an annunciator panel which indicates the location and type of alarm that has been triggered. Building fire and Building Owners and Code Administrators International, Inc. (BOCA) codes now require that elevators automatically return to the first-floor level where they are isolated in the event of a fire alarm. This prevents their use in an emergency by anyone other than the fire department. If full-time staff are available, they should be instructed to immediately contact the fire department to confirm the emergency in the building. The staff may further assist by showing the location of the alarm and stating the location of residents who may need assistance.

Emergency Generators. Most building codes now require emergency generator systems, or at a minimum, battery-operated lighting packs to allow ample time for vacating the premises in the event of a major system failure or a general power outage. Emergency generators are vital to life safety, and should, therefore, be under a regular maintenance program. This must include weekly testing that may be done automatically via a seven-day time clock mechanism. However, even automatic testing should be monitored by a designated person. Battery-activated emergency lighting should also be tested weekly.

Lifesaving Techniques. The usage of cardiopulmonary resuscitation (CPR) techniques has dramatically improved lifesaving for many. Everyone in the community should be somewhat prepared to save another person's life. Some associations sponsor courses in CPR. High-rise buildings may also provide portable oxygen systems as an added life-sustaining measure while awaiting the arrival of paramedics.

Evacuation Plans. Many municipalities now require buildings of four stories or more to have a detailed written plan of evacuation. This must be reviewed on a regular basis by the fire prevention bureau or fire marshall, as the case may be. The plan should include emergency exit locations; the proper fire department telephone numbers; the method of evacuation; and procedures for assisting the handicapped. A fire warden may be appointed to each floor to assure that all residents have evacuated the building in an emergency. Most fire departments will aid in the preparation of such a plan.

Building staff must be prepared to take proper steps in the event of a bomb threat. Upon receiving such a threat the local police and fire departments should be notified immediately. They will advise as to what steps should be taken. Residents must be kept calm during such situations. Therefore, a bomb threat evacuation plan should be devised. Full knowledge of all areas of a building where any explosive device could be hidden, such as crawlspaces, storage areas, boiler rooms, or stairwells, is required of the management agent, and certain board members.

Storm Warnings. Areas that are subject to tornados, hurricanes, or similar natural disasters require a community to have a plan to handle such emergencies, by assisting resident evacuation where necessary. This may be coordinated with the local police, weather authorities, or local Civil Defense Agency. Arrangements may be made for boarding over windows or securing areas where flooding or wind damage can occur.

9
MANAGING
THE HUMAN
ELEMENT

A condominium community may be made up of buildings, parking lots, swimming pools, and trees. But above all, it is made up of people. The men, women, and children who live in a condominium form a community bound by a common social and financial interest. They want to enjoy living in the community, and they want the value of their property to be protected. They are the people who create the condominium's social environment. They alone have the ability to make that environment harmonious or discordant.

Buildings, parking lots, and trees are easy to manage. There are certain accepted ways to paint a building or patch a hole in a road or trim a tree. People are quite a different matter. Each resident has a unique disposition and interacts in his or her own unique manner with neighbors. Most of the association's problems evolve from managing this human element.

Condominium associations manage the human element primarily by establishing a set of mutual promises. When a condominium purchaser signs the deed to the unit, he or she promises to observe the covenants of the association. The association, in turn, promises to provide the use of and maintain common areas and facilities. There also are implied, unstated mutual promises. For example, each unit owner agrees to keep noise at reasonable levels, especially in the later hours. In return there is the implied promise that other residents will do the same. Cooperation, the key to enjoyment of high-density living, thrives when the positive value of social interdependence is recognized.

The most important step in alleviating some of the human problems is to establish a strong internal network for informing all residents of what is going on within the community. People cannot be interested in association activities if they are unaware of them. They cannot be expected to abide by rules that they do not know about. Even with the best system of information exchange, however, there still will be complaints and disputes. The board of directors must establish procedures for handling these grievances and enforcing the rules and regulations.

Communications

Internal communication is the lifeline of any association. The board of directors is responsible for creating this lifeline. Through open channels of communication, the board can establish an environment of friendly cooperation. If it is successful in doing this, human problems will diminish. To the degree that it is unsuccessful, problems will increase.

The best way to foster a climate of common care and concern is through a continual exchange of ideas and issues. Everyone who is involved in the association—unit owners, board members, the management agent, maintenance and service contractors, and any others who serve the community—should be linked by this vital communications system. Because there cannot be direct interaction among all of these persons, the board of directors or, in some cases, the management agent, must act as the gatherer and transmitter of information.

Strong lines of communication should be established immediately, even as early as the prospective buyer's first visit to the property. Many ill feelings that evolve between unit owners and developers could have been prevented if the developer had told the buyer what the responsibilities as a unit owner would be. In the same manner, during the sale of a condominium unit, a representative of the developer should inform the prospective buyer of the declaration and rules and regulations of the association before the buyer signs a purchase contract.

The governing documents should be furnished by the association's board or management agent and become a part of the sales package that is presented to prospective purchasers. Too often a buyer of a condominium finds, after moving in, that an existing rule—such as no pets, mobile homes, or motorcycles—conflicts with his or her needs as a resident of that community. The only choices at this point are to change one's lifestyle to conform to the rule, to sell the unit, or to challenge the association's governing body regarding the legality of the ruling. In those cases where the latter course is taken, hard feelings are generated. If the buyer had been informed of all rules prior to purchasing the unit, the choice would have been easier and the later confrontation would have been avoided. *(See Appendix A for sample Consumer Checklist for Buying a Residential Condominium.)*

A problem common to many condominiums is that buyers do not really understand what a condominium is or what their obligations to it are until it is too late. Even those who have read the governing documents may not fully comprehend that a condominium association requires their participation. In addition, they do not realize that there are rules and regulations by which they must live and social courtesies that they must observe. The association may be able to do little about a poor communications link established by the developer. However, once the owner-controlled board of directors has been elected, it should assign top priority to establishing effective vehicles of communication. The process of creating an atmosphere of neighborliness and cooperation originates through this mechanism.

Personal contact is, without a doubt, the best form of communication. There is simply no substitute for it. In small condominiums with few residents, informal discussions may be the best way to relay information. Even in larger condominium developments where common areas form natural gathering places, groups will meet informally to talk about issues that are important to the association. Although personal communication may be preferred, its one large drawback is that some owners may be excluded from the communication if they are not readily available. The association must guard against this weakness in personal contact by making certain that every owner is informed of each issue through a well-organized formal program of communication.

How formal the communications program must be depends in large part on the size of the association. A small association, one that comprises 25 units or less, may need to prepare only those written notifications that are specifically required by the governing documents. Other information to be relayed to unit owners can probably be conveyed informally. For example, volunteers may go from door to door to pass along pertinent information, or they may telephone each unit owner. Boards of directors of larger associations must consider adopting more formal communications techniques. In fact, every association is in need of a tailor-made, effective program for spreading the word to all its members.

The welcoming committee

The condominium needs the support of all of its members. The best time to enlist that support is when someone new moves into the community. Moving into a new home can be a trying experience. A helping hand and a friendly face can make that experience less difficult. When a representative of the association personally welcomes the newcomer, the association gains support and forges a link in the chain of communications.

The association's communications program should emphasize the importance of greeting new members. The board of directors should form a committee to welcome new residents into the condominium community. One or more of its representatives should personally visit each new resident. Information on schools, churches, shopping areas, and other facilities should be furnished, along with a list of phone numbers for hospitals, fire, police, and a community representative. The committee should use this visit to explain the condominium association and make certain that new residents have been given all documents pertaining to the association.

The newsletter

Although personal communication is very effective, the association newsletter is a more practical and more productive means of communication. The newsletter should be delivered to resident owners, renters, and absentee owners. It is the logical means of telling the members of the association what is going on in the community, and can be a very positive force in the community. It can arouse interest, invite participation in association activities, and contribute greatly to the creation of a neighborly environment. It should be the vehicle for transmitting official information on board, committee, and membership meetings and public hearings. It may report on committee activities and policy changes and publish annual financial statements. Space may be allocated to a regular column written by the association's president or other officers.

Less official in nature, but certainly of interest to many residents, are classified advertisements and announcements of neighborhood events. In this way, the newsletter serves as a community bulletin board. To further the sense of neighborliness, the newsletter might contain a column of personal news about residents—births, marriages, and similar information—and the names and unit numbers of new members to the community.

The newsletter need not be a stale, boring information sheet. Newsletters that only communicate new rules or scold residents about past problems lose their effectiveness. The residents in these associations get tired of reading nothing but lists of "don'ts," and soon tend to lose enthusiasm or interest in such media. The newsletter can contain things such as feature stories on residents and their interesting jobs or hobbies. Illustrations can be used to give it vitality. The goal should be to publish the most attractive and informative newsletter possible within the confines of the budget. The most successful community newsletters are those that disseminate useful information or news along with reports on the actions of the board. It can also be used as a questionnaire to poll owners on their desires and opinions about certain issues that affect the association.

The association budget usually dictates what method of printing may be used. A newsletter made up of mimeographed sheets is likely to be least costly, and a local school may have equipment that it can lend to the association. Alternatively, a member of the association or the management agent may have an office copier available for board use. Large associations may publish a small tabloid newspaper. Even larger ones may be able to sell advertising space to local merchants, thereby making a comprehensive newspaper that is partially or totally self-supporting.

The board of dirctors must study the needs of its association to determine the most effective size and frequency of publication of the newsletter. While one association may require a one-page mimeographed sheet each week, another association may find its needs better met by a four-page monthly newsletter. It is of utmost importance that directors, owners, and the management agent or on-site manager have input in the newsletter if it is to be meaningful.

An editor is of equal importance. The editor's main role, in addition to normal editorial duties, is to encourage input from those involved in the operation of the association. Neither the management agent nor the board members should be given the responsibility of editing, as their views may not be totally representative of the owners. It is common in any size association for some homeowners to have talents that will enable them to serve as editors. Homeowners may be former high school, college, or neighborhood newsletter editors or staff members. There may be people with journalism backgrounds or free-lance writers. The editor, working with the board and management agent, determines the size of the newsletter. Newsletter editors must keep in mind that a newsletter that is too long may discourage readership, thereby defeating its purpose.

The newsletter, whatever its form, can help create the positive environment necessary to the success of any association. If it is written well and reflects favorably on the community, it can become the main cohesive force in the condominium, fostering a spirit of cooperation among members.

Meetings

Meetings provide the best forum for discussing association-related issues. There are three steps that the board should take to assure that meetings realize their greatest potential. The first step is notification; the second, discussion; the third, follow-up.

The governing documents usually require formal notification of membership meetings, but all other meetings of the board, committees, or other groups may be announced through the newsletter, community bulletin board, or by mail. Announcements of meetings should be presented so as to spark interest in them, making members eager to attend. A subject of great concern to many members that will be discussed at a meeting should be given special emphasis. If, for example, there is dispute over the location of playground equipment, the announcement of a meeting might state: "What is the best location of playground equipment? Discuss this subject at the board meeting, 7:30 P.M. Friday, September 17, in the recreational building." This meeting announcement should draw participation if the issue is really important.

Although a number of business items may be on a meeting's agenda, it is important that time be set aside for open discussion. The order of business can be maintained without stifling democratic participation. *(See Chapter 5 for a more complete discussion of agendas.)* Many associations have found it good practice to set aside 15 to 30 minutes, usually at the end of each board meeting, for open debate. Members should submit their debate topics to the board secretary prior to the meeting. The topics of discussion can be announced, encouraging those interested in a specific subject to attend. The board should consider limiting discussion to one or two subjects per meeting to assure that each issue receives adequate discussion. Although participation is encouraged, the board must make it clear that discussion will end at a certain time to properly control the meeting. Rules need to be established and followed to govern the open portion of meetings. The reasons for this are obvious: to limit discussion; to avoid debate, defense, or justification; to allow input to and from the board; and to limit time.

Follow-up of all meetings is essential to effective communication. Not everyone who is interested in the association will be able to attend all meetings. Therefore, a report on the meeting should be published in the newsletter or posted in highly visible locations following each session. Although a complete set of minutes need not be publicized, a synopsis of the business that transpired should be.

Special communications problems

Major issues that require special communications tactics will occasionally come before the board. In anticipation of these occasions, the board should develop careful plans for presenting and discussing highly controversial issues. The board must never attempt to evade an important issue or bypass other members of the association, as it will generate resentment or, worse, mistrust.

One such sensitive issue is the need to increase assessments. Once the board has agreed that a decision must be made on this issue, it may notify the membership that a budget discussion will take place. The governing documents of some condominiums provide that assessments can be changed only with the agreement of a certain percentage of unit owners. Therefore, this subject might best be brought up at the annual membership meeting, which residents are more likely to attend. To streamline discussion and decision making, notice of the meeting should be given far enough in advance to give members adequate time to consider the issue. It is also advisable to outline the topics on the notice.

A board's strategy should be to inform residents at regular intervals throughout the year about the association's financial standing. Members who understand how assessments are set will be less likely to object when the board recommends an increase if they have had an ongoing dialogue on financial matters.

One way to improve communications on financial issues is to present information creatively. For example, instead of presenting residents with a set of technical data that may never be read or understood, the board should consider presenting the breakdown of the assessment in terms of a pie diagram, showing how large a slice of the whole pie is allocated to utilities, how much to insurance, and so on. A careful and meaningful presentation of pertinent facts is essential to effective communication. *(See Appendix A for sample Pie Diagram Assessment Presentation.)*

The same kind of strategy should be adapted to other special issues facing the board. Keeping the lines of communication open will decrease the potential for surprise and hostile reaction when issues are put before the membership.

The overall communications plan

The board of directors should use any and all methods of communication that are appropriate for the condominium community. It should not overlook any possible channel of communication, and it should survey every possible means for getting news of the association to its members. The conventional bulletin board in the laundry room, the lobby, or other public place should be considered as a way to relay information. An association that employs parking attendants in its garage may have them pass out printed notices, while a smaller association may use volunteers, or "block captains," to distribute news bulletins door to door. Board members should exercise the effectiveness of personal contact when they have an opportunity to discuss association activities with other residents on a one-to-one basis.

In setting up the communications program, the board should consider appointing one person to coordinate all forms of communications to assure that the program is properly executed. There are two main ways in which the program may be undermined when central coordination is poor or entirely lacking: everyone believes someone else has done a job, or several persons takes on the same job. The first situation may result in no information being relayed, the second in costly duplicated efforts that reflect poorly on the board. The communications coordinator should develop a schedule of activities and decide how they should be carried out. The coordinator should work closely with the newsletter committee to make sure information is relayed promptly and accurately to association members.

Certain communications responsibilities may be assigned to the management agent or on-site manager, such as responsibility for notifying members of meetings, distributing copies of the annual budget, or printing and distributing the newsletter. Some management firms use computer billing mailout or Addressograph systems which may be used to mail monthly meeting notices and information bulletins if costs are reasonable.

The importance of an open and well-planned communications program cannot be overemphasized. The board of directors cannot afford to lock itself in a room, make all decisions behind closed doors, and fail to inform other residents of its decisions. At a very minimum, minutes of the board meetings and periodic financial reports should be made available at a central point or points in the association complex for review by the unit owners. The board demonstrates through this that it cares about the residents, is hiding nothing, and is acting to the best of its ability for the mutual benefit of all. No matter how good the board's intentions, leaders who do not inform unit owners of plans will be unsuccessful. Board decisions affect everyone who lives in the community. Therefore, it has a responsibility to keep residents informed of developments. The condominium association serves as a form of government to the condominium. Like any government, if it is to be trusted, its administrative body must be accessible, open to suggestions, and candid about its activities.

Complaints

No matter how good a job the board is doing and how well it is communicating with other residents, complaints about the maintenance and services provided by the association are inevitable. Some complaints may be petty, while others will be legitimate. Human relations programs are incomplete unless they provide a means to air grievances.

The board of directors should attempt to avoid complaints by recognizing potential problem areas and correcting them before a complaint results. All problems cannot be anticipated or easily resolved. To assure association members of a way to bring problems to the attention of the board, grievance forms indicating the name of the unit owner, unit number, and nature of the complaint should be made available to all residents. *(See Appendix A for sample Grievance Form.)*

Complaints related to the association's management of common areas or provision of services should be directed to the appropriate board liaison or committee chair. For example, a complaint about the frequency of garbage pickups, when the association provides this service, should go to the chair of the maintenance committee. If a management agent is employed, the complaint may be directed to the management agent for action or forwarding to the board. A management agent will usually have the necessary experience to resolve problems, but the agent should not be used as a scapegoat. Similarly, the management agent should not give the board excuses for failure to resolve a problem.

After all facts have been gathered, the person assigned to handle a complaint should try to resolve it personally. A committee chair may try to correct it before referring the complaint to the committee. If the attempted correction is unsuccessful, the committee should then try to resolve the matter. If this fails, the committee should make appropriate recommendations to the board of directors, which is ultimately responsible for problem solving. If the same complaint recurs frequently, the appropriate committee and/or the board should study it carefully for a long-term remedy, perhaps adopting new house rules. *(See Appendix A for sample Condominium Association Complaint Log.)*

No matter how trivial a complaint may seem to the directors, committee, or management agent, it must never be ignored. Small problems often grow into large ones if they are not handled promptly. As an act of courtesy, the person who files a complaint should be given an acknowledgement of receipt of the grievance and be kept informed of any action taken on it. Actions taken to resolve complaints about the association's operation should be publicized. This is critical when a resolution results in the adoption of new rules.

The board of directors may find it helpful to form a community relations committee to act as liaison between complaining residents and the board. The responsibility for establishing grievance procedures may be assigned to this committee, and it should be sure that the procedures conform to state law and/or the condominium's governing documents.

Rules, Regulations, and Restrictions

Constructing many dwelling units on relatively small areas of land allows a condominium to fill a vital economic need. The obvious financial benefit, however, is accompanied by certain social disadvantages derived from people living quite close together. As residential density increases, individual complaints will increase—fortunately not in direct proportion. Not everyone has the temperament suitable to condominium living since many persons cannot tolerate living in close quarters. Some are unwilling to abide by the rules and regulations required if condominium living is to be pleasant. Unfortunately, there are always a few persons living in every condominium community who do not care about others in the association. They may make loud, unnecessary noises after permitted hours. They may fail to put garbage cans in their proper location. They may park in unauthorized areas. Such behavior cannot be allowed to continue. If house rules and regulations are reasonable and do not infringe on individual rights and freedoms, they must be respected and properly enforced. By purchasing a condominium unit, the buyer has agreed to respect and adhere to the rules and regulations of the association. Hence, an uncooperative unit owner should not be allowed to disrupt the community by ignoring the rules and regulations established by the association.

It is critical that the board not adopt rules that are arbitrary or capricious. The management agent also shares a responsibility to ensure that this does not occur. Rules and regulations should be formulated with the understanding that they must enhance condominium living and be of mutual benefit to all owners and residents.

Architectural controls

Although all condominium owners have a right to the exclusive use of their units, they do not have the right to make changes to the exterior that affect the outward appearance of the condominium community. Architectural controls are enacted for the benefit of the individual owners and the community as a whole. These controls are necessary to protect the integrity of the condominium community and, in turn, protect the property value of each unit. It is easy to see that an association without such controls—where an owner is free to change colors, use different styles of doors, to make additions to patios and balconies, etc.—could soon become a hodgepodge of design. Its appeal to the public would be greatly diminished, and the market value of the units would be reduced. Many problems will arise if unit owners fail to understand the need for such controls and do not cooperate by adhering to them.

Most governing documents require the establishment of an architectural control committee to review all proposed architectural changes and give guidelines as to how the committee should function. In most cases the board remains ultimately responsible for the final decision on architectural changes, although the committee is given the power to recommend approval or rejection of proposed changes. In some cases the committee may have full power of approval or rejection.

The first step in the approval process should be to require each unit owner who wishes to modify the exterior of a unit to make formal application to the committee. Associations should provide standard architectural control applications and review forms for unit owners who request approval for changes. The forms should provide space to write a complete description of the change being considered. When applicable, the unit owner should be requested to include a sample of paint color, construction plans, drawings, or any other specifications that describe the change more fully. *(See Appendix A for sample Architectural Improve-*

ment Application and Review Form.) The governing documents usually require that the owner receive a formal response to such a request within a specified number of days, usually 30 to 90 days. If no response is made within that specified time, the change is approved automatically. Any change approved by such default on the part of the board or committee could result in serious morale and legal problems.

To accelerate the review process and assure consistent decisions, the committee should adopt basic architectural standards. These standards may relate to such things as approved colors, fences, patios, gardens, exterior patio covers, and porch railings. In other words, anything done by an owner to a unit that can be seen from outside the unit. In most cases, the governing documents will provide guidelines for the architectural committee to use in adopting standards. However, the committee may be assigned the task of developing a more comprehensive set of specifications that are compatible with the overall theme of the community. Some associations also provide a list of unapproved modifications submitted in the past.

Once architectural standards have been adopted, the review process is systematic. Standards are especially important because they ensure that all unit owners will be treated equally. A well-written set of standards should tell unit owners which changes probably will be approved by the architectural control review committee and which probably will not be. Again, owner participation should be solicited when standards are developed to encourage acceptance of the standards. *(See Appendix A for sample Guidelines for the Architectural Control Committee.)*

On occasion, approval of an application may carry with it the requirement that the owner requesting the change be responsible for any increased maintenance due to that change. One example might be an owner who wishes to add a skylight in his or her unit through a common area roof. The board might approve this change, making the owner or any successor responsible for the repair of any leaks in that section of roof. The agreement should be recorded so it can be enforced in the future.

Care must also be taken by the architectural committee

or board when approving landscape changes. Existing sprinkler systems, overall drainage patterns, access by landscaping crews, and ongoing maintenance should be considered.

Problems in enforcing architectural controls are likely to arise. The board may be plagued with such infractions as doors painted in unapproved colors or patios that extend into common areas. Although requests for all exterior changes should be submitted to the architectural control committee, some unit owners may bypass this requirement. To strengthen the authority of the architectural control committee, some associations keep a log of violations and issue strong warnings that legal action will be brought against persons who violate design regulations and refuse to take appropriate steps to remedy them. *(See Appendix A for sample Architectural Control and Use Violation Log.)* Of course, any enforcement measures must be within the framework of both state and local law and the governing documents.

Announcing rules and controls

The job of any board of directors does not end simply with the adoption of a new rule. The rule must be publicized. Having rules that have not been properly announced is no better than having no rules at all, and compliance cannot be expected or legally enforced.

Various methods of posting new rules, regulations, and controls have been found to be successful in various condominium associations. Some associations publish them in the association newsletter. Others send a copy or new rules to each unit owner. Others merely post them on association bulletin boards. Some associations have a handbook of rules and regulations. Others put the necessary information in a letter. Each method works. The important point is that each association must publicize rule changes.

Whenever an association makes changes in its restrictions, it should send a complete copy of the revised rules and regulations or architectural controls to each member. The board may adopt this as a routine policy to be done once a year if the rules change frequently. Publishing rules and regulations in a small, easy-to-use handbook increases the chances that they will be read and kept. A system to inform new owners of all rules, regulations, and restrictions must also be established. As mentioned earlier, this may be done through a welcoming committee, the management agent, or the board.

Customarily, when a unit is being sold the title company or lender must request a resale certificate from the association that indicates status fees on the selling unit. When this request is filled by the management agent or board, a copy of the rules and regulations should be included in the packet, which is usually provided at the time of settlement, and given to the new owners.

In addition to the house rules, regulations, and restrictions, some associations adopt additional sets of rules for the use of particular facilities. Such rules should be posted at the facility itself. As an example, swimming pool rules should be displayed in a prominent place in the pool area. The bulletin board on which such rules are posted should be attractive and eye catching. Rules must be written simply to avoid unnecessary misunderstanding.

Enforcing rules and controls

Most governing documents offer limited guidelines on rules enforcement, except for loss of certain privileges such as voting rights, use of recreation facilities, or reduction of services. Guidelines for enforcement and administration of disciplinary action against violators should be comprehensively developed by the board and either a covenants committee or a rules committee. Solving the problem of a broken rule or regulation may be approached in several ways.

The first step should be to have someone discuss it informally with the violator—preferably the management agent, if one is available. Having the management agent be the objective party hired to administer the rules is a good alternative, and it is less personal than having a board member, who lives in the area, do it. In the absence of a management agent, or in certain circumstances even with one available, a board or committee member may be asked to discuss the matter with the offender. In any event, an informal discussion may permit the matter to be disposed of quickly and quietly.

If the first approach does not work, the board should schedule a hearing with the violator present to hear the dispute. The hearing allows the accused person an opportunity to defend his or her actions. It should take place before the covenants or rules committee, with the infractions clearly defined for all who are present. Once the hearing has been completed, the committee should make its recommendations to the board, which then will take any necessary action. It is critical that in any such procedure the principle of due process of law and fairness to the offender be always exercised.

Another method of enforcing regulations is via the lender, or mortgagee if the unit is mortgaged. Deeds of trust—the document giving the lender the right to foreclose in the event of certain happenings—may provide that notice is to be given to the lender if the borrower/owner violates any of the rules or covenants of the association. This notice of violation to the lender, along with the lender's ability to take back the unit, may result in the offender's taking steps to correct the problem.

Some documents provide for imposing monetary penalties on persons found guilty of breaking the covenants. If the violator refuses to pay the penalty, some jurisdictions authorize a board to sue to collect it. Keep in mind, though, that a suit is worthwhile only if the penalty is reasonable and has been imposed with due process. The wisdom of selecting this route is determined by the seriousness of the violation and the monetary significance of the fine.

As a last resort to collect the fine, the penalty can be assessed against the unit. Usually, if it remains unpaid, the same carrying charges will be added to it as are added to other unpaid assessments. If the penalty remains unpaid at a time when the unit is offered for resale, the penalty can serve as a lien. Clear title cannot be passed to the new owner until satisfaction of the lien.

The various court rulings on resident violations in condominium associations are too numerous to go into in this text. However, a few rules of thumb in adopting association rules and regulations may help, should a dispute end up in court.

Historically the courts have applied the rule of reasonableness in their decisions. When rules are based upon fairness and reasonableness and when their enforcement is to the benefit of *all* residents, rather than arbitrary rulings made for the benefit of a few, their enforcement is usually upheld in the courts.

Documents filed by the developer will contain numerous restrictions. The board of directors, however, has authority to make house rules and regulations governing the day-to-day operation of the condominium. When residents are given a chance to be involved in establishing these rules, a more cooperative and compliant attitude evolves. This involvement of others may strengthen the association's case in a court of law. Bringing residents into the rule-making process encourages their abiding by the rules.

Good rules have two major characteristics: reasonability and enforceability. Rules should be reasonable so as not to infringe unfairly upon personal freedom. Rules should be practical to be enforceable. A rule requiring absolute silence between certain hours probably exceeds the bounds of reason and is unenforceable. On the other hand, rules that require dog owners to walk their pets in restricted areas or drivers to park in prescribed locations are regarded as both reasonable and enforceable. *(See Appendix A for sample House Rules and Regulations.)*

There is some legal question as to which restrictive documents are more legally binding. The courts tend to rely more heavily upon restrictions written into the declaration and bylaws than on house rules and regulations. This is based upon the fact that the first two documents are accepted by all unit owners upon purchase settlement, while house rules and regulations may have been adopted subsequent to such settlement, and do not necessarily reflect a consensus of owners. For this reason the declaration and bylaws should be amended to include house rules and regulations if they were not part of the original documents.

Enforcing the rules and regulations may be especially

difficult when a high percentage of units are rented by absentee owners. Tenants, historically, have not been interested in association activities and are therefore more likely to ignore the rules than resident owners. The association should handle renters' complaints and violations through their respective landlords. In developments where there are a large number of renters, the association may wish to form a renter's committee. This committee may serve to involve tenants in association functions, make them feel more a part of the association, and demonstrate board concern for their affairs. Tenants who are involved are more likely to live within the rules, regulations, and restrictions of the association. An additional benefit is that their absentee landlords will tend to have fewer problems with them as tenants.

No matter how simple or elaborate the procedure for handling rules violations, the covenants must be enforced. They must be enforced from the very beginning, and in a uniform, consistent and nondiscriminatory matter. If one unit owner breaks a rule and is not reprimanded, another is sure to follow suit. A precedent for ignoring rules and violators must never be set, as there would soon be chaos. The inevitable result is a decrease in the value of the property, a diminished quality of lifestyle, and the onset of a negative environment. Failure to enforce a rule over a long period of time may prevent the board from legally enforcing that particular rule.

10
ESTABLISHING
SOUND FISCAL
POLICIES

The governing documents of a condominium association charge the board of directors with numerous responsibilities to preserve and maintain the development's common areas and administer the overall operation of the association. Obviously, it needs money to fulfill these obligations, and this money must come from the unit owners through assessments. Because of its fiduciary responsibilities, the board must operate according to sound fiscal policies and procedures.

Virtually all condominium documents require that the board elect a treasurer to be responsible for financial and accounting records. In a small association the treasurer may do the actual bookkeeping, but this is not recommended. More often these duties are performed by a professional accountant or a management agent, who has the experience, staff, and systems to provide these services competently and efficiently. The board also may appoint a budget and finance committee to work with the treasurer, management agent, or accountant, and to keep abreast of the association's financial operations.

Even if the services of an outside professional are retained, the board of directors is ultimately responsible for all custodial and fiduciary duties. Therefore, even though the board members may not personally prepare the budget, keep the records, or prepare the assessment bills, they must understand the basic principles of record keeping, accounting, and budgeting. The board members are not expected to become accountants, but they should have a rudimentary understanding of the fundamentals of financial reporting. The benefits of this knowledge far exceed the burdens of obtaining it. Understanding accounting principles and reasons for internal controls along with an ability to analyze financial statements will assist board members in the management of the association's affairs.

Each condominium association is unique in size, resources, staff, and kinds of common areas. The following discussion of common financial procedures is presented with this fact in mind. The condominium's unique characteristic must be taken into consideration when adopting the following concepts to the association's specific needs. Financial policies should be molded to fit those needs, and the board must recognize both the uniqueness of its association and the importance of protecting the association's capital resources.

The Budgetary Process

A *budget* is a summary of estimated expenditures and income for a given period of time, usually one year. Although a budget typically extends through one fiscal year, it is an ongoing entity. A first unit owner-controlled board of directors will have a budget—usually prepared by the developer —from which to work. If a management agent is employed by the association, the agent probably will be responsible for recommending a budget to the board. Even though the board may not personally prepare the budget, it must know how it was developed. If the board merely approves the management agent's budget and sends it to the membership for a vote without analyzing every aspect of it, the board, in effect, is permitting the management agent to decide how the association is to spend its money.

The budget reflects the needs and desires of the unit owners in regard to common areas, common services, and the association's ability to adequately finance these needs and desires. Because the principal source of association income is derived from unit owner assessments, the budget sets the common expense assessments for the year. Since assessments are a direct result of projected common expenses, and are thereby the revenue to meet these expenses, understanding of the revenue section of an association's budget is fairly clear cut. The expense side of the budget represents that portion where considerable time and budgetary experience are required. The assistance of a management agent who has managed condominiums in the past and has actual experience on which to base budget estimates can be invaluable. Preparing an accurate budget is a difficult job, especially for those unfamiliar with the task. It is not uncommon even for self-managed associations to employ a management agent to assist in the preparation of an operating budget.

Scheduling budget preparation

The fact that a condominium association's budget reflects many variables requires that adequate time be allocated for its preparation. A budget that is hurriedly drafted and fails to properly estimate and match expenses with income can leave an association financially vulnerable. A timetable should be established for preparing the budget, usually no more than four months. Within this time frame a well-thought-out budget for the coming fiscal year can be adequately planned and adopted.

The governing documents usually require the casting of a new budget reasonably in advance of the end of the current fiscal or calendar year; that is, 30 to 60 days prior to the beginning of the new fiscal or calendar year. These documents may also require that association owners be given advanced notice of the proposed budget so they have time to comment on it prior to its fiscal approval. Other documents require association approval of the proposed budget before it can be passed. Both of these methods are cumbersome and time consuming. The simplest method for final budget approval is one in which a board of directors has the power and responsibility for budget adoption. Regardless of the approval process required by the governing documents, advanced planning and adherence to a realistic schedule is imperative.

The calendar for preparing the budget must be planned according to the fiscal year under which the association operates. The governing documents may prescribe the fiscal year period, with many requiring that the fiscal year run concurrent with the calendar year, January 1 through December 31. Others begin the fiscal year at the date on which transfer of control occurs. Still other documents give the board of directors discretion to determine the fiscal year.

Since the money to operate the association comes from the unit owners, these owners should be given a chance to voice their opinions about how it is spent. The treasurer, usually with the assistance of an accountant, budget committee, and/or a management agent, may be responsible for drafting the budget. Participation of all association members should be sought. The best method for soliciting input is through a committee, especially the budget and finance committee. An open committee hearing may be advisable— those who are interested will attend. If a management agent is responsible for drafting a proposed budget, these recommendations should be submitted after such a hearing has been held. Where acceptance or rejection of a budget hinges on approval by the association at large (which may be very cumbersome and counterproductive), participants must be given an opportunity for input.

The budget calendar should provide ample time in which to complete all of the steps necessary before the budget can officially take effect. This must include adequate time to coordinate all committee and individual responses, submit the recommended budget to the board of directors, incorporate revisions made by the board, submit the final working budget to the membership, and print and distribute the approved budget to all unit owners. *(See Appendix A for sample Budget Preparation Calendar.)*

Estimating expenses

Budgeting is in essence economic guesswork, but the guesswork must be based on historical or factual data. The challenge is to secure enough information by which to reasonably calculate costs. The persons responsible for preparing the budget should know the governing documents, what common areas the association is responsible for repairing and maintaining, and what, if any, additional or unusual maintenance or improvements are required.

An imperative early step is to carefully examine all past invoices, audits, contracts, and financial records, especially those related to the previous year's financial performance. This review provides a basis for estimating expenses. Of course, changes will occur in expenses from year to year; however, fixed rate contracts which are binding throughout the coming fiscal year can be projected accurately. If a service contract expires before the end of the fiscal year, any increase in the cost of that service must be considered in order to adequately forecast new contractual expenses. Any possible or proposed price increases should be discussed with contractors, vendors, and suppliers prior to budget preparation.

Although the previous year's records may provide a relatively accurate account of utility costs, utility rates are also subject to change. Therefore, utility companies should be contacted to determine what rate increases are anticipated in the coming year's actual expenses. In short, preparing a budget requires looking into the future and anticipating all possible changes in expenditures.

Condominium associations throughout the country experience similar problems in establishing expenditures with inadequate information. Although each association is somewhat unique and slightly different from another, an exchange of financial experience can be valuable. A comparative summary of the operating expenses of one association may be informative to a similar association that is preparing its first budget. Publications of the property management industry are designed to encourage and facilitate this kind of information exchange. One that may be helpful is the *Expense Analysis: Condominiums, Cooperatives, & Planned Unit Developments,* published annually by the Institute of Real Estate Management (IREM).

Itemizing expenses

A budget may classify items of expense in one of two ways: by *line item* classification or by *program* classification. A line item budget lists expenses by type (for example, salaries, office supplies, insurance, taxes). A program budget lists expenses according to the program or activity for which they will be disbursed (for example, payroll, administration, maintenance, operations, reserves). A program budget may be somewhat more difficult than a line item budget to prepare because some costs, such as staff salaries, must be distributed, that is, broken down and allocated to several programs or functions. To some the program budget is preferable because it may more accurately identify actual costs of specific services, and the advantage of this may far outweigh the additional work required to prepare it. While this budget form has its own advantages, a combination of the two where line items are subordinated to a major account (program) heading often meets the needs of the association.

Since the expense requirements of different condominium associations vary, the degree of detail required in listing expenses will also vary. The treasurer and/or management agent should tailor an expense format to the association's particular needs, establishing expense categories based on those needs. A master list of all suitable account categories will be prepared allowing the management agent or treasurer to establish the appropriate line items for the condominium budget. These will then also be used in preparing the monthly statements and audited financial statements. Once established, these financial categories should be used consistently in all of the association's financial records. *(See Appendix A for sample Budget Worksheet.)*

Although there is no one "right" way to list expenses, IREM has developed a set of program expense categories that are used by real estate managers in filing reports for IREM's Experience Exchange research program. These categories are administrative expenses, operating expenses, repair and maintenance expenses, fixed expenses, and reserves. (These are defined and explained more fully in the following pages.)

While neither inclusive nor exclusive, these categories may offer an association reference points for use in preparing a budget. They may be used on the budget worksheet without change or adapted to fit the association's unique requirements. The names of categories are less important than their being used properly and consistently.

Payroll Expenses. Although smaller associations may depend primarily on volunteer efforts to administer the association, larger associations probably will require staff to handle details. *Personnel salaries* must be accounted for in the budget and classified as payroll expenses or as administrative expenses. Payroll expenses should include current wages, vacation and sick pay, holiday pay, group medical benefits, and anticipated wage increases. As employee benefits become increasingly recognized as part of employee retention, these benefits (social security taxes, unemployment compensation, insurance, and pension benefits) are best separately itemized under *employee benefits and payroll taxes.* These supplementary personnel costs could be as much as 12 to 20 percent of the actual salaries.

Administrative Expenses. Expenses attributable to management of the affairs of the condominium association should be classified as administrative expenses.

Every association will have *office expenses,* including those that use volunteers to perform administrative activities in their homes. Office expenses may include such things as postage, supplies, printing, equipment rental, photocopying, and newsletter preparation. Telephone expenses that are directly attributable to the management of the association, such as a telephone for association business, may be paid as an administrative expense. If an association has a telephone switchboard for unit owners the costs are attributable to operating expenses.

If the condominium is managed by a management firm or agent, the *management fee* is usually considered as administrative expense. On-site managers' salaries may be an administrative expense or a payroll expense.

The association may need the services of other professionals. *Legal expenses,* including regular and special fees paid by the association for an attorney's services, typically are categorized as administrative expenses. An attorney may be retained to provide ongoing legal advice to the board of directors in matters ranging from service contract negotiations to the adoption of rules and regulations. In addition, legal counsel may be needed if the association has to file liens to collect delinquent assessments from unit owners. Most governing documents require an audit of the association's financial records at least annually, and the cost of hiring the accountant to perform this service is considered an administrative expense.

A *miscellaneous* account classification can cover other items of administrative expense, such as room rent for an annual meeting, hiring a consultant, or sending board members to educational seminars on condominium management. However, wherever possible the use of the miscellaneous expense category should be minimized, placing such expenditures into more specific accounting categories such as *educational expense,* and *dues and subscriptions.*

Operating Expenses. The overall operation of a community requires providing certain services, including utilities, to the common areas and, in some projects, to the individual units. Regular or cyclical services are often performed on a contractual basis, and these expenses can be budgeted with a fair degree of accuracy. Irregular operating expenses may be more difficult to estimate.

Costs relating directly to the upkeep of an *elevator* are operating expenses. Where the payroll is distributed by job function, elevator operators' wages may be allocated to elevator expense.

The cost of *heating fuel* may represent a large portion of the overall operating expenses budget, especially in colder climates. Depending on the mechanical plant of the building, fuel may represent the cost of heating common areas only or it may include the cost of heating the entire structure, including the individual units.

The total cost of all *electricity* used in the common areas —including that used to operate equipment and facilities— is an operating expense. The units themselves usually have individual meters so the unit residents pay the cost of their own electricity.

All *water and sewage* costs for the condominium must be considered when the budget is planned. The cost of *gas* used to heat water or boilers is another utility expense in many associations. Gas used for heating the building should be budgeted as a heating fuel.

As crime against property and persons increases, *security* measures ranging from telephone entry systems to door attendants and on-site security personnel represent an expense of growing magnitude. This expense should be reflected as a separate item. Some condominium associations consider it appropriate to add a security classification as a separate budget item to indicate to unit owners how much this costs on an annual basis.

Exterminating services may be a regular monthly expense or a special expenditure for nonrecurring problems. Exterminating expenses should include both the associated wages and the cost of exterminating supplies. If the work is done under contract, the contract price should be used in preparing the budget.

Rubbish removal costs should include not only the cost of actual trash removal, but also expenses related to incineration, trash bags used in compactors, trash cans, dumpsters, and special hauls.

Window washing done under contract should be listed as an operating expense. If the on-site staff is responsible for cleaning windows, window washing should be considered a repair and maintenance expense.

Repair and Maintenance Expenses. A primary responsibility of a board of directors is to preserve the physical environment of the condominium. It is therefore imperative that expenses for repair and maintenance be estimated carefully. Dividing each repair and maintenance expense category into payroll, material, and/or contract costs may be desirable. For example, if money is budgeted for painting the exterior of a building by the association staff, the estimated cost of surface preparation, paint, and brushes may be budgeted under a materials category, and the cost of the labor under salaries. If the work is contracted for and the vendor provides paint as well as labor, the total contractor's cost would be listed under the contract category.

Grounds and paved area maintenance may relate to gardening, landscaping, sidewalk upkeep, street sweeping, snow removal, sprinkler maintenance, and light maintenance. These jobs may be done by employees of the association or by contractors. Incidental supplies used in performing such maintenance also must be budgeted for.

All payroll costs and supplies used to perform routine policing and housekeeping jobs may be listed as *custodial expense* items, while *general maintenance* expenses can include the cost of minor repairs which may occur on a continuing basis. General maintenance may include such things as the replacement of light bulbs, repair of holes in roofs, and fence mending. Costs that relate directly to running and maintaining *heating, ventilation, and air conditioning* systems must also be budgeted. Frequently overlooked are building circulating fans and pumps, which represent high capital costs, and proper regular maintenance of these are vital to the successful operation of the building. If not done by in-house maintenance personnel, contractors are usually available for such service.

Painting interior and exterior common areas, along with costs of plastering, stucco repair, and other related work, also should be considered when preparing a budget.

Expenses for maintaining and repairing all *recreational amenities*, including swimming pools, tennis courts, golf courses, recreational buildings, and so on, must be anticipated. These expenses should include the costs of supplies and equipment, payroll, and contracted services.

With energy costs escalating at such a rapid rate, *energy savings* systems are now being installed in buildings. These systems vary of course, depending upon the geographic location of the property, type of building, and the metering of the utilities. Master-metered properties are more adaptable to energy savings systems, and many such properties have already installed these systems. Some require maintenance; others, such as solar heating, require little or no maintenance. Where energy savings systems requiring specific maintenance have been installed, such maintenance costs must be included in the budget.

Fixed Expenses. Although fixed expenses may not

remain as stable as their name implies and may change from year to year, they usually remain relatively constant and can be anticipated with reasonable accuracy.

Any local and state *real estate taxes* paid through the condominium association must be planned for in the budget. If taxes are segregated and allocated directly to the individual units, they are not included in the budget. The association may have to pay *other taxes*, such as personal property taxes on furnishings and equipment owned by the association, franchise taxes, licenses and permit fees, or other taxes necessary to the operation of the condominium.

Although sometimes considered an administrative expense, *insurance* is often classified as a fixed expense. Insurance should be budgeted to include all costs of fire, liability, compensation, theft, boiler explosion, and any other appropriate insurance coverage for the building structure and the common areas. Blanket fidelity bonds and directors' and officers' liability coverage must also be included. If the condominium documents provide for insurance appraisals, it is necessary to include this cost when casting a budget. Another item which is sometimes overlooked is the deductible paid per occurrence. Where the deductible is a large amount, provision should be allowed for this in the budget. The association policy may be written on a multiyear basis at a fixed premium, in which case the total premium should be prorated for budget purposes. Serious effort must be given to estimating the current replacement cost of the building, mechanical equipment, appurtenant facilities, and landscaping.

If the association lacks certain amenities, it may rent them. In this case annual fees paid for the *leasing* of certain facilities must be contained in the budget. Where the municipal or state tax authorities levy real or personal property taxes on these leased facilities, and such taxes are passed on to the association, this expense is part of the budget.

In certain localities, an association pays *ground rent* for the right to occupy the land on which the condominium development rests. If the association is assigned the ground rent right, this rent must be budgeted as a common expense. In other areas ground rent for the individual unit is a separate contractural agreement between the unit owner (the lessee) and the ground owner (the lessor). In this case the ground rent is not an association obligation and is not to be included in the budget-making process.

Reserves. Most governing documents require the board of directors to maintain reasonable levels of reserves for operations, replacements, and emergencies. Monies set aside for this purpose are to be treated in the budget as an expense, since reserves are paid for through unit owner assessments.

Establishing reserves

Eventually every property will need major repairs and replacements. Preserving and protecting common areas requires that a condominium association be prepared for both expected and emergency repairs or replacements. Establishing adequate reserves will help to assure unit owners that they may not encounter large special assessments which they are unable to pay. More and more boards of directors are establishing appropriate reserves for working capital, operations, contingencies, and replacements by reassessing the cost to replace and the useful life on an annual or semi-annual basis.

Replacement Reserves. Although most boards recognize the need to establish reserves for replacement expenditures (sometimes referred to as capital reserves), determining what amount should be set aside can present difficulties. Some jurisdictions require that a mandatory percentage amount of the total annual assessment collection be held in escrow in a reserve fund for replacement or repair of large equipment and building items. This method rarely proves successful and is considered an inadequate means of arriving at a replacement reserve amount, which is more accurately arrived at through the whole life/remaining life formula. *(See Appendix A for sample Replacement Reserves Worksheet.)*

In the life formula, the first step is to list all major component items for which the association is responsible. Then determine how long these capital items, such as the carpeting, furniture in the lobby, the central heating unit, or emergency generators, can be expected to last (live). Major decorating requirements—primarily, the painting of interior and exterior common areas—should be itemized if they qualify as replacement, and not regular maintenance expenditures. (Contractors, engineers, manufacturers, the management agent, and the developer or an appraiser may be able to help estimate reserve life.)

Once the base life is established, the remaining useful life of each of these items is determined. The remaining useful life is determined by the following formula:

$$\text{Whole life of equipment} - \text{Number of years in use} = \text{Remaining useful life}$$

The remaining life is then factored on the then new replacement cost of the equipment. The most fiscally sound approach to determining cost is to establish a new replacement cost annually or semiannually, so that inflation and cost escalations are taken into consideration.

The third step is then to divide replacement or repair costs (as adjusted) by the remaining years of useful life. The result tells the board how much should be set aside in reserve each year, by equipment identification, to meet repair or replacement costs when they are incurred.

Take as an example a condominium that has a $142,000 heating and air conditioning unit that has a life expectancy in year 13. To be prepared to replace the unit in year 13, $11,833.33 ($142,000 ÷ 12 years) should be placed in reserve each year. Further, if the replacement cost is reevaluated to $160,000 in year 4 of the 12 year life, then in year 5 the reserve should be:

$11,833.33 × 4 years = $47,333.32 replacement reserve accumulated
$160,000 − $47,333.32 = $112,666.68 to be accumulated in 8 years
$112,666.68 ÷ 8 years = $14,083.34 to be reserved in fiscal year 5.

By using this method, inflation, increased cost, and most other factors are considered in establishing the new reserve level. An engineer or appraiser is most useful in helping to establish the new costs.

Another example is lobby carpeting that has an expected life of 7 years with an original cost of $18 per square yard. The lobby is 7 yards wide and 8 yards long, requiring 56 square yards of carpeting at a cost of $1,008 (56 yards × $18 per yard). The first year reserve requirement for this time therefore would be $144 ($1,008 ÷ 7 years). In year 3 a reassessment of the reserve is done. It will still require 56 yards of carpet but the cost now will be $22.50 per yard. The computation would be:

$144 × 2 years of accumulation = $288
56 yards of carpet × $22.50 = $1,260 cost to replace
$1.260 ÷ 5 years remaining useful life = $252 to reserve for carpet in year 3

It is important to note that this is simply an example. For practical purposes most reserve items usually have a minimum first-time or one-time cost of $5,000 and a minimum life of 3 years. Otherwise, the item is simply regarded as routine maintenance.

Replacement reserves need not anticipate the cost of every item that eventually may need to be replaced. Certain items whose replacement costs would be extremely high, such as replacement of an elevator in a high-rise condominium, would be a major expense. Assuming that the elevator has a useful life equal to the building it serves, and that it will undergo periodic improvement such as new panels or trim, an elevator need not be totally reserved for. Only the capital planned improvements estimated to be necessary should be reserved for. (Also, full-service maintenance contracts of major components of equipment will prolong useful life.) Because periodic improvements will be made and proper service will be given, reserves are established for major equipment that should have a useful life of five years or more.

Replacement items should be listed separately on the replacement reserves worksheet to indicate how much will be needed for painting; roofing; streets and driveways; swimming pools and tennis courts; furnishings and equipment;

and other items. Most governing documents and the Internal Revenue Service require that these reserves be segregated in the financial records, prohibiting the association from using them to meet current operating costs.

Contingency Reserves. Since no one can precisely forecast every operating expense that an association will have during a fiscal year, to cover major unexpected emergencies, and avoid special assessments, the board may establish a contingency reserve.

The Federal Housing Authority (FHA) recommends that a contingency reserve equal to three percent of the annual budget be established. For example, if the total operating budget is $120,000, a contingency reserve of $3,600 ($120,-000 × 3%) should be established under the FHA guidelines. Older condominium developments, especially those converted from rental apartments, may have more unforeseen problems than new developments. Therefore, these associations may wish to set aside a greater percentage of the budget for contingency purposes. A contingency reserve of five percent of the total budget is considered sufficient for an older condominium.

Determining and itemizing income

The principal source of association income comes from *unit owner assessments*, and the governing documents specify how assessments may be used. From a practical standpoint, assessments are to be used to meet the financial needs of the association. This includes general administration, repair and maintenance of common areas, and programs and services that are available to all residents. Where a swimming pool within a condominium development is maintained as a common expense, it is open to all unit owners. If unit owners must pay a membership fee to use the pool, general assessments cannot, in fairness, be used to run the pool.

Although regular assessments provide the bulk of the association's income, other sources of revenue are found in amenity rental fees, interest, or special assessments.

Amenity rental fees are special fees paid by unit owners or their guests for the use of certain condominium amenities or limited common areas, including clubhouse rentals, facilities user fees, tennis court and golf course greens fees, and rental of parking spaces and storage lockers.

Interest received on association funds held by lending institutions, banks, brokerage liquid asset accounts or United States government obligations should be budgeted as revenue. Interest may generate from any association account, including accounts set aside for reserves.

Special assessments may be levied against the unit owners to cover unexpected expenses. They will as a rule be included in the budget. However, budgets should be reviewed during the fiscal year and modified to take into account any unexpected major expenses which may be offset by special assessments. This income should be treated separately in financial statements, distinguishing it from budgeted income.

Additional sources of income, such as those generated from vending machines and social and recreational activities, should be grouped in a *miscellaneous* or "other" income category.

Financial Statements

Regular comparisons must be made between the financial activity as budgeted and the actual resulting financial performance. From such a comparison the board of directors can gauge the success and accuracy of their forecasting, thereby evaluating whether the budget objectives are being met. The economic status of an association is capsulized in a set of financial statements prepared either by the treasurer, the management agent, or an accountant. The board should study these statements to determine the association's financial strengths and weaknesses and use this information to evaluate the association's operations. Before any financial statements can be prepared, a decision must be made as to which system of accounting is more appropriate to the operation of the association.

Systems of accounting

There are two basic systems of accounting: the *cash method* and the *accrual method*. The cash method records actual cash as it is received or paid out. The accrual method is a more sophisticated method of accounting that keeps track of expenses as they are incurred and income when it is due, rather than when the bill is paid or the revenue is received.

The cash method is the easier method both to understand and to maintain accurately and consistently. Most people use a cash method of accounting in balancing a typical checkbook. Assuming there are no outstanding bills, a cash system lets the association see if it has enough cash to meet its current financial obligations. This accounting method works very well for many condominium associations, and is especially useful to smaller associations with smaller revenue and expense requirements. A cash basis system will meet the needs of a number of boards because it will meet their accounting requirements.

The accural method matches revenue when due (but not necessarily collected) with expenses that have been incurred (but not necessarily paid for). More simply stated, the accrual method of accounting records the expense of buying an item at the time bought and records the revenue to pay for it at the time the revenue is due to be received. Many condominiums may not require this method if their revenue and expenses are at an annual dollar amount of less than $500,000. However, larger associations will definitely want to consider accrual-basis accounting.

It is important to note that in many cases the accrual accounting concept is especially effective as it relates to the expense side of an operation. Since collection of assessment revenue is rather strictly guarded or controlled by the documents, accrual of revenue is not as critical as the accrual of expenditures. It is especially important to accrue major one-time expenses of say, $500 in a month, and ongoing contract payments that are amortized monthly, such as landscape maintenance, elevators, trash removal. If a board and/or committee does not understand accrual accounting and it is used in its association, it is important that the management agent explain it to them.

Most condominium associations require an annual audit by an independent auditor or a certified public accountant (CPA). This audit, or examination of an association's financial transactions, obligations, and statements, is a report to the owners separate and apart from the financial reporting by the board, staff, or management agent. Associations should require the auditor to prepare the audit based on the accrual method to accurately reflect that year's transactions.

The statement of income and expense

The *statement of income and expense* provides a board with the information they need to run their association financially and is the only statement that usually is needed by an association utilizing the cash method of accounting. This statement, utilizing either the cash or accrual method of accounting, indicates how much income has been earned or received, and what expenses have been incurred or paid within a certain period of time (usually each month). Known in the corporate world as the profit and loss (P&L) statement, this report provides an overview of the association's financial status. A statement of income and expenses must be prepared at least once a year for the purpose of computing income tax returns. However, it is good business practice to prepare and review a quarterly or monthly financial statement. Since the cost of providing such statements increases with the frequency in which they are produced, a board should decide if it requires quarterly or monthly financial reports. Boards use a monthly statement to track the month's activities, but should focus more directly on the year-to-date activities, which gives the real trend of financial behavior.

The statement of income and expenses shows both budgeted and actual figures for the current month or quarter and for the year to date. Comparison of the variance between budget and actual figures permits the board to track the association's financial performance and make adjustments as necessary to ensure the association's financial solvency.

The accounting equation for the statement of income and expense is:

$$\text{income} - \text{expense} = \text{net income (or deficit)}$$

The statement should list revenues and expenses in the same account categories used in the budget to facilitate comparison of actual and budgeted income and expense. *(See Appendix A for sample Statement of Income and Expense Worksheet.)*

Other financial statements

Associations that use the accrual method of accounting will require additional financial statements, among them a *balance sheet*, a *cash flow statement*, and a *statement of members' equity* (on the balance sheet), and sometimes an *investment summary*. Cash-basis accounting also utilizes these supplemental statements. Such statements are usually prepared by the management agent or an accountant.

While the statement of income and expense presents information about financial performance over a given period of time, the balance sheet tells the association where it is financially at a specific time by listing its assets, liabilities, and members' equity.

The cash flow statement records actual inflow and outgo of cash during a given accounting period. It is needed for both the accrual system and the cash system of accounting to determine the ability of the association to meet its obligations at a given time. Since the accrual system records income due and expenses incurred, it augments the cash flow statement by including actual receipts or disbursements with receipts due and disbursements made.

The statement of members' equity tells the unit owners what their vested interest in the association is on a specific date. This interest does not necessarily refer to a sum of cash. Rather, it represents the value of the property to the members after all liabilities have been subtracted, based on their percent of ownership interest. The formula is:

$$Assets - Liabilities = Owners'\ equity$$

The investment summary is an attachment to the other financial summaries of operations. It indicates the amount of investments, tells where they are invested, details the interest rates, and states the maturity dates where applicable.

Financial record keeping

Financial record-keeping procedures must be established to gather all necessary information needed to prepare a statement of income and expense, along with supplemental statements that may be required. The board of directors does not need a detailed understanding of bookkeeping methods, but it should understand fundamental principles and terminology to enable it to recognize any errors or omissions in the association's records and to follow simple accounting transactions.

Five basic records should satisfy the financial record keeping needs of most associations. These are: cash/accrual receipts journal; cash/accrual disbursement journal; the payroll journal; the billing journal; and, the general journal which is used to record all entries that do not fit into the other four books. These five records of original entry are summarized at the end of each accounting period. The results are posted in a general ledger, which contains accounting entries for each transaction shown in the statement of income and expense. The accounting transactions in the general ledger are totaled and balanced to prepare the financial statements.

In addition to the statement of income and expense, certain other reports may periodically be given to the board. They are: accrued accounts payable, aged accounts receivable, reserve fund analysis, insurance tickler or inventory. Some boards may request a schedule of prepayments and delinquents. The *accrued accounts payable* listing reflects unpaid obligations, indicating more accurately the association's financial condition. The *reserve fund analysis* reflects the current placement of reserve funds in their various forms of investment, indicating dates of maturity, amount, and interest yield (this is also reported in an investment summary). Reinvestment instruction for maturing investments is the responsibility of the board, usually the treasurer.

The *insurance inventory file* is a listing of all forms of insurance carried by the association with policy expiration dates shown. A licensed, qualified insurance agent should be used to perform insurance placement counseling and renewal, although the final responsibility for adequate insurance coverage and placement rests with the board of directors.

The chart of accounts

Along with selecting a format in which to present the financial statement, the association should design a *chart of accounts* to facilitate the preparation of useful economic reports. A chart of accounts is a system of coding by number and title each income and expense category used in the budget and financial reports. Its purpose is to provide uniformity in the accounting system.

The particular needs of a condominium association will dictate the detail and amount of information the board will need in its chart of accounts. As a general rule, an account series will be needed for each balance sheet and income and expense statement account. The Department of Housing and Urban Development (HUD) has adopted a chart of accounts for use by its insured multifamily projects, and these expense accounts can be adapted to the needs of most associations. The HUD system is more extensive than most associations will need, but it provides a standard and uniform method of accounting that complements the set of categories used by property managers to file reports for the IREM Experience Exchange program. *(See Appendix A for HUD Chart of Accounts.)*

The HUD chart uses a four-digit series for coding accounts. Numbers ending in 000 designate general types of accounts; numbers ending in 00 designate groups of accounts within each general type; and, numbers ending in 0 or another number designate specific ledger accounts. The following illustrates this account number method, with *N* representing a whole number:

N000	General type of account
NN00	Group of accounts
NNN0 or NNNN	Ledger accounts
	For example:
6000	All expense accounts (General type of account)
6300	Administrative expenses (Group of accounts)
6311	Office expenses (Ledger account)
6320	Management fee (Ledger account)

The association should adopt a chart of accounts to fit its own operational needs. This can be accomplished with the help and guidance of a management agent who has probably already developed a chart of accounts adaptable to the accounting system of the association. The modular nature of a number-coded chart of accounts permits it to be revised and expanded with relative ease as the needs of the association change.

Fiscal Controls

No association can afford to take an "it can't happen here" approach to error or fraud. The board of directors and the management agent or on-site manager will be entrusted with a great deal of money. A system must be adopted that will provide regular checks and balances on the exactness of accounting data, protect the assets of unit owners, and encourage efficiency. Most condominium management firms have developed tried-and-tested controls, but an association that manages itself will have to develop its own. These controls should outline the methods of recording all transactions, directing the flow of cash, and preparing financial documents. How expanded these fiscal controls are will depend upon the unique characteristics of the given association. Extreme caution is advised in setting up proper financial controls. The association that plans to self-manage must seek the help of a CPA to establish correct, adequate accounting records (with proper controls) and reporting procedures.

Collecting and recording assessments

Since an association derives most of its income from unit owner assessments, it is essential that procedures for billing, collecting, and recording assessments be adopted and followed.

If the association is not on a computerized collection system, individual ledger cards should be prepared for each unit owner to serve as the official record of each owner's assessment status. Each card should list the unit owner's name, the address of the unit, the billing address if an absentee owner, a legal description of the unit, and the regular monthly assessment. The card also may be used to record other useful information, such as the owner's telephone number, the number, names and ages of children, and the number and kinds of pets. At each pay period, entries should be made of the assessment due, the period the assessment covers, and any additional charges, such as late payment fees or interest. *(See Appendix A for sample Unit Owner Ledger Card.)*

Several methods may be used for billing unit owners for regular assessments, although direct billing is not recommended for monthly collection. Very large associations may have unit bills prepared based on information shown on the ledger cards. As invoices are prepared and mailed, and the total amounts billed are posted in a billing journal. When all invoices have been posted, the assessment, late charge, and interest columns of the billing journal should be totaled, and the totals posted in the general ledger.

Massive billings are very cumbersome and increase both fees for management agents and the association. Therefore, many associations do not send out individual monthly bills. Instead, most associations send each unit owner an annual notice of the regular assessment, indicating the amount due and when it is due, much the same as a mortgage company. The unit owner is then responsible for making sure certain payments are made on time. Other associations use a coupon book system, supplying coupons to be returned with each assessment payment. A combination of the annual notice with a coupon book saves time, confusion, and often, costs. Some associations and management firms have abandoned the no-billing or coupon-billing system due to problems within a specific area or property. Where frequent ownership turnover occurs, the seller often transfers the coupon book to the new owner without advising the management agent of the transfer of property.

Specific procedures for handling assessment payments as they are received should be established. Each check should be reviewed to make sure it shows the correct date, amount, and signature. If it does not, the check should be returned to the sender with a request for a replacement. If the check is correct, the return stub or duplicate bill (if used) should be dated and attached to the check. The back of each check should be stamped "For deposit only" to the association's bank account or the agency account. Then, each check should be listed in the cash receipts journal by date, name, and unit number, and the total of the check posted in the cash column with additional payments for late charges or service charges being shown in separate columns. The total of each recorded income account column should be added, and should equal the cash receipts column so that each equals the total of the checks (called reconciling).

Checks should be deposited daily and the amount of the deposit entered into the checkbook immediately. When each assessment is paid, the appropriate information should be entered on the individual ledger cards. It is a good practice to file all duplicates of bills or stubs in an envelope, recording the date and amount of the deposit on the outside. If any problems arise, deposits can then be checked easily.

At the end of each accounting period (usually the last day of the calendar month) the cash receipts journal should be balanced. The total should be posted to the appropriate account in the general ledger. Individual ledger cards should be balanced for further verification. The total amounts shown paid on the cards should equal the amount shown in the accounts receivable column of the general ledger. Delinquent payments are recorded on the individual ledger cards and tied to the end balance of the general ledger as accounts receivable.

When an association has other sources of revenue, this income should be handled with procedures similar to those used to collect and record regular assessments.

Developing delinquent assessment procedures

The board should refer to the association's legal documents for guidance in collecting delinquent assessments. If the documents do not provide sufficient guidelines, the association must adopt formal procedures to be strictly followed in all cases of delinquent assessments.

The first step in establishing collection and payment procedures is to set a time period after which an assessment is considered delinquent. Some associations consider a payment late if it is not received within 10 days of the due date; in others a payment is late when it is 30 days past due. As soon as a payment is delinquent, a reminder notice should be sent to the unit owner. If the assessment remains unpaid after a predetermined period, such as the end of the month, the delinquent unit owner should be notified a second time by certified mail, or registered mail for all Canadian or non-United States resident owners, and given the date by which payment must be made to avoid legal action.

If payment is still not received, the matter should be turned over to the association's attorney for legal action, as prescribed by the governing documents. Usually the attorney writes a letter demanding payment, prescribing what actions will follow if the demand for payment is not satisfied. A lien action can be the severest action taken, resulting in the mortgage holder paying the outstanding amount, the lien being discharged, and then resolving it with the owner. At times it can lead to foreclosure or forced sale to collect monies due.

Where a management agent is employed, the management agreement should specify the extent of the agent's authority to collect delinquent payments. The agent's authority may be limited to mailing a reminder notice, or extend as far as instituting the filing of a lien through the association's attorney.

Although adopting incentives, such as discounts for prompt payments, may at first appear a good idea, "negative" incentives are the only realistic collection alternatives. These negative incentives are late fees, percentage penalty fees, and similar penalties. Discount incentives for prompt payment takes revenue from the association and rewards owners for fulfilling an obligation they have already agreed to. The important criteria is that the board fully enforce its collection procedures so that it is not later found derelict in its fiduciary responsibility to the association.

Controlling expenditures

Internal fiscal controls are needed for the payment of expenses incurred by the association in carrying out its responsibilities, and it is important that a system for processing invoices be established. Each invoice should be date stamped at the time of receipt and checked for mathematical accuracy. It should be verified that the invoice has not already been paid. If it has not, then it should be stamped with a stamp that provides for: a space to record the number and date of the check by which it is paid, the account number or category to which it is to be charged, the name of the person approving payment, and the date of approval.

Once approved for payment, the bookkeeper or management agent writes the appropriate expense account code number or category in the space provided. If the invoice is for goods or merchandise, the person who received the goods or merchandise will have signed a delivery ticket indicating the goods or merchandise were received in good order or in the right quantity. The person authorized by the board to approve the invoice (usually the treasurer in a self-managed association, or the management agent) should sign it in the appropriate space. The invoice is then filed in the accounts payable file to be paid. All invoices should be paid on time to maximize discounts and to maintain a good credit rating.

As each invoice is paid, it should be noted in the cash disbursements journal. This journal is balanced at the end of the accounting period; the total is then transferred to the general ledger. Invoices remaining unpaid at this time should be listed in the general journal as payable.

Checks should be prenumbered to ensure that each is accounted for. Checks that are voided should be marked so that they cannot be used again; blank checks should be kept in a safe place where only authorized persons have access. When a check is drawn, the check number and the date should be entered on the invoice. After the check has been signed and mailed, the invoice is filed in a paid invoice file for future reference and the audit.

The governing documents may outline certain procedures for signing checks. In a self-managed association, an officer or some other designated person may be required to sign all checks. Some associations require two signatures on all checks; others require two signatures only on those checks that exceed a certain amount (usually $1,000). When a management agent is employed, the board should give the agent authority to endorse checks. This authority may be limited, requiring countersignature on checks in excess of set amounts. Such procedures must be outlined in the management agreement. Countersignature requirements should be looked at closely, as they can be a time-consuming practice. They can hamper the orderly flow of funds and may require additional bonding. Since a management agent is bonded, and the cost of the bond is included in the management fee, the board is better off to assign signature rights to the agent.

The audit

Most association documents require that the financial records be audited at least once a year, usually by a CPA. Even if this requirement is not spelled out, the board of directors should have this important service performed. The members of the association provide most of the association's income, and they have a right to know how their money is being spent and if it is being handled properly. An audit is a thorough examination of the records and accounts to ensure their accuracy and determine if the financial statements fairly illustrate the association's financial status. It provides assurance to the association members of the propriety of its money management.

One of the key considerations in choosing an auditor should be his or her degree of experience in auditing condominium association records. Associations differ greatly from manufacturing companies or grocery stores, and the auditor must recognize their unique nature. Familiarity with the governing documents, the budget, the method of setting assessments, the bookkeeping process, tax requirements, depreciation of common areas, and reserve escrows is essential. In selecting auditors, the board should request CPAs to prepare proposals, listing their services and estimated fee schedules. Since most accountants will charge either a flat fee or a daily rate, it is best to secure a flat fee to complete an audit.

Even though a management agent is employed by the association, an audit is usually required by the documents, mandating it be performed annually. The use of a management agent may result in lower audit costs because the agent's formal, organized bookkeeping system saves the accountant time and facilitates the audit.

Because it is costly and impractical, a complete, detailed analysis of every financial transaction is never undertaken by an auditor. The board, therefore, must define carefully the scope of the audit. In general, the auditor should review fiscal controls, test procedures used in handling cash receipts and disbursements, make sure that all assessments are billed and collected in accordance with the documents, and verify that all financial requirements as set forth in the documents are being met. The period covered by the audit, the date the report is to be delivered, and the number of copies to be distributed is determined by the board of directors.

An officer of the association, and the management agent where applicable, should meet with the auditor in order to transmit all the information (receipts, records, ledger, disbursement journal) required to complete the audit. The board may instruct the auditor to prepare the report using the same classifications as used in the budget and statement of income and expense. This will facilitate comparing the audit statement with the budget and the financial statement. All of the terms of the audit should be stated in a formal, signed agreement.

As the auditor nears the completion of the audit, he or she should meet with the board, bookkeeper, or management agent to review the draft of the audit report. The board should ascertain that it is presented in an easily understandable manner. The board should seek recommendations from the auditor on the adequacy of fiscal controls executed by the staff or management agent in the administration of association funds. The board should take immediate action to correct any deficiencies cited by the auditor. Upon completion, an encapsulized copy of the audit report should be sent to each association owner.

11
INSURING
THE CONDOMINIUM
COMMUNITY

People who choose to own and live in condominium units are faced with certain problems that owners of single-family houses do not have. One such problem concerns *insurance*, which relieves the fear of financial loss due to a disastrous event by shifting the risk of such an event to an insurance company. In exchange for assuming this responsibility, the insurance company receives a payment, known as an *insurance premium*. To fully relieve all unit owners of the fear of loss, adequate property and liability insurance must be obtained both for the areas that are owned in common by all unit owners and for the individually owned units.

Securing a complete insurance program is one of the most important tasks assigned a condominium association board of directors by the condominium's governing documents. No matter how large or how small the community, its need for adequate insurance is great. An uninsured loss may be not only emotionally traumatic to all those involved but could undermine the soundness of the association as well. In view of the association's inability to withstand significant unbudgeted expenses, the board must insure it against potential loss. The board is directly responsible for seeing to it that the association is sufficiently protected against all insurable catastrophes. Although a management agent may assist the board by recommending coverages and seeing to it that the insurance policy is maintained in force, assuring that the association has proper insurance coverage ultimately is a responsibility of the board.

The governing documents should indicate what type of insurance the board should obtain. They also may provide some guidelines for determining how much coverage is required. Because state laws tend not to be specific about insurance requirements, the insurance provisions of one set of documents may differ from the insurance provisions of another. Insurance requirements in declarations and bylaws may be extensively detailed or only superficially outlined. Although some provide detailed insurance guidelines, many are sketchy at best. The board that merely complies with loose requirements may fail to provide its association with a sound condominium insurance program. The board must satisfy the requirements specified in the governing documents but also must use its own discretion in determining how much and what kind of insurance coverage is adequate. The first step in tailoring an insurance policy to the needs of a condominium association is to define which potential liabilities belong to the association and which belong to the unit owner. This is not an easy thing to do. Because the condominium concept is somewhat new to the United States, a number of complicated legal questions have yet to be answered.

Some of those who have studied the housing industry believe the modern condominium concept to have been born before its time. Certainly, not all of the complexities of condominium life had been worked out before high-rise and garden condominiums began springing up throughout the country. One wrinkle that needed to be ironed out was the method for writing an insurance policy for condominium property. Major difficulties arose in condominiums where the boundaries of one unit formed the boundaries of other units. If neighboring unit owners both insured the wall separating their units, coverage would be expensively duplicated. If neither insured the wall, there would be a potentially disastrous gap in coverage. The question was: How can interconnecting structures of individually owned units be insured adequately without either leaving major gaps in coverage or duplicating it?

In response to this problem, a system was devised that placed the full burden of insuring the condominium's structure on the association while simultaneously recognizing that every unit owner has the right and obligation to obtain full personal property and liability coverage. Thus, there are two kinds of condominium insurance policies: a master *association insurance policy*, and a *unit owner's insurance policy*. The association policy generally combines property and liability coverage for the common areas into one package, serves as the main coverage for the structure of the condominium, and takes precedence over a unit owner's policy in the event of duplicate coverage. The unit owner's policy, which can provide for coverage of real and personal property and liability of the unit owner, was conceived as a complement to the broader association policy and was intended to neither supplement nor replace it.

It is important that the board of directors recognize that various insurance carriers have arrived at various interpretations of how the association can be insured most appropriately and completely. Well-conceived, well-planned association and unit owner insurance policies still may leave gaps or provide overlapping coverage, but experienced condominium carriers do offer integrated programs that can provide a maximum amount of coverage for both the association and the individual unit owner. The board of directors should seek a professional insurance agent who is experienced in drafting condominium insurance policies and who will be able to read the documents and determine the liability exposures of the association based on his experience. The insurance agent also should keep abreast of all changes in the law that apply to condominium ownership and the responsibilities of association boards of directors.

There is no one standard insurance policy that is right for all condominiums. Operating systems differ greatly among, say, suburban townhouse and downtown high-rise condominiums, while resort condominiums at the seashore have different insurance needs from those high in the mountains. Obtaining specialized, customized service and policies is the key to maximum protection for condominium communities. Board members are not expected to understand the complicated machinery of condominium insurance; only a specialist experienced in writing policies tailored to the service needs of various clients can be depended upon for this kind of expertise. However, to enable them to deal intelligently with such a specialist, board members should have a basic understanding of condominium insurance needs.

The Association Insurance Policy

Drafting an insurance policy of any kind is a difficult, confusing task. Because of the uniqueness and intricacies of joint ownership and operation, drafting an association policy is doubly difficult. To answer its basic insurance questions, the board should consult with a specialist in condominium insurance who has developed a reservoir of expertise in this area. Although various insurance agents represent different underwriters and therefore offer different coverages, there are a few similarities in the kinds of association coverage that are provided.

Insuring the condominium property

In determining the kind of real and personal property coverage the association needs, the board of directors must deal with three primary considerations. It must determine what hazards it needs to protect against, what property requires coverage, and how much coverage is adequate.

What Are the Risks? In determining what perils it should insure the condominium against, the board first must look to its documents. Although fire is the major threat to a condominium, the governing documents may require the board to obtain coverage against a broader range of risk. If there is no such requirement, the board of directors itself may consider it a sound practice to provide additional coverage.

The standard fire insurance policy usually covers direct loss by fire, lightning, and damage by "removal from premises endangered by a peril insured against" (as stated in the New York State Standard Fire Policy, which generally is considered the national standard). Damage by removal can result from breakage, exposure to the elements, or virtually any other cause. Obviously, this basic coverage is incomplete. The board might consider, and possibly be required by the governing documents to consider, *extended coverage*, which expands coverage to include damage caused by seven additional perils: windstorm, hail, explosion, riot and civil commotion, aircraft, vehicles, and some types of smoke.

Coverage can be extended even further with *all-risk coverage*. Many governing documents require this kind of policy, which provides the most comprehensive protection. However, all-risk may be one of the most abused phrases in the insurance industry. Instead of listing the perils that are insured against, the all-risk policy protects the association from losses arising from any cause other than some that specifically are excluded. The term "all-risk" would seem to imply that the association is protected against any direct physical loss to the property, but, because of the exclusions, that is not the case. To further complicate the matter, not every insurance carrier defines all-risk in the same way. However, when all-risk coverage is provided, it is the responsibility of the insurance carrier to prove that coverage does not exist (by way of one or more of the exclusions listed in the policy), otherwise they must pay for the loss. In contrast with the *named perils* policies described above, the burden of proof that coverage exists is on the insured (the association). Typically, however, all-risk coverage does not protect against damage resulting from wear and tear, earthquake, flood, sewer back-up, war, water seepage, boiler explosion, or nuclear contamination.

The board of directions must know what is excluded from all-risk coverage and understand what the exclusions could mean to the association and how it can fill in the gaps with *endorsements* or riders attached to the policy that extend or otherwise alter its coverage. For example, few all-risk policies cover damage caused by water that is not a result of damage to the exterior of the building. Although this may be a small, recurring liability, it could involve a major expense. For example, a violent thunderstorm could drive rain water under the sliding glass doors of a recreational room and destroy the carpet. *Water damage insurance* policies are available that would cover such a loss, and the board should consider obtaining such coverage (even though it too may list certain exclusions). Similarly, *sprinkler leakage insurance* may be obtained to cover a loss caused by water leaking from an automatic sprinkler system when the discharge of water is caused by something other than fire.

All-risk coverage does not cover earthquake and flood damage. Although this may not present a problem to many condominiums, it will to those built-in areas vulnerable to these perils. In those cases, *flood and earthquake insurance* often is available and should be considered if the protection package is to be adequate. Loss due to floods may be especially catastrophic and certainly is worth insuring against if the condominium is situated on a lakefront or in a low-lying area where river flooding may occur. The National Flood Insurance Program provides property coverage in designated and approved areas. Associations may have other local concerns for which they require special coverage; for example, sinkhole insurance in Florida.

Another gap in insurance protection can be filled with an endorsement to cover damage caused by vandals or as the result of malicious mischief. Again, the board should consider this endorsement for *vandalism* and *malicious mischief insurance* and any other endorsements that may be appropriate to obtaining the most complete property insurance policy for the association.

What Should Be Covered? Even an all-risk association insurance policy may not adequately cover every piece of property that is the responsibility of the board of directors. However, the appropriate endorsements to the policy can provide a complete blanket of protection.

Many condominiums are built with a great deal of exterior glass. However, all-risk coverage does not always adequately insure against plate glass breakage. There may be glass in common area exterior walls that is the responsibility of the association and should be insured against breakage. Also, in some condominium associations the board of directors is responsible for glass in individual units that forms outside walls. Although many policies include coverage for glass breakage, this coverage usually is limited to $50 per pane and $250 per claim. This limited coverage is scarcely adequate to cover the hundreds of windows in many condominium properties. *Plate glass insurance* policies covering breakage to the full amount of the actual loss, subject to a deductible, are available.

Because all-risk coverage does not protect against boiler explosion, the board should consider obtaining an endorsement to the association policy that would fill this gap. *Boiler and machinery insurance* may provide protection against loss arising out of the operation of pressure, mechanical, and electrical equipment, including damage or destruction of air conditioning and other similar equipment.

Many board of directors are responsible for swimming pools, fences, signs, piers, light poles, auxiliary buildings, driveways, walkways, and other elements of common property. These items may not be covered under the basic association policy, but coverage can be included in the policy if the appropirate endorsements are added. The same is true of coverage of trees, plants, lawns, and shrubs.

The association also may be responsible for providing coverage for personal as well as for real property. The board must be sure it does not forget to adequately protect lobby furniture, laundry room washers and dryers, office, maintenance, and recreational equipment, and any other association personal property. Damage and destruction of these items are covered by most policies if the equipment is used to service the buildings. Otherwise, coverage for personal property must be purchased to cover these items. Many policies depreciate these items for age. However, for an additional premium, it is possible for a policy to be written that would cover these items to their replacement value rather than at their depreciated value. Nor do all policies cover theft. Because items that are used in the common areas frequently disappear, it is wise to have theft insurance.

How Much Coverage Is Needed? After deciding what kinds of property coverage are needed, the board must decide how much is needed. The governing documents may provide the board with guidelines for determining adequate levels of insurance. The association needs to have enough property coverage to permit it to replace all of the common areas and personal property for which it is responsible. Therefore, in selecting coverage, the board should look for coverage that is related to replacement cost rather than actual cash value.

Actual cash value is defined as a replacement cost less depreciation, and, at the time of a loss, usually is less than the cost of returning the condominium to its original status. Replacement cost can be determined by an independent appraisal of the property or be projected based on the original cost of construction plus inflation. Depreciation takes into consideration a condominium's age, obsolescence, and degree of deterioration. When a condominium is insured to its replacement cost, the insurance company (assuming that the association has purchased enough insurance) agrees to repair or replace the damaged building without making an allowance for depreciation. To realize the benefit of replacement cost coverage, some policies require that the association must actually replace the damaged building on the same premises after a loss.

In fact, many condominium documents require the board to insure the condominium at its replacement cost rather than at its actual cost. Although this is the wisest course in most cases, there are exceptions. For example, the actual value of an older apartment building that has been converted to a condominium may be two or even three times less than the replacement cost. Replacement cost refers to the cost of returning a structure to its status prior to damage.

Most association policies contain a *coinsurance* clause, which restricts the amount the association may recover on a partial loss if the condominium is not insured for at least a certain percentage—usually 80 or 90 percent—of its actual cash value or replacement cost, depending on the kind of coverage. If the policy contains a coinsurance clause with an 80 percent requirement, the board must insure the condominium to 80 percent of its actual value or replacement cost. In return for compliance with the requirement, the association benefits from a reduction in its premium rate. If it does not comply with the coinsurance clause and a loss occurs, the association will not be fully compensated for the loss. The formula used to determine the amount of recovery after such a loss would be:

$$\frac{\text{Amount of insurance carried}}{\text{Amount of insurance required}} \times \text{Loss} = \text{Recovery limit}$$

The coinsurance clause therefore places the responsibility for buying the proper amount of insurance on the buyer—in this case, the board of directors.

For example, let us say that a board of directors had purchased $700,000 worth of coverage, which it considered to be in compliance with an 80 percent actual value coinsurance requirement. Thereafter, a fire causes $30,000 worth of damage. If an appraisal then shows that the actual value of the condominium prior to the loss was $1,000,000, the insurance company would not have to pay the full amount of damages since the board did not meet the requirement and the condominium was not insured to 80 percent of its actual value, or $800,000 ($1,000,000 × 80 percent). Instead, the insurance company would pay for only a portion of the damages, based on the previous formula:

$$\frac{\$700,000}{\$800,000} \times \$30,000 = \$26,250$$

The association members therefore would have to pay the difference between the loss ($30,000) and the amount collectible ($26,250), or a $3,750 penalty.

Penalty for possible noncompliance with the coinsurance requirement can be avoided by waiving the coinsurance clause and replacing it with an *agreed amount* clause. This clause represents an agreement by the insurance company to pay the association the face amount of the policy in the event of insured destruction. This face amount is based on the value of the condominium as agreed upon by the board of directors and the insurance company. In effect, the board can partially shift the responsibility for making a correct decision regarding adequate coverage to the insurance company. When a policy includes the agreed amount clause, the insurance company is obligated to pay claims on a replacement cost basis if partial losses should occur. There should be no additional cost for this protection, since, under the agreed amount clause, the property must be insured to at least 90 percent or, most often, 100 percent of its value.

Even if the condominium association's insurance policy includes an agreed amount clause, it is good business practice to require frequent reappraisals of the property. (Some governing documents require such reappraisals to be conducted annually.) Coverage should be updated from time to time to take into account any appreciation of the property indicated by the appraisal. An inflation guard endorsement may be added to assure that the coverage keeps pace with inflation.

Most association policies provide for *deductibles* of $100 or more. Deductibles in an association policy will apply either on a per-occurrence basis or on a per-building basis, the former being easier to administer in the case of multiple-building condominium projects. Although the board should be wary of extremely large deductibles, which might negate the purpose of obtaining insurance, inclusion of deductibles in a policy usually results in lower premiums by eliminating numerous small claims that can be relatively expensive for the insurance company to process. Therefore, deductibles may be considered by cost-sensitive associations as a method of lowering premiums.

Repair or Reconstruction? If some calamity results in a complete or near-complete loss of the project and the owners cannot agree whether or not to rebuild, highly emotional debates are sure to erupt. Some association policies require reconstruction to occur on the same site; others do not. Some state laws make reconstruction mandatory unless a certain percentage of a condominium project is destroyed. New York, for example, requires reconstruction unless more than three-fourths of the structure is damaged, in which case the proceeds from the insurance policy are divided among the unit owners according to their percentages of interest. If only a small portion of the condominium is damaged, a unit owner may wish to *partition* the association, that is, to bring legal action to divide the recovery compensation so that the unit owner may recover his or her share individually. Governing documents should prohibit this.

The Insurance Trustee. Most master policies require that an *insurance trustee* be designated by the condominium association. The trustee (often a bank or trust company) collects funds from the insurance company and disburses them according to the contracts let for repair or replacement of the common areas. State laws outline trustee requirements. In Maryland, a typical example, the trustee clause is invoked only in the event of losses in excess of $25,000. Trustees, of course, never handle compensation for damage to the interior of a unit insured by an individual unit owner's policy.

Protecting against liability

To achieve maximum protection for the association, the board must obtain an insurance package that includes liability coverage, as required by most documents. While property insurance is to protect the association from losses of direct damages to the property itself, *liability insurance* should protect it from paying damages to a third person for bodily injury or damage to his or her property. This could result from a civil action charging negligence on the part of the association. The association liability policy should provide coverage for all liability hazards related to the common areas and facilities, as well as offer sound, realistic liability coverage for the administration and operation of the association.

What Are the Liability Hazards? The board of directors should select a *comprehensive general liability insurance* policy, the most complete liabilty policy available. This policy provides broad coverage for *bodily injury liability, property damage liability,* and *medical payments* and, in addition, can be written to include other liability hazards including many of the coverages discussed in this section below. The board must understand what kind of protection such a policy offers.

First, with bodily injury liability coverage, the insurance company agrees to cover all sums which the association is legally obligated to pay as damages because of bodily injury, illness, or death.

Second, with property damage liability coverage, the insurance company agrees to pay the association's liability for legal damages awarded because of damage to or destruction or loss of a person's property as a result of an accident.

Third, it voluntarily pays the medical costs of any guests who have accidents in the common areas for which the association is not legally liable. Such payment does not affect the right of the injured party to bring tort action, that is, to file civil suit, against the association. However, this medical payments coverage is essential to maintaining the good will of the unit owners, since an injured party may be content to have the incurred medical expenses paid and not take legal action to claim damages. (It should be noted that medical payments coverage applies only to guests and does not cover unit owners who have accidents in the common areas.)

Even with these three basic liability coverages, the association still will be vulnerable in some areas. The board of directors should be aware that its comprehensive general liability policy can be tailored to cover other liability exposures. For example, if automobiles of unit owners or their guests are parked on common area parking lots or in a garage, the association may become liable for damage to these vehicles. *Garagekeepers' legal lability* coverage is available to protect the association in such a situation. This coverage can be written to cover (sometimes subject to deductibles) loss resulting from fire, explosion, theft, vandalism, and collision.

The board also may consider it wise to carry *completed operations and products liability* coverage, which protects against liability related to manufactured products or workmanship. An association may need this kind of protection even though it does not manufacture products. For example, it may sponsor a bazaar at which homemade items may be sold, and claims could arise out of alleged injury caused by any such products that are improperly made or improperly labeled.

It is not unlikely that the association at some time will sponsor a social event at which liquor will be distributed on the condominium premises at no charge. Claims could arise from such an occurrence. There is even a chance that the association may be held liable for accidents arising out of the use of liquor dispensed at private parties held by unit owners in common areas, such as in a social room. To avoid such problems, the board of directors should add a *host liquor liability* endorsement to the association policy. This endorsement will cover the association in these situations.

If an employee or a board member has an accident in his or her own automobile while on company business and the accident involves a third party, a claim could be brought against the association by the third party. This could occur if, for example, there is no or insufficient liability coverage on the employee's or the board member's car. *Automobile hired and nonownership liability* coverage could protect the association in such a situation if the person is an employee. *Hired car* coverage is needed to protect the association for using cars of nonemployees.

Many condominiums, especially those in warmer climates, either own, hire, or otherwise are involved with boats. The board of directors of such a condominium should see to it that its policy contains an endorsement for *watercraft liability*.

Contractual liability coverage should be included if the association has entered or plans to enter into any contracts that contain indemnification or hold harmless clauses. Under the hold harmless clause, the association assumes the liability of the person with whom it has such a contract. Contractual liability coverage will protect the association against the liability it assumes in this way.

If the association plans to undertake any new construction or extensive repairs, it will need additional protection to cover bodily injury or property damage liability that may result. *Contractor's protective liability* provides the protection that is needed when construction goes beyond routine maintenance or minor alterations.

Insurance companies usually assess a flat charge for *personal injury liability* coverage, and the association should consider obtaining such coverage because its cost is reasonable, while any personal injury liability claims against the association could be quite large. This endorsement covers the association against claims for false arrest, libel, slander, invasion of privacy, or wrongful eviction, claims for which could result from the actions of an employee or board member.

A condominium might have additional liability hazards that can be covered in the association policy. An insurance agent familiar with problems unique to associations should be able to recognize the areas of risk and suggest appropriate endorsements to protect against losses resulting from them.

Many of these coverages can be automatically included by using the broad form general liability endorsement, with which a knowledgeable insurance agent will be familiar. Broad form general liability covers many items, thus replacing writing separate endorsements.

Special Problems. Because there are certain condominium insurance problems that rarely are associated with the insurance of other kinds of properties, the association policy should contain provisions that address the condominium's unique circumstances. One is a provision that all unit owners be named individually as insureds. Such a provision protects all those named as insureds against personal claims arising out of the ownership, maintenance, or repair of the common areas.

Almost all insurance policies contain a *subrogation* clause, which gives the insurance company the legal right to take action against a third party responsible for damage for which it has made payment. This could create problems in a condominium association, where the company could pay a claim of the condominium management or third party and then, in turn, file suit (subrogation) against an individual unit owner. To prevent this from happening, the association policy should contain a *waiver of subrogation*. This waiver, which recognizes that each unit owner is insured by the policy, protects a unit owner from being held personally liable for something that happens within his unit that causes damage to the entire development.

Another unique situation may occur in the event unit owners are injured in a common area. The law usually prohibits people from successfully making claims against liability coverage that they provided for themselves, and this, in fact, would be the situation should a unit owner file suit against the association of which he or she is a member. Such a case was tested in California in 1971, and the appeals court ruled that a condominium unit owner could indeed sue the condominium management for injuries sustained when the unit owner fell over a water sprinkler in a common area. The court held that "unincorporated associations are entitled to general recognition as separate legal entities and that as a consequence a member of an unincorporated association may maintain a tort against his or her association." Many states have failed to address this issue, and it still is uncertain to what extent the California ruling will apply elsewhere. Some condominium declarations require the association's policy to include a *cross liability* endorsement and, in view of the California precedent, even if such an endorsement is not required, a board should include it in the policy.

Protecting the Board of Directors. Should the board be protected and, if so, how? The personal liability of board members is one of the most frequently overlooked areas of association risk exposure. The board is a unique group. Its members may have had little experience in the administration of a small business. Nevertheless, they are obligated to deal with unfamiliar administrative duties in addition to their involvement in the social and political community. Therefore, there is a great need for *directors' and officers' liability insurance,* a kind of errors and omissions insurance.

The board members and officers of a condominium association are as liable for their acts, or failure to act, as the members and officers of boards of directors of corporations. They are responsible to fellow unit owners, as well as to the public and, as a result, are subject to suit by individual unit owners, prospective buyers, accountants, and others who have business relationships with the association. Among areas of dispute that could result in lawsuits are conflicts of interest; mismanagement of funds; failure to exercise good judgment, diligence, or good faith in the execution of their official capacities; exceeding the authority granted by the declaration or the bylaws; misstatement of the association's financial condition; and failure to obtain competitive bids. Any decision made by the board may be challenged in court, subjecting its members to defense costs as well as to the cost of any financial settlements that may result.

The temptation to sue is particularly strong in condominium communities. Unlike the boards of many nonprofit organizations, the condominium board actually is in business and thus is responsible for major decisions, as well as for substantial dollar amounts. Unfortunately, many board members assume that the association's nonprofit status and the fact that the board serves without pay eliminates financial liability for its decisions. This misunderstanding can lead and has led to disastrous financial predicaments.

To add to the confusion, some condominium documents contain a hold harmless clause that attempts to shelter the board from legal liability for its actions. That such a provision will be upheld in court is questionable. If a board that is "held harmless" by the association is judged liable, responsibility is merely shifted to all members of the association. Therefore, the hold harmless clause found in many declarations is not to be considered sufficient protection for either the individual board member or the total board. Furthermore, even if the hold harmless clause protects the board, the defense and loss costs are then just spread to the association members as a whole.

Directors' and officers' liability policies are written on either a *claims made* basis or an *occurrence* basis. Associations buying this coverage should be aware of this difference before purchasing their contracts. The claims made policy will assign the date of a claim as the date it is reported, while an occurrence policy will assign the claim date as the date of the incident for which claim is being filed. An event or action for which the board is being sued may have taken place well prior to the effective date of the current directors' and officers' policy, in which case the claims made form would respond only if *prior acts* coverage is purchased. The occurrence form would respond if a policy was in effect at the time the event occurred that caused the injury. Again, it is most important to deal with an insurance agent knowledgeable in this class, who would be able to identify the different types of policies and help the association purchase the correct type for their particular needs.

Although the term "directors' and officers' liability" is commonly used, different insurance companies define the term differently. Carriers use their own exclusionary languages. Typically, however, a directors' and officers' liability policy does not cover dishonesty, fraud, personal injury, wrongful decisions as they relate to insurance, undue enrichment, or losses resulting from the denial of the civil rights of an individual, or other nonmonetary damages.

The Blanket Fidelity Bond. Board members and employees of the association (excluding contracted property managers) should be covered by a *blanket fidelity bond*, a requirement that may or may not be spelled out in the declaration. It is important to note that such a bond ordinarily does not cover a contracted property manager, unless specifically identified in the policy. Because the treasurer of the board and certain employees are responsible for overseeing the disbursements of funds, the association needs to be protected against loss resulting from fraudulent or dishonest acts of employees. The bond should be in an amount as designated by the governing documents or slightly in excess of the total funds that the employees or treasurer can be expected to have access to at any time. The bond would reimburse the association for any loss it sustains, up to the amount of the bond, by reason of a dishonest act of a person covered by the bond.

Workers' Compensation. Providing *workers' compensation* is a statutory requirement. Therefore, any condominium association that employs building or grounds maintenance or other personnel, whether they be full- or part-time regular employees or only incidental workers, must be covered by workers' compensation to relieve it of any claims for work-related injuries. Workers' compensation insurance provides for the cost of medical care and weekly income payments to persons injured while carrying out association business. Workers' compensation laws vary greatly from state to state, so again, it is important to be able to depend on your insurance agent to know what is required to meet the association's individual needs.

For further protection in this area, associations should be aware that they have an exposure when any worker is on the premises performing a job. If an employee of an independent contractor or subcontractor is injured and his or her employer does not provide workers' compensation coverage, the association may have to pay workers' compensation benefits to the injured person. Therefore, certificates of insurance as evidence of in-force workers' compensation insurance protecting those workers should always be required prior to having a job performed by an independent contractor or subcontractor.

How Much Coverage Is Enough? Governing documents seldom stipulate the minimum amount of liability coverage required. Since property damage and bodily injury liability could involve substantial figures, the board should be careful not to underinsure the association. There are no statutory limitations on the amounts that potentially could be recovered for bodily injury and property damage. The board therefore should act prudently and buy adequate insurance to cover any probable circumstances.

While it is important for the board to select a comprehensive general liability policy, coverage can be extended under an *umbrella liability* policy. This provides coverage for claims that exceed the limits of the comprehensive general liability, and also might cover losses not listed in the basic association policy. Umbrella liability coverage usually is available in increments of $1 million and may be subject to a self-insured retention. The board of directors should consider appropriate coverage, depending on its own needs. While such needs cannot be accurately anticipated, the board should consider all possibilities and work with an expert in determining a realistic amount of liability coverage.

Contracting for the association policy

After the board has learned what kinds of coverage are available, it should draw up a bid specification, taking into account any insurance requirements specified in the governing documents and the association's peculiar insurance needs. If an annual evaluation of the property is performed, it should be included in the bid package. All other pertinent data, including floor plans and governing documents, should be added to the package. An insurance agent with experience in insuring condominiums should be selected. The agent should be capable of recommending and giving advice on certain coverages specifically applicable to condominiums.

Before making a final selection based on the bids it receives, the board should investigate the potential agents' and carriers' ability to serve the association properly. The companies should be checked for financial management skills through such guides as *Best's Key Rating Guide: Property–Casualty*. The board should also inspect the carriers' records of claims services and staff capabilities. Unit owner's policies that the agency offers should be considered and reviewed along with unit owner's billing services, if applicable.

The board should endeavor to select an agent with a high premium volume in that class and one who has a close working relationship with carriers in that class. The agent should have the ability to bridge the natural adversarial relationship that may develop when handling claims. This can be checked through references to other associations that the agent represents.

The knowledgeable agent will ask for certain association information, such as recent appraisals, definitions of terms as they appear in the governing documents, the method of handling improvements and alterations, and other information necessary to the underwriter. The agent must demonstrate familiarity with local and state regulations. He or she should be willing to attend either annual membership meetings or insurance committee meetings and be familiar with the interaction of the unit owners, board, and the management agent or on-site manager. The agent will also want to be informed of policy issues such as who is responsible for the payment of deductibles.

Once the insurance company has been selected, a method for handling large claims should be established. Such an agreement will expedite claims and protect the interests of all persons involved.

After an insurance company has been selected by the board of directors, it is the agent's responsibility to prepare, in clear, understandable language, a statement of coverage. This statement should outline the association insurance policy and communicate to owners exactly what the building policy covers and what is the responsibility of the individual unit owners. This information may be disseminated through a written form letter sent to each unit owner or through the board. It is the obligation of the agent to respond to any inquiries that unit owners have concerning the master policy and its relation to the individual unit owner's policies. The agent should be expected to be able to assist the individual unit owner in the selection of an appropriately integrated personal policy. The agent should also inform mortgagees of the coverage on the association.

It also is a good idea for the board of directors to contract with the insurance carrier to provide engineering assistance in reducing hazards within the development. Most insurance companies will provide this service without charge because it reduces their risk. Special attention should be paid to structural problems and those that could result from use of the swimming pool.

The Unit Owner's Insurance Policy

Because coverage provided by the master condominium association policy is limited to those losses involving only common areas, individual owners are responsible for losses affecting their own units. Until recently, most condominium unit owners purchased the kind of insurance sold to rental apartment dwellers. However, because of the many differences between the two types of tenancy, this kind of insurance was inadequate to cover the unit owner's unique needs. A condominium unit owner's policy in various forms now is available throughout the country, and unit owners should be sure that they are covered by a policy designed especially for them.

The condominium unit owner's policy may cover five areas: the personal property of the unit owner (with some exceptions, as noted in the policy); unit realty that may not be covered by the association policy; additional living expenses incurred by the unit owner in the event he or she is forced to live elsewhere temporarily while repairs to damage are made or new permanent quarters are found; personal liability, including legal defense against suits arising from bodily injury or property losses sustained by another; and medical payments to others for injuries resulting from accidents on the owner's premises.

However, the unit owners may not be adequately protected by these coverages and may need to endorse their policies to provide the missing protection. If the condominium association policy covers the entire physical structure, the unit owner's policy should cover the remainder of his or her needs. However, although most association policies cover all real property, not all do. In some cases it may be the unit owner's responsibility to insure some real property within his or her unit, such as permanent fixtures or additions or alterations made at the owner's expense. The unit owner's policy may be endorsed to provide insurance coverage beyond the limits of the basic policy.

The basic owner's policy, like the association package, can be endorsed to cover all risks, with certain exclusions. Here again, the comprehensiveness of the all-risk coverage depends upon the carrier. This all-risk approach is particularly desirable because, in the condominium structure, a unit owner has relatively little control over events that may originate in a neighbor's unit.

Some condominium owners rent their units to others. If a rented unit is furnished, an endorsment is available to cover theft of personal property belonging to the individual unit owner. Also, such appurtenant structures as poolside cabanas, hobby shops, or storage sheds often are installed at the owner's expense, and that unit owner may endorse his or her individual policy so that these structures are properly and adequately covered.

Unit owners also may want to consider obtaining *loss assessments coverage* to cover the requirement that losses incurred by the association and not otherwise insured must be met through a special assessment of the unit owners. Let us say, for example, that a condominium association carries only $450,000 liability protection for occurrences within the common areas. Then, a guest is fatally injured by falling down a stairway, the guests inheritors sue the association for $1 million, and the courts eventually award them $650,-000. In this instance—and such large judgments are not unlikely—the insurance company would pay the $450,000 covered by the association policy, but the association still would owe $200,000. If there were 60 unit owners in the association, each would be assessed a share of the amount owed based on the percentages of ownership, or about $3,-300 each. The loss assessment endorsement, however, should cover the unit owner's portion of this amount, as well as provide protection against certain other kinds of special assessments. To keep premiums low, payment under this coverage may be subject to a deductible.

A tenant who rents an apartment and is displaced by fire or other damage resulting from some other occurrence usually will relocate in a relatively short period of time, but a condominium unit owner probably will need to wait until repairs are made and the original unit can be reoccupied. Considerable time may elapse before the unit is once again livable. A family that must spend many weeks or months in a hotel or other temporary living quarters may find bills running up quickly. Although the basic unit owner's policy may provide some protection against such an occurrence, an appropriate endorsement can provide increased protection of cover excessive expenses through *additional living expense insurance.*

Condominium unit owners may have additional needs that may be made by special endorsements to their policies, and an insurance agent should be able to provide advice as to coverage of these other unit owner liabilities.

12

TAX CONSIDERATIONS

*F*illing out tax returns, receiving tax bills, and paying all kinds of taxes are inescapable facts of American life. The new condominium unit owner will need to know both how the property will be taxed and how he or she will be treated by the Internal Revenue Service (IRS). Understanding the federal income tax status of the total condominium community requires the unit owner to think on two separate and distinct levels. On the one hand, the owner should know how he or she will be regarded as the owner of an individual condominium unit; on the other, the owner should understand the tax treatment of the condominium association, of which all unit owners are members.

The Federal Tax Status of the Condominium Association

Finding a way to tax the income of condominium associations was a very complicated and lengthy process. The very purpose of the association clouded the issue. The difficulty of trying to apply federal income tax laws to a nonprofit organization formed to operate and manage property owned by all of its members raised some interesting and unique questions. The federal tax treatment of the condominium association was blanketed in confusion until the passage of the Tax Reform Act of 1976.

The Tax Reform Act changed the way condominium associations and other homeowners' associations are taxed by making it possible for them to be treated as tax-exempt organizations. Prior to the adoption of the act, one of a condominium association's main concerns usually was its federal income tax status. Of course, there was no problem if money collected from assessments was spent on the condominium's operation during the tax year. The issue of how to treat reserves held for capital improvements and operating expenses, however, raised serious questions. If income tax had to be paid on reserve funds, condominium unit owners, in effect, were being taxed on money they were setting aside for maintenance of their homes. The Tax Reform Act resolved many of these questions, allowing the condominium association to elect tax-exempt status if it met certain qualifications and regulations.

Electing tax exemption

Under Section 528 of the Internal Revenue Code, corporate surtax exemption, a condominium association that is organized and operated to provide for the acquisition, construction, management, maintenance, and care of a condominium's common areas can qualify for tax exemption if (1) at least 60 percent of the association's gross income comes from unit owner assessments, (2) at least 90 percent of its expenses go for managing, maintaining, and caring for common areas, (3) substantially all of the units are used as residences, and (4) no part of the net income benefits any individual member of the association.

If it meets these requirements, an association can elect tax-exempt status by filing federal income tax return Form 1120-H, the U.S. Income Tax Return for Homeowners Associations. This must be done annually. If Form 1120-H is not completed and the tax-exempt option is not taken, the association will be taxed as a corporation.

Section 528 of the Internal Revenue Code requires the condominium association to distinguish between income that is exempt from taxation and income that is taxable. In general, any regular membership dues, fees, and assessments received from residential unit owners for operations reserves are considered exempt income and can be applied toward meeting the 60 percent qualification. Sources of income that are not exempt and are subject to federal income tax are (1) interest earned on reserve funds, (2) fees received from nonmembers for the use of association facilities, such as a swimming pool, tennis court, or social room, (3) assessments for work done on a privately-owned portion of a condominium unit, (4) income received from members as customers for services, such as house cleaning, rather than in their roles as unit owners, and (5) fees received from unit owners for special use of facilities that is not normally available to association members, including such things as hourly tennis court fees, laundry room and vending machine income, and rental fees for use of a social room. To further define the latter category, the Internal Revenue Code makes this distinction: If regular membership assessments do not entitle a member to use a particular facility, then income generated by that use is subject to tax. For example, if a unit owner pays a $110-a-month assessment but, in addition, must pay $1.50 each time he or she uses the swimming pool, the money collected in the form of swimming pool user fees is taxable income.

The condominium association should be aware that obtaining tax-exempt status does not necessarily mean that it will not have to pay any income taxes at all. Income that does not come from unit owner assessments still will be subject to tax. However, Section 528 does permit it to take two deductions. First, it can deduct any expenses that are directly related to producing any of the association's income. For example, if a condominium realizes $1,500 in amenity rental fees for the use of the swimming pool, the $1,500 would be subject to tax. But if the association spends $300 to print identification cards for the pool's users, the $300 could be deducted and only $1,200 of this income would be taxable. Second, every tax-exempt condominium association is allowed a specific deduction of $100 from its taxable income. This $100 deduction is allowed so that associations with only a small amount of otherwise taxable income will not be subject to tax.

When an association elects tax-exempt status, its entire taxable income is taxed at the rate of 30 percent. As an example of how this works, consider the hypothetical condominium association that had the following income and operating expenses one year:

Income	
Assessments	$ 98,000
Interest	1,100
Amenity rental fees	900
Total income	$100,000
Operating expenses	$ 92,000
Income over expenses (reserves)	$ 8,000

If expenses of $120 could be allotted to the amenity rental fee income, the income tax would be determined as follows:

Nonexempt income (interest + amenity rental fees)		$ 2,000
Deduction of expenses to		
generate amenity rental fees	$120	
Specific deduction	100	
Total deductions		220
Taxable income		1,780
Tax rate		30%
Tax due		$ 534

Tax-exempt status or corporate status?

If a condominium association does not elect the tax-exempt status, or if it does not qualify under Section 528 to do so, the association must file a tax return in the same manner as a corporation and be taxed at the corporate tax rate of 17 percent (in the case of a tax year ending after December 31, 1980) of income over expenses, including reserves. This is how the corporate tax rate would affect the same condominium association:

Income	$100,000
Operating expenses	92,000
Taxable income	8,000
Tax rate	17%
Tax due	$ 1,360

Obviously, this association would benefit from electing the tax-exempt status.

If the association elects tax-exempt treatment, it is not permitted to benefit from special deductions provided for corporations or the net operating loss deduction. Thus, the association that elects tax-exempt status under Section 528 will not be able to deduct from its taxable income any losses that it may have had in the previous year. Accordingly, in some situations, an association might lower its income tax by not electing tax-exempt status and by being taxed as a corporation.

To understand how this factor can affect an association, consider its impact on the same hypothetical condominium association. For example, in the previous year the association had operated at a $9,000 loss (such losses are not unusual for fledgling associations). In effect, its operating expenses exceeded its income by $9,000. If this condominium association filed its tax return as a corporation, its $8,000 net income in the same year could be entirely offset by the previous year's net operating loss and the association would not have to pay any taxes. In addition, because net operating losses incurred in tax years ending after 1975 may be carried forward seven years following the taxable year of the loss, the remaining $1,000 would be available as a deduction in the next six years, provided the association filed its return as a corporation.

Although it does not often occur, it is possible for an inexperienced condominium association to operate at a loss but still have to pay income tax. If the association elects the tax-exempt status for the year it operated at a loss, any revenue that is not tax-exempt—such as user fees and interest—would be subject to the 30 percent tax-exempt organization tax rate. This could be avoided if the association filed its return as a corporation.

In addition, there is a way that an association can file as a corporation and avoid income tax even if its assessments exceed its expenses. If the excess assessments are refunded to the unit owners or are applied to the next year's regular assessments, they will not be subject to corporate tax. Either action requires a special vote of the membership. Of course, this alternative does fail to recognize the importance of establishing reserve funds.

There is yet another method for avoiding income tax on certain reserves. If an association chooses the corporate tax treatment, special assessments designated for specific capital expenditures are not included in the gross taxable income, provided that they meet certain requirements. These special assessments can be excluded from taxation if the assessment has been appropriately approved, if the funds are set aside in a special bank account and not commingled with regular assessments, and if the funds are used for the purpose for which they were assessed. In effect, this alternative excludes capital reserves from being treated as income for tax purposes. To successfully isolate capital reserves from income to avoid taxation, such reserves may only be used for capital items. If reserves are used for expense items, the reserves, upon an IRS audit, may be taxed as income. To understand how this works, again consider a hypothetical condominium:

Income	
Assessments (operations)	$ 91,000
Assessments (capital reserves)	7,000
Interest	1,100
Amenity rental fees	900
Total income	$100,000
Income subject to tax	
Assessments (operations)	$ 91,000
Interest	1,100
Amenity rental fees	900
Total income subject to tax	$ 93,000
Operating expenses	$ 92,000
Taxable income	$ 1,000
Tax rate	17%
Tax due	$ 170

Since the election for tax-exempt treatment must be made each year, a condominium association should review its financial status annually. An election under Section 528 might be advantageous one year, while the assocation might be in a better tax position by accepting the corporate tax treatment the following year. The condominium association should weigh all of the variables before it reaches a decision. There are ways to avoid or lower the tax bill, if all of the alternatives are known and understood. Certainly, no condominium association should pay federal income taxes on assessments collected to operate and maintain the condominium community.

Although the Tax Reform Act of 1976 resolved certain issues, it also created some new questions that will be answered only as Section 528 is interpreted by the courts. Because of these questions, obtaining the assistance of a qualified tax attorney or a certified public accountant—preferably one who has had experience in condominium legal practices—is essential to making the right decision about the association's tax status.

The Federal Tax Status of the Unit Owner

The person who owns a home has certain advantages that the apartment renter clearly does not have. Specifically, the home owner can benefit from a set of federal income tax shelters. In the eyes of the Internal Revenue Service, there is no essential difference between a condominium unit owner and single-family home owner. As a result, families and individuals can turn to condominiums as a way to take advantage of income tax incentives.

Taking advantage of deductions

The person who owns and uses his or her condominium unit as the principal residence throughout the year can enjoy the same tax benefits as the person who owns a conventional house. Assuming that both itemize their deductions, the three principal tax deductions available to both the condominium owner and the single-family home owner are deductions for interest, property taxes, and casualty and theft losses.

Because condominium unit owners obtain their own individual mortgages on their units, they can deduct any mortgage interest paid during the tax year. Similarly, if an owner has a mortgage on his or her share in the common areas of the condominium, the interest paid on that mortgage can also be deducted. Although it is very rare for individual unit owners to obtain a blanket mortgage, if they did, each unit owner could deduct his or her portion of the interest on that common mortgage. And any time that a unit owner borrows money to make repairs, improvements, or additions to an individual unit, the owner can deduct the interest that is paid on that debt.

Like home owners, condominium unit owners also can deduct property taxes for the year in which they are paid. They can deduct real estate taxes assessed against their individually owned units, they can deduct their share (based on percentage of ownership interest) of any real estate taxes assessed against the condominium's common areas, and they can deduct real estate taxes on any other separate interest that they own in the condominium project. Under some state laws, for example, condominium unit owners may hold title to a parking space or a storage locker. If so, they can deduct real estate taxes levied on such a piece of property.

Unit owners should keep in mind that deductions for property taxes are available only if they have a fee simple absolute interest in the land. (*See Chapter 1 for a discussion of this term.*) If they have a leasehold interest, they are not entitled to deduct the real estate taxes that are assessed against the land, even though they are obligated to pay these taxes. However, real estate taxes assessed against any buildings or additions and improvements can be deducted.

Again like conventional home owners, unit owners whose property is damaged or destroyed by fire or other casualty, in excess of $100, may have incurred a deductible loss, and the same is true of losses due to theft. A deductible casualty loss is determined by comparing the value of the property in question immediately before the casualty with its value immediately after the casualty. If there is no better way to determine this difference in value, it may be based on the cost of repairing or replacing the property to the condition it was in just before the casualty occurred. If the decrease in the value of the property as a result of the casualty is less than its *adjusted basis,* in other words, its original cost, the decrease in value is used to determine the deductible loss. If the decrease in value is greater than the original cost, then the latter is used. If an item is stolen, either its *fair market value* at the time of the theft or its original cost, whichever is less, is used to determine the deductible loss. In all cases, any insurance compensation and a $100 loss limitation is subtracted from the total loss to arrive at the deductible loss.

A single example should illustrate how the deductible loss is determined. Let us say that a fire has damaged an interior wall that is part of the unit owner's property, a sofa that was originally purchased for $900, and a painting purchased for $25. It is established that the value of the sofa just before the fire was $300, but after the fire it was worth only $10. The painting, which was totally destroyed by the blaze, had greatly appreciated since it was purchased and, just prior to the fire, was valued at $750. The decrease in the value of the sofa (the value before the fire minus its value after the fire) was $290 ($300–$10), and of the painting, $750 ($750–$0). The wall was repaired for $565. Since the loss is based on either the adjusted basis or the decrease in value, whichever is less, the loss on the sofa would be $290 and the loss on the painting would be $25. The loss on the wall, set by the repair cost, would be $565. Thus, the total loss would be $880. If the unit owner received $330 from the insurance company, the owner's casualty loss deduction for income tax purposes would be $450. The method for determining that figure is shown on the next page.

People who use their condominium units as their primary places of residence cannot deduct personal expenses, such as maintenance assessments, assessments for the use of recreational amenities, cost for repairing and maintaining their units, insurance, depreciation, utility fees, or wages of

		Sofa	Painting	Wall
(1) Adjusted basis (original cost)		$900	$ 25	—
(2) Value before casualty or theft (if available)		300	750	—
(3) Value after casualty or theft (if available)		10	0	—
(4) Decrease in value (Line 2 minus Line 3) or Repair or replacement cost (if Line 2 and Line 3 are unavailable)		290	750	$565
(5) Loss		$290	$ 25	$565
(6) Total loss (if more than one item of property is damaged, or destroyed, or stolen)	$880			
(7) Insurance or other recovery compensation	$330			
(8) $100 limitation	100			
(9) Total Line 7 plus Line 8		430		
(10) Casualty loss deduction (Line 6 minus Line 9)		$450		

domestic help. Nor, like home owners, can they deduct depreciation on their units. However, if condominium unit owners use their units as income-producing property and rent their units to tenants, then the property can be depreciated for income tax purposes. Unit owners also can claim the normal landlord deductions for expenses related to maintenance. These deductible expenses could include regular assessments and fees, insurance, repairs, maintenance, and utilities. Of course, all rents that are collected on a rental unit must be reported by the owners as income.

Selling a condominium unit

Just like home owners who sell their houses and make a profit on the sale, owners of condominium units used for residential purposes who sell them at a gain will have to pay a *capital gains tax*. A loss on the sale of a condominium unit has no effect on individual income tax and no deduction for it is allowed.

However, again like the home owners, condominium unit owners who realize a gain can defer payment of the capital gains tax if certain qualifications are met. Specifically, (1) a new residence, no matter whether it is a house, mobile home, houseboat, cooperative, or another condominium, must be built or bought; (2) this residence must be purchased and moved into within 18 months of the sale of the condominium unit (additional time is allowed for occupancy of a home that is being built); and (3) the *adjusted sales price* of the new residence must be equal to or greater than the adjusted sales price of the unit that was sold. This postponement also is available to a home owner purchasing a condominium unit as a residence.

Unit owners should be mindful that, while this capital gains tax may be postponed, it may not be forgotten or ignored. The long-term advantage of postponing this tax is that a home owner can indefinitely defer the capital gains tax by continually reinvesting in more valuable homes. If it is postponed until the owner reaches the age of 55, all or part of the gain up to $100,000 may be excluded from his or her gross income in accordance with certain requirements set forth in the Internal Revenue Code.

When the capital gains tax is postponed, the gain is subtracted from the cost of the new residence to determine the income tax basis of the new residence. For example, if a unit owner realizes a gain of $17,000 on the sale of his or her condominium unit and six months later purchases a new unit for $52,000, the nonrecognized gain of $17,000 is subtracted from the purchase price of the new unit, making its *basis* or value for tax purposes $35,000.

Energy tax credit

Under the Energy Tax Act of 1978, certain tax credits toward personal federal income taxes are available to individual unit owners when a condominium association spends money for energy conservation or the installation of renewable energy sources such as solar and wind energy equipment. When qualified expenditures are made by the association, the individual unit owner may take a proportionate share as a tax credit subject to certain limitations.

Qualified expenditures for energy conservation include:

(1) Insulation materials whose primary purpose is the reduction of heat loss or gain. (It should be noted that such items as carpeting, drapes, or wood paneling, which have an insulating effect, are excluded from this category since their primary purpose is decoration. Other items that serve a significant structural function, such as extra-thick walls, also will not qualify since their primary purpose is not reduction of heat loss or gain.)

(2) Furnace replacement burners designed to save fuel.

(3) Storm doors and windows.

(4) Furnace ignition systems which replace pilot lights.

(5) Clock thermostats that reduce energy consumption by regulating the demand for heating or cooling.

(6) Other expenditures that are specified by IRS regulations.

(7) Equipment which uses solar or wind energy to heat, cool or provide energy for residential purposes, such as windmills and solar collectors. (It should be noted that this type of equipment does not need to be attached directly to any dwelling unit in order to qualify for the tax credit.)

To obtain an energy credit, any of the above items must be new and must be reasonably expected to remain in use for a minimum of three years. Further, expenditures concerning swimming pools are specifically excluded from this tax credit category.

Each resident condominium unit owner may take a tax credit of 15 percent of the first $2,000 of his or her share of qualified expenditures made by the association for energy conservation and 40 percent of the first $10,000 of the owner's share of expenditures for renewable energy sources. Non-resident owners are not entitled to the energy tax credit, although they may be entitled for a deduction for their entire share of these costs if the unit is designated as income-producing property.

There are, of course, limitations on the energy tax credit. The minimum credit that can be claimed is $10. Prior expenditures for the same condominium unit reduce the amount of maximum qualified expenditures available for the current year. The credit cannot exceed the tax liability on the individual's return, but excess credits can be carried over to any tax year prior to 1987. In the case of ownership of a condominium unit by two or more individuals, the allowable credit must be prorated between the individuals.

The following example will demonstrate how the energy tax credit is calculated: A condominium association with 100 dwelling units (each entitled to ownership of one percent of the common areas) enters into a contract for roof repairs and installation of insulation in all units at a cost of $100,000. The contract specifically provides that the cost of installing the insulation is $60,000. The available residential energy tax credit for an individual unit owner who has taxable income of $15,000 on which a tax of $2,000 must be paid is computed as follows:

Individual unit owner's portion of the total expenditure	$1,000
Individual unit owner's portion of qualifying expenditure for insulation	600
Tax credit of 15 percent	$ 90

The credit of $90 is then applied to the individual owner's total tax liability of $2,000. This leaves a tax of $1,910. To claim an energy conservation tax credit, the individual unit owner must fill out an IRS Form 5695.

The individual unit owners should consult with a qualified accountant or tax attorney when determining the allowable energy tax credit.

The Condominium's Real Estate Tax Status

In addition to paying federal income taxes, unit owners also will be faced with paying real estate taxes. One of the characteristics of condominium ownership is that the individual units are taxed separately; the project is not taxed as a single piece of property.

Because real estate taxation practices have their roots in state condominium laws, there are likely to be some differences from state to state in the method used to access condominium properties. Most state laws consider each condominium unit and its undivided interest in the common areas as one parcel of real property. In such cases, the unit owner's property is subject to an individual assessment and individual taxation as if it were any other kind of real property. Although this is the usual practice, it is not uncommon for assessors to value the entire project as though it were a single property and then determine the individual real estate tax assessments based on the percentages of interest. Even when this is done, however, separate tax bills are sent to each unit owner.

The condominium association usually does not receive a tax bill. However, the general guidelines is that if a parcel can be sold, it can be assessed, and the association may hold title to a property that can be sold, such as an office for use of the on-site manager or the management agent, an apartment used by a janitor, or a garage. In these cases, the association may, at least in some states, receive a tax bill.

Because each unit owner can deduct all property taxes paid—including his or her share of the property taxes on the condominium's common areas—the association should document each owner's portion of an assessment whenever taxes are assessed against common areas and paid by the association as a common expense, to support each owner's deduction claim.

APPENDIX A:
SAMPLE FORMS AND
CHECKLISTS

Governing Document Content Checklist

SUBJECTS TREATED IN GOVERNING DOCUMENTS	DECLARATION	ARTICLES OF INCORPORATION	BYLAWS	UNIT DEED	HOUSE RULES AND REGULATIONS
Definitions of Units and Common Areas					
Assignment of Percentages of Ownership Interest					
Establishment of Administrative Procedures					
Outline of Maintenance Responsibilities					
Establishment of Fiscal Procedures					
Delegation of Management Authority					
Outline of Insurance Requirements					
Establishment of Rules, Regulations, and Restrictions					
Method for Transferring Controls					

Condominium Association
Record of Administrative Requirements

Condominium Association _____

RECORDATION OF DOCUMENTS

Declaration

Date _____ Municipality _____ Book _____ Page _____

Bylaws

Date _____ Municipality _____ Book _____ Page _____

Articles of Incorporation

Date _____ Municipality _____ Book _____ Page _____

ANNUAL MEMBERSHIP MEETING REQUIREMENTS

Date _____

Notice Required _____ Proxy Due Date_____

VOTE REQUIREMENTS

Amend Declaration _____ Amend Bylaws _____

Decide Operational Issues _____ Approve Special Assessments _____

SPECIAL MEETING REQUIREMENTS

Notice Required _____ Limitation of Issues _____

Board Vote Needed to Call_____ Owner Vote Needed to Call_____

BOARD OF DIRECTORS REQUIREMENTS

Number_____ Initial Terms _____

Offices _____

Requirement to Remove Officer _____

Requirement to Remove Director _____

Method for Replacement of Director _____

BOARD MEETING REQUIREMENTS

Minimum Number of Meetings _____

Notice Required _____ Votes to Pass Motion _____

Policy Resolution

Policy of _____Condominium Association

Adopted by the Board of Directors _____
(Date)

Topic _____

Resolved: _____

_____

_____

_____

_____

_____

_____

Filed in Minute Book Page _____

Attested by _____
(Secretary)

Ballot

To elect _____ Directors of the Board of Directors of

_____ Condominium Association

Date _____   Vote _____times

Candidates   Indicate
(list alphabetically)   Vote Here

_____   _____

_____   _____

_____   _____

_____   _____

_____   _____

_____   _____

_____   _____

_____   _____

_____   _____

Nomination Application

I, _____
(Print Name)

hereby submit my name for consideration for nomination for the Board of Directors

of _____ Condo-

minium Association, the election of which is to be held at _____ on
(Time)

_____ at _____ .
(Date)   (Location)

Occupation _____

_____

Education _____

_____

Experience _____

_____

Outside Activities _____

_____

I think I would be an asset to the Board of Directors because _____

_____

_____

Endorsements

Name	Address	Signature
_____	_____	_____
_____	_____	_____
_____	_____	_____
_____	_____	_____
_____	_____	_____

Signed _____

Address _____

Date _____

Notice of Annual Membership Meeting

The annual membership meeting of _____

Condominium Association will be held at _____ on _____
(Time)   (Date)

at_____ for the purpose of electing_____
(Location)

Director(s) and the transaction of such other business as may properly come before

the meeting.

Signed_____
(Secretary or Management Agent)

Proxy

I/We, _____ being the owner(s)

of the condominium unit located at _____

in the _____ condominium do hereby

authorize and appoint _____
(Name of Proxy)

of _____ to be my/our proxy,
(Address of Proxy)

to represent me/us on the issues to be discussed at the membership meeting of

_____ Condominium Association

to be held on _____at _____
(Date)   (Location)

and to vote on my/our behalf on the issues submitted to vote at this meeting or, in the

event a quorum shall fail to attend, at such time and place as the adjourned meeting

shall be resumed. This proxy shall remain in full force and effect until such time as it

shall be revoked by me/us in writing.

_____   _____
(Date)   (Signature of Owner)

_____   _____
(Date)   (Signature of Owner)

Notary Seal

Parliamentary Rules Governing Motions

Name of Motion	Can Speaker Be Interrupted?	Is a Second Needed?	Can It Be Debated?	Can It Be Amended?	What Vote Is Needed to Pass?	Can It Be Reconsidered?
Ranking Motions						
Privileged Motions						
Fix the Time to Adjourn	No	Yes	No*	Yes	Majority	No
Adjourn	No	Yes	No	No	Majority	No
Recess	No	Yes	No*	Yes	Majority	No
Question of Privilege	Yes	No	No	No	Chair Rules	No
Orders of the Day	Yes	No	No	No	Enforceable on Demand	No
Subsidiary Motions						
Lay on the Table	No	Yes	No	No	Majority	No
Previous Question	No	Yes	No	No	Two-thirds	No; unless vote on question has not been taken
Limit Debate	No	Yes	No	Yes	Two-thirds	Yes
Postpone Definitely	No	Yes	Yes	Yes	Majority	Yes
Refer to Committee	No	Yes	Yes	Yes	Majority	Yes
Amend	No	Yes	Yes	Yes	Majority	Yes
Postpone Indefinitely	No	Yes	Yes	No	Majority	Yes
Main Motions						
General Main Motion	No	Yes	Yes	Yes	Majority	Yes

Parliamentary Rules Governing Motions, *cont.*

NAME OF MOTION	CAN SPEAKER BE INTERRUPTED?	IS A SECOND NEEDED?	CAN IT BE DEBATED?	CAN IT BE AMENDED?	WHAT VOTE IS NEEDED TO PASS?	CAN IT BE RECONSIDERED?
Nonranking Motions						
Main Motions to Renew Questions						
Take from the Table	No	Yes	No	No	Majority	No
Rescind	No	Yes	Yes	Yes	Two-thirds	Yes; If Negative Vote
Amend Something Previously Adopted	No	Yes	Yes	Yes	Two-thirds	Yes; If Negative Vote
Discharge a Committee	No	Yes	Yes	Yes	Majority	Yes; If Negative Vote
Reconsider	Yes	Yes	Yes	No	Majority	No
Incidental Motions						
Point of Order	Yes	No	No	No	Chair Rules	No
Suspend the Rules	No	Yes	No	No	Two-thirds	No
Object to Consideration	Yes	No	No	No	Two-thirds in Negative	No
Division of Question	No	Yes	No	Yes	Majority	No
Division of Assembly	Yes	No	No	No	Enforceable on Demand	No

*Not debatable when another question is before the assembly.

Committee Interest Questionnaire

Please complete this questionnaire if you are interested in playing an important role in the activities of _____Condominium Association.

Name _____

Address _____

Telephone _____ Date _____

I would like to work on the following committee (in order of preference):

_____ Architectural Control Committee

_____ Landscape and Grounds Committee

_____ Budget and Finance Committee

_____ Insurance Committee

_____ Maintenance Committee

_____ Rules and Regulations Committee

_____ Social Committee

_____ Newsletter Committee

_____ Welcoming Committee

_____ Recreation Committee

I would accept chairmanship of the committee I am volunteering for:

_____ At this time

_____ In the future

I have a (considerable) (moderate) (small) amount of time to devote. The most convenient time for me is (weekends) (days) (evenings) (whenever needed).

I have the following skills which may be of value to the operations and activities of the community (typing, shorthand, specific vocational experience, etc.): _____

_____

_____

Preventive Maintenance Schedule

Item _____ Date _____

DESCRIPTION OF MAINTENANCE JOB	FREQUENCY			
	INSPECT	CLEAN	LUBRICATE	REPLACE

*Frequency Code: D–Daily; W–Weekly; M–Monthly; Q–Quarterly;
S–Semiannually; A–Annually.*

Appendix A: Sample Forms and Checklists

Emergency Telephone Number Checklist

Condominium Association _____

Address _____

		TELEPHONE	
	OFFICE	HOME/NIGHT	
Board of Directors	_____	_____	_____
	_____	_____	_____
	_____	_____	_____
	_____	_____	_____
	_____	_____	_____
	_____	_____	_____
Association Employees	_____	_____	_____
	_____	_____	_____
	_____	_____	_____
	_____	_____	_____
	_____	_____	_____
Accountant	_____	_____	_____
Attorney	_____	_____	_____
Architect	_____	_____	_____
Developer	_____	_____	_____
Insurance Agent	_____	_____	_____
Management Agent	_____	_____	_____
Service Contractors	_____	_____	_____
Air Conditioning	_____	_____	_____
Heating	_____	_____	_____
Fuel	_____	_____	_____
Equipment	_____	_____	_____

Emergency Telephone Number Checklist, *cont.*

	TELEPHONE		
	OFFICE	HOME/NIGHT	
Elevators	_____	_____	_____
Antennae	_____	_____	_____
Electrician	_____	_____	_____
Glass	_____	_____	_____
Landscaping	_____	_____	_____
Lawn Service	_____	_____	_____
Laundry	_____	_____	_____
Locksmith	_____	_____	_____
Painter	_____	_____	_____
Pest Control	_____	_____	_____
Plumber	_____	_____	_____
Roofer	_____	_____	_____
Security Service	_____	_____	_____
Security System	_____	_____	_____
Snow Removal	_____	_____	_____
Street Lighting	_____	_____	_____
Trash Removal	_____	_____	_____
_____	_____	_____	_____
_____	_____	_____	_____
_____	_____	_____	_____
Miscellaneous			
Fire Station	_____	_____	_____
Police Station	_____	_____	_____
_____	_____	_____	_____
_____	_____	_____	_____

Custodial Maintenance Schedule

AREA	DESCRIPTION OF MAINTENANCE JOB	FREQUENCY
Lobby		
Laundry		
Halls and Corridors		
Elevators		
Stairways		

Frequency Code: D–Daily; W–Weekly; M–Monthly.

Service Contract Record

COMPANY	TYPE OF SERVICE	FREQUENCY OF SERVICE	TERMINATION DATE	AMOUNT (MONTHLY)	CANCELLATION PROVISION
	Pool				
	Gardening				
	Janitorial				
	Elevator Maintenance				
	Security Services				
	Trash Removal				

Grounds Care Program
Specifications for Bid

LAWN CUTTING

(1)   Initial cut in first week of April; final cut in middle of November.
(2)   Total cuts: Thirty (30); additional per cut cost should be indicated.
(3)   Cut height: Two and one-half (2½) inches.
(4)   Grass clippings: Swept and removed from all streets, curbs, sidewalks, and entrance ways and from surfaces of any walls, windows, or doors to which adhered with such cutting; grass clippings are to be raked and removed from all lawn areas if their length shall exceed three (3) inches.
(5)   Inability to cut due to weather: Credit for incomplete cuttings or cuttings not performed shall be prorated on the basis of the percentage of the area incompleted with adjustment made at the close of the season.
(6)   Lawn cutting shall be confined to between the hours of 8:30 a.m. and 5:00 p.m. and shall be performed on weekdays only unless otherwise agreed to by the Board of Directors.
(7)   Grass around all buildings, flower beds, trees, and other obstacles within the lawn area shall be hand trimmed with each cutting, and the cuttings raked and removed.

EDGING

(1)   Inclusive of all sidewalks, entrance ways, and curbs.
(2)   Complete edging is to be accomplished in single operation during the first week of June, August, and October and in the last week of November.
(3)   Depth of edging: Minimum of two (2) inches.
(4)   Width of edging: Minimum of one-half (½) inch.
(5)   Edged dirt and grass is to be swept up and removed as generated.

PRUNING

(1)   All shrubs and trees are to be pruned upon completion of their growth season to maintain proper shape and uniformity of appearance.
(2)   Clippings are to be removed as generated.

Grounds Care Program
Specifications for Bid, *cont.*

LAWN CARE PROGRAM

Early Spring: Soil test for nitrogen, phosphorous, and potassium needs; soil test for pH requirements; lime and fertilize as required: aerate and roll; apply chemicals for weed and fungus control; milky spot treatment for Japanese beetles.

Early Summer: Fertilize; aerate and roll; apply chemicals to control weeds, fungus, cinch bugs, sod webworms, and pre-emergence crabgrass control; spray trees for beetles and webworms.

Late Summer: Fertilize; roll; apply chemicals for weeds, cinch bugs, sod webworms, and pre-emergence crabgrass control.

Fall: Fertilize; lime; seed; aerate and roll; apply chemicals for weed and fungus control.

MULCHING OF TREES AND FLOWER BEDS

(1)   Turn monthly.

(2)   Apply and spread additional mulch as needed.

GENERAL SPECIFICATIONS

(1)   Contractor agrees to maintain Workers' Compensation and Public Liability insurance in the amounts of $50,000; $100,000; $300,000 in full force throughout the term of the contract and to furnish vendee with certificates of said insurance in evidence thereof.

(2)   Contractor shall furnish vendee with one estimate for application of the above program to the condominium development grounds for one season.

(3)   Contractor shall furnish all tools, equipment, materials, and labor at his expense.

Bid Amount   _____

Consumer Checklist
for Buying a Residential Condominium

(1) Is the building well constructed throughout?
  (a) Do the corners meet?
  (b) Are the floors level and tight?
  (c) Do the roof joists sag?
  (d) Do the gutters drain away from the building?
  (e) Do the windows or the walls leak?
  (f) Are there signs of plaster failure?
  (g) Is the bathroom and/or kitchen plumbing noisy enough to be heard through walls?
  (h) Is the electrical system adequate?
  (i) Is there space to install air-conditioning systems inside the unit?

(2) Does the building meet all of the requirements that are important to you?
  (a) Are the size and layout of the unit suitable for your needs?
  (b) Is the floor covering provided?
      What type is required?
  (c) Are there restrictions on draperies or window coverings?
  (d) Are the elevators and trash disposals conveniently located?
  (e) Are the laundry facilities conveniently located, well maintained, and sufficient to service the building?
      Is there an adequate number of washers, driers, tables, and chairs?
  (f) Are there enough closets?
  (g) Have security provisions been made?
      Does the building provide peepholes, intercom systems, door chains, dead-bolt locks, door attendants, or a security patrol?
  (h) Are the parking facilities convenient and adequate for the number of automobiles of the building?
      How are guest parking requirements handled?
      Are domestic employees and contractors able to park on the premises?
      Can boats and trailers be parked on the property?
  (i) Is the building well located to shopping, transportation, parks, schools, etc.?
  (j) How are utilities metered?
      If master metered, what energy-conserving measures are being implemented?
  (k) Are any of the following amenities available to you?
        pool (indoor or outdoor)
        health club
        storage lockers (location, size, ventilation, number)
        air conditioning (central or individual)
        appliances/fixtures
        balconies
      If so, who owns them and who is responsible for their maintenance?

Consumer Checklist
for Buying a Residential Condominium, *cont.*

Are residents required to pay special charges for use privileges?

Which amenities, if any, are available for use by guests or outsiders? Under what conditions?

(l) Are children permitted?

(m) Does the condominium permit pets?

If so, what type?

What sorts of restrictions are placed on pets?

(3) Is the condominium association well organized and effective?

(a) Is the board of directors effective and decisive?

(b) Are unit owners willing to invest their time and take a firm, businesslike approach to community self-government?

(c) Is an on-site manager or property management firm employed?

(4) Are you in complete agreement with the governing documents of the association (declaration, bylaws, individual unit deeds, articles of incorporation, and rules, regulations, and restrictions)?

(a) Is the process of amending the declaration or regulations acceptable to you?

(b) Do you agree with the definitions of common maintenance obligations versus owner obligations?

(c) Are the liability provisions acceptable?

(d) Are the rules, regulations, and restrictions acceptable?

(5) Does the condominium have adequate insurance against fire, liability, theft, or boiler explosion?

(a) What personal property insurance should an owner have?

(b) Is the unit owner liable for the deductible portion of the association's policy?

(6) Is the proposed budget for the operations of the building provided?

(a) Who prepared the budget?

(b) Are maintenance fees sufficient?

(c) Are reserves sufficient?

(7) Does the building have a policy on absentee owners?

(a) Are leases permitted as a general practice, on a hardship basis, or not at all? Are leases long term or short term?

(b) What is the accepted percentage of renters?

(c) Is there a standard condominium lease form that gives the association the right to collect rents if unit owners fail to make monthly assessment payments? Does it give the association the right to evict tenants who fail to follow the rules and regulations?

(8) Is the developer reliable?

(a) Are the sales personnel the developers or independent brokers?

(b) Who is responsible for misrepresentations?

Pie Diagram
Assessment Presentation

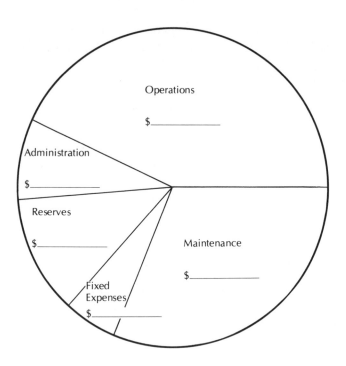

Grievance Form

Date _____

Nature of Complaint_____

_____

_____

_____

_____

Filed by _____

Address _____

Phone _____

Condominium Association Complaint Log

DATE	TIME	OWNER	ADDRESS	TELEPHONE	FORM OF COMPLAINT	DESCRIPTION OF COMPLAINT	DISPOSITION	COMPLETED

House Rules and Regulations

(1) Any common sidewalks, driveways, entrances, or passageways shall not be obstructed or used by any unit owner for any other purpose than ingress to and egress from the units.

(2) Except as to the areas termed limited common areas, no article shall be placed on or in any of the general common areas except for those articles of personal property which are the common property of all the unit owners.

(3) Unit owners, members of their families, their guests, residents, tenants, or lessees shall not use sidewalks, driveways, entrances, or passageways as play areas.

(4) No vehicle belonging to or under the control of a unit owner or a member of the family or a guest, tenant, lessee, or employee of a unit owner shall be parked in such manner as to impede or prevent ready access to any entrance to or exit from a building.

(5) No owner, resident, or lessee shall install wiring for electrical or telephone installation or for any other purpose, nor shall any television or radio antennae, machines, or air conditioning units be installed on the exterior of the project, nor shall any similar improvements that protrude through the walls or the roof of the condominium be constructed, except as may be expressly authorized by the Association.

(6) No work of any kind shall be done upon the exterior building walls or upon the general or limited common areas by any unit owner. All such work is the responsibility of the Association.

(7) Owners and occupants shall exercise reasonable care to avoid making or permitting to be made loud, disturbing, or objectionable noises and in using or playing or permitting to be used or played musical instruments, radios, phonographs, television sets, amplifiers, and any other instruments or devices in such manner as may disturb or tend to disturb owners, tenants, or occupants of other units.

(8) Disposition of garbage and trash shall be only by the use of garbage disposal units or by use of common trash and garbage facilities.

House Rules and Regulations, *cont.*

(9) No rugs or other materials shall be dusted from windows, balconies, decks, or patios by beating or shaking.

(10) No cats, dogs, or other animal, bird, or reptile (hereinafter for brevity termed "animal") shall be kept, maintained, or harbored in the development unless the same in each instance is expressly permitted in writing by the management agent or, if there is no management agent, then by the Board of Directors. Where such written permission is granted, such permission is revocable if the animal becomes obnoxious to other owners, in which event the owner or person having control of the animal shall be given a written notice to correct the problem, or if not corrected, the owner, upon written notice, will be required to dispose of the animal. The written notice provided for herein shall be issued by the management agent or, if there is no management agent, then by one or more of the members of the Board of Directors.

(11) The Association assumes no liability for nor shall it be liable for any loss or damage to articles stored in any common or other storage area.

(12) Any damage to the general common areas or common personal property caused by a unit owner or a child or children of a unit owner or their guests or the guests of a unit owner shall be repaired at the expense of that unit owner.

(13) No unit shall be occupied by more than four persons, which number shall not include more than two children, without the consent of 100 percent of the percentage ownership of the units as that term is defined in the Declaration of this Condominium. For these purposes the term "children" refers to persons who have not attained the age of 13 years.

(14) No owner shall display any sign visible from the exterior of any unit, nor place on or remove from the project grounds plants of any description without the prior consent of the Board of Directors.

The foregoing House Rules and Regulations are subject to amendment and to the promulgation of further regulations.

Guidelines for the
Architectural Control Committee

The Architectural Control Committee (hereafter referred to as the Committee) shall be made up of volunteers appointed by the President of the Board of Directors. The Committee will help to administer the rules and regulations as set forth in the Declaration and Bylaws. The Committee shall vote on requests for all external changes and shall present its recommendations to the Board of Directors (hereafter referred to as the Board) for its approval or disapproval.

APPLICATION PROCEDURES

(1) A written request describing any improvements to be made to the property must be sent to _____

(2) The descriptions must include all vital information pertaining to the changes to be made.

(3) When a color change is requested, a color swatch is required.

SPECIFIC PROJECT REQUIREMENTS

(1) Awnings and above-ground decks of any kind are not felt to enhance aesthetic qualities of the community and therefore shall be prohibited.

(2) Any additions to the parent structure shall be prohibited.

(3) Any exterior paint change must be approved by the Committee.

(4) Any extensions of the rear patio must be approved by the Committee.

(5) All front and side iron railings must remain the original black color. The back railings and porches may be painted a different color if approved by the Committee. All iron railings and porches must be well kept and be attached properly to the unit.

(6) All fences must be wood and be of a natural wood color or stain. Fences that enclose a yard must be no higher than five (5) feet and be of a natural wood color or stain.

(7) Hedges are considered fences and therefore are not generally allowed forward of the rear line of the house. Chicken wire may be used to reinforce a hedge only for the first growing season of the original hedge, then it must be removed.

(8) A privacy fence that is perpendicular to the unit may be erected to a height of six (6) feet and a depth of twelve (12) feet. This fence may not enclose an area but must be along the side of property lines.

Guidelines for the
Architectural Control Committee, *cont.*

(9) Any type of plastic, metal, or wood flower bed fencing that does not exceed a height of twelve (12) inches may be used to enclose a flower bed that does not extend to the sidewalk. If a front yard has been turned into a flower bed, it must be enclosed by brick-in-the-ground edging or be left unedged.

(10) Exterior lighting shall not be directed in such manner as to create annoyance to neighbors.

(11) Trash containers shall not be permitted to remain conspicuous except on days of trash collection. No trash containers may be kept on general common areas.

(12) No pools other than small wading pools that can be put in storage nightly shall be used on any lot at any time.

(13) No structures such as dog houses, storage sheds, etc., shall be constructed on any lot at any time.

(14) Children's play equipment such as small plastic slides is permitted so long as it can be stored at night.

(15) Small portable sandboxes are permitted so long as they are well kept, covered at night, and removed at the end of the summer season. If not kept in good condition, the Committee will request repair or removal.

(16) Swing and gym sets on individual lots shall not be permitted.

(17) No outside televisions or radio antenna shall be permitted.

(18) Realty signs shall not be permitted on general common areas. No realty sign shall be attached to a unit. Realty signs must not remain on individual lots after sale of units.

(19) No clothes lines of any kind shall be permitted.

(20) All latticework must be against the surface of the rear or sides of the building. It may be left the natural wood color or painted a harmonious color with Committee approval.

(21) No garden shall be bordered with chicken wire. Vegetable gardens are restricted to the rear portion or yard of the limited common area of any unit and shall be limited in size to one-third (⅓) of that area.

(22) Small wooden bird feeders shall be permitted so long as they are placed on poles between five (5) and eight (8) feet high and are kept presentable. Multibird houses shall not be permitted.

(23) Minibikes shall not be permitted on any common area per local law.

(24) No motor vehicle shall be kept on any common area except the parking area.

(25) No boat or trailer shall be parked on any parking area or street.

Approval of any project does not waive the necessity of obtaining a county building permit.

Architectural Improvement
Application and Review Form

Unit Owner_____Date _____

Address of Unit _____Phone _____

Nature of Improvement _____

_____

_____

_____

Color (if applicable) _____

Location (if applicable) _____

Dimensions (if applicable) _____

Construction Material (if applicable)_____

Supplier_____Approximate Cost _____

(A sketch of all improvements must be attached to the application to show location and dimensions.)

Send to _____

Address _____

Date Submitted_____Signed _____

For Internal Use Only

Date Received _____

Inspected on _____Inspected by _____

Approved on _____Disapproved on _____

Reason for Disapproval _____

_____

_____

Architectural Control and Use Violation Log

Unit Address	Unit Owner	Description of Violation	Date Noted	First Notice	Inspection	Second Notice	Second Inspection	Attorney	Comments

Budget Preparation Calendar

DATE	ACTION TO BE COMPLETED
	President assigns members of Budget and Finance Committee to work with standing committees in preparing appropriate budget requests.
	Committees submit budget requests to treasurer.
	If association employs staff, treasurer submits salary recommendations to board of directors.
	Public hearings conducted, at which time committee chairmen formally make their requests, explain them, and answer questions regarding them. All unit owners invited.
	Budget conferences between board and committee chairmen conducted.
	Final budget decisions, including official estimates of revenue from assessments and other sources, are made by treasurer with assistance from management agent.
	Treasurer submits proposed budget to board.
	Modifications made by board are incorporated into budget.
	Printing of budget with amendments completed under treasurer's supervision.
	Board reviews final budget and passes resolution to adopt it.
	Fiscal year begins, and budget takes effect.

Replacement Reserves Worksheet

ITEM	REPLACEMENT ÷ COST	REMAINING USEFUL LIFE	= ANNUAL RESERVE REQUIREMENT
Painting, Interior	_____	_____	_____
Painting, Exterior	_____	_____	_____
Water Heater	_____	_____	_____
Carpet and Flooring	_____	_____	_____
Street and Driveway	_____	_____	_____
Heating-Air Conditioning System	_____	_____	_____
Swimming Pool	_____	_____	_____
Tennis Court	_____	_____	_____
Furnishings and Equipment	_____	_____	_____
Light Fixtures	_____	_____	_____
Fire Extinguishers	_____	_____	_____
_____	_____	_____	_____
_____	_____	_____	_____
_____	_____	_____	_____
_____	_____	_____	_____

Total Annual Replacement Reserves Requirement _____

Budget Worksheet

		TOTAL ANNUAL	TOTAL MONTHLY
EXPENSES			
Administrative Expenses			
Office Salaries		————	————
Office Expenses		————	————
Management Fee		————	————
Legal		————	————
Audit		————	————
Telephone		————	————
Miscellaneous		————	————
Operating Expenses			
Elevator		————	————
Heating Fuel		————	————
Electricity		————	————
Water/Sewer		————	————
Gas		————	————
Exterminating		————	————
Rubbish Removal		————	————
Window Washing		————	————
Miscellaneous		————	————

Repair and Maintenance	Pay-roll	Mate-rials	Con-tract	TOTAL ANNUAL	TOTAL MONTHLY
Security	———	———	———	————	————
Ground Maintenance	———	———	———	————	————
Custodial	———	———	———	————	————
General Maintenance	———	———	———	————	————
Heat/AC/Vent	———	———	———	————	————

Budget Worksheet, *cont.*

	Pay-roll	Mate-rials	Con-tract	TOTAL ANNUAL	TOTAL MONTHLY
Painting, Interior	___	___	___	___	___
Painting, Exterior	___	___	___	___	___
Recreational Amenities	___	___	___	___	___
Miscellaneous	___	___	___	___	___
Fixed Expenses					
Real Estate Tax				___	___
Other Tax				___	___
Insurance				___	___
Recreational					
Facilities, Leased				___	___
Ground Rent				___	___
Reserves					
Capital Replacements				___	___
Operating Contingencies				___	___
Total Expense Budget				___	___
INCOME					
Regular Unit Assessments				___	___
Rental Fees				___	___
Interest				___	___
Special Assessments				___	___
Miscellaneous				___	___
Total Income				___	___

Statement of Income and Expense Worksheet

	MONTH ACTUAL	MONTH BUDGETED	YEAR-TO-DATE ACTUAL	YEAR-TO-DATE BUDGETED
INCOME				
Regular Assessments				
Rental Fees				
Interest				
Special Assessments				
Miscellaneous				
Total Income				
EXPENSES				
Administrative Expenses				
Office Salaries				
Office Expenses				
Management Fee				
Legal				
Audit				
Telephone				
Miscellaneous				
Operating Expenses				
Elevator				
Heating Fuel				
Electricity				
Water/Sewer				
Gas				
Exterminating				
Rubbish Removal				
Window Washing				
Miscellaneous				

Statement of Income and Expense Worksheet, *cont.*

	MONTH ACTUAL	MONTH BUDGETED	YEAR-TO-DATE ACTUAL	YEAR-TO-DATE BUDGETED
Repair and Maintenance				
Security				
Ground Maintenance				
Custodial				
General Maintenance				
Heat/AC/Vent				
Painting, Interior				
Painting, Exterior				
Recreational Amenities				
Miscellaneous				
Fixed Expenses				
Real Estate Tax				
Other Tax				
Insurance				
Recreational Facilities, Leased				
Ground Rent				
Reserves				
Capital Replacements				
Operating Contingencies				
Total Expenses				
Net Gain (Loss)				

Chart of Accounts
from the U.S. Department of Housing and Urban Development

6300 ADMINISTRATIVE EXPENSES

6310	Office Salaries
6311	Office Expenses
6312	Office Rent
6320	Management Fee
6330	Manager or Superintendent Salaries
6340	Legal Expenses
6350	Auditing Expenses
6360	Telephone and Telegraph
6370	Bad Debts
6390	Miscellaneous Administrative Expenses

6400 OPERATING EXPENSES

6410	Elevator Payroll
6411	Elevator Power
6420	Fuel
6421	Engineer Payroll
6430	Janitor Payroll
6431	Janitor Supplies
6440	Bus Operator Payroll
6441	Gasoline, Oil, and Grease
6450	Electricity
6451	Water
6452	Gas
6460	Exterminating Payroll
6461	Exterminating Supplies
6462	Exterminating Contract
6470	Garbage and Trash Removal
6490	Miscellaneous Operating Expenses

6500 MAINTENANCE EXPENSES

6510	Protection (Security) Payroll
6511	Protection Fee, Costs, or Contracts
6520	Grounds Payroll
6521	Grounds Supplies and Replacements
6522	Grounds Contract
6530	Cleaning Payroll
6540	Repairs Payroll
6541	Repairs Material
6542	Repairs Contract
6543	Repairs—Extraordinary and Nonrecurring
6550	Elevator Maintenance
6551	Air Conditioning Repair and Maintenance
6560	Decorating Payroll
6561	Decorating Supplies
6562	Decorating Contract
6570	Motor Vehicle
6580	Maintenance Equipment Repairs
6590	Miscellaneous Maintenance Expenses

6700 INSURANCE AND TAXES

6710	Taxes
6720	Insurance

Unit Owner Ledger Card

Unit Owner _____

Address of Unit _____

Billing Address _____

Monthly Assessment _____

DATE	DESCRIPTION OF PAYMENT	BILLED	RECEIVED	BALANCE

Miscellaneous Information

Telephone Number _____

Children _____   Pets _____

Other _____

_____

_____

APPENDIX B:
CONDOMINIUM LEGISLATION—
RECOMMENDED CRITERIA

NATIONAL ASSOCIATION OF REALTORS®
Condominium Committee
Condominium Legislation—Recommended Criteria

PREAMBLE

Condominiums are and should remain an important form of ownership. As applied to homes, the form affords an apartment dweller both the opportunity for the efficiency and convenience of that type of dwelling and the security and benefits of being an owner. To a detached or townhouse owner, the form provides an organized method of control by all owners over the conduct of the affairs of an entire project. The industry has just begun to explore the use of this type of ownership in commercial and industrial situations. However, the popularity of condominiums has revealed abuses, inequities, and problems affecting the consumer. Further, an analysis of the present statutes reveals inadequacies not only in "consumer protection" but in other areas affecting the formation, operation, and use of this form of ownership.

The person who forms a condominium to sell units as part of his ordinary business or in contemplation of a profit is often referred to as a "developer." A person forming a condominium of a pre-existing building is often described as a "converter." As used herein, the term "sponsor" connotes both these entrepreneurs.

Based upon this analysis, the Condominium Committee of the NATIONAL AS-SOCIATION OF REALTORS® recommends the following:

DIVISION I—BASIC CONSUMER PROTECTION—RESIDENTIAL CONDOMINIUMS

1.   Disclosure—Filing

(a) Statement—The consumer needs education about and information on the scope and nature of the residence he is about to purchase and the costs involved. Certain "abuses" have come to light and must be eliminated; they are dealt with in other paragraphs in this Division. In many areas, disclosure will be sufficient to protect the consumer and acquaint him with the facts he requires to make an informed decision.

Disclosure of material information is to be made by the sponsor.

(b) Filing with an Agency—Not all jurisdictions will find filing with a governmental agency necessary. It must be emphasized that there are great costs involved and that ultimately those costs will be borne by the consumer.

Before the sponsor may sell any unit, the disclosure statement must be filed with a state governmental agency.

(c) Scope of Applicability—The condominium form of ownership has applicability to many situations which makes it a useful device. It is most commonly employed as the method of establishing the apartment dweller/home owner type of unit. It is in these projects that consumers have suffered abuses and the thrust of remedial efforts must be focused in this area.

"Residential condominiums" are to be governed by disclosure/filing requirements and other provisions outlined under these criteria. A residential condominium is a project or portion of a project devoted to and used primarily for residential purposes, each apartment or unit being intended for use by a single family.

(d) Small Condominiums Exempt—Not all residential projects should be covered; however, it is not intended that "loopholes" be permitted. A series of small buildings grouped together by a sponsor which are in reality one large development under an umbrella association should not escape the more stringent requirements. The most salient criteria might be that of the contiguity of the land on which the projects or units are built.

Disclosure/filing should not be applicable to condominium projects containing twelve units or less.

2.   Budgeting and Reserves

(a) Pro Forma Operating Statement

A statement shall be prepared and certified to by an independent professional experienced in such matters projecting the anticipated actual operating costs (and income) adjusted for full occupancy for at least one year beginning with the anticipated date of the initial occupancy. Such statement shall fairly present in clear language the basis upon which it was prepared, indicating that it assumes full occupancy and the factor, if any, used for inflation. In the case of a phased condominium, the statement shall disclose the estimated amount of the effect, if any, of an increased number of units in the condominium and the basis upon which such estimate was made. Further, these statements shall be revised annually.

(b) Creation of Reserves

Initial reserves are to be established and funded by contributions to be made by the individual unit owners either at the closing of each purchase by a lump sum payment or after closing by monthly payments as part of the regular assessment.

(c) Sponsor's Assessment

The sponsor shall pay all the expenses of the condominium and receive all rental income from the common areas, if any, until the association makes assessments against the units. Thereafter all unit owners, including the sponsor, shall pay the assessments made by the association and the association shall receive all rental income from the common areas. Assessments to be paid by the sponsor for unfinished or unoccupied units shall be reduced by the proportionate amount of savings on common expenses, if any, realized by the association due to the unfinished or unoccupied status of the sponsor's units.

3.   Management Agreements and Service Contracts

(a) Length of Term—Under paragraph 7 below, it is contemplated that the association will be in the control of the individual unit owners no later than three years after the sale of the first unit (except for the "expandable condominium"). Accordingly, under the rule suggested in this paragraph 3, the individual unit owners will have an opportunity to choose their own management. The same rule would apply to contracts for landscape maintenance, fuel supply, and similar routinely needed services. It is the experience of the Institute of Real Estate Management, an institute of the NATIONAL ASSOCIATION OF REALTORS®, that a three-year term is a reasonable period for these types of contracts in the initial stages of a condominium's formation. Longer terms may not necessarily be of benefit to the project and are not always justifiable. However, a shorter term may be too restrictive on the sponsor or the management company or service contractor he might employ. In any event, there should be termination for just cause.

> Management agreements and service contracts entered into by the sponsor or the condominium association while the sponsor controls its decisions shall have a termination date or be cancellable three years after the closing of the sale of the first unit, except for "expandable condominiums" which are referred to below.

4.   Recreational Leases

A residential condominium project constructed around and focused on an amenities package (which might even include a golf course) designed to meet the needs of that project should not be burdened with a device where a sponsor can enjoy a future benefit in a disguised fashion. On the other hand, where a given project is adjacent or close to a recreational facility and an individual unit owner can decide not to participate and thereby incur no charge, there is no hidden cost.

(a) Prohibited—Exception

> Leases of recreational or other facilities to the residential condominium association by the sponsor or related parties should be prohibited unless all of the cost of operations are payable on a "membership" basis and "membership" is not compulsory or part of the regular monthly assessment to the unit owner.

(b) Disclosure of Certain Leases

> Any "tie-in" between the sponsor and a related party in a permitted recreational lease must be disclosed in the statement required in paragraph 1.

5.   Leases to the Sponsor or Others of Portions of the Common Elements or Association-Owned Units (such as Food Shop or Restaurant)

A merchant or restaurateur may be reluctant to invest in the trade fixtures needed to make his establishment of high quality, knowing that it may be years before the given project would reach a sustaining level, which may be well after all the units are sold out. It is not unusual to see leases providing for up to five years' free rent for such tenants. Disclosure will reveal those leases designed to hide a benefit to the sponsor as contrasted to those that are legitimate business transactions.

(a) Disclosure of Lease Terms

> The terms and identity of the lessee and any relationship to the sponsor must be disclosed in the statement required in paragraph 1 above.

6.   Warranties of Quality for Newly Constructed Condominiums

(a) Required—It is contemplated that all assignable manufacturers' and contractors' warranties will be assigned in addition to the warranty.

> Warranties by the sponsor should be required as follows:
>
> (i) For the individual unit and limited common elements, one year from the date of closing.
>
> (ii) For the common elements, six months from the date the association is "turned over" to the individual unit owners or two years from the substantial completion of the common elements, whichever is earlier; but in no event less than one year from the closing of the first sale.
>
> (iii) For the common elements, until the association is "turned over" to the individual unit owners, the individual unit-owner members of the

association board may enforce the warranty in the name of the association, and if there be no individual unit owners on the board, then the
individual unit owners may enforce the warranty in the name of the
association.

(b) Warranty or Insurance Program—The NATIONAL ASSOCIATION OF REAL-
TORS® Home Protection Committee has established criteria for a warranty-type program.
It is intended that a program meeting such criteria base will be offered by private industry.

*The sponsor can discharge his obligation under this paragraph by furnish-
ing a warranty insurance policy of a financially responsible institution
affording coverage for the matters to be warranted.*

7.   Control by Individual Unit Owners

During the period before the control passes to the individual unit owner, it is recommended that sponsors as a matter of good practice encourage the formation of an
"Advisory Council" to meet with the official board in a consultative capacity. In this
way several of the individual unit owners become knowledgeable in the operation of
the condominium and are prepared for the eventual "transfer." "The inexperience of
unit owners in self-government" is at the heart of many consumer complaints regarding
condominiums. If this approach is followed, the individual unit owners will develop
the expertise necessary to the proper administration of the board's affairs.

(a) Time and Units Sold

*Control of the condominium association must be transferred to the indi-
vidual unit owners no later than three years after the closing of the first
unit or when 75 percent of the units are sold and closed, whichever is the
first to occur, except for the "expandable condominiums," which are
governed at paragraph 9 below.*

(b) Rights of Individual Unit Owners

*Prior to the transfer of control referred to above, the individual unit own-
ers shall have the right to elect at least one board member after 25 percent of the units are sold and closed, and after 50 percent of the units are
sold and closed the individual unit owners shall have the right to elect a
"full" minority of the board, a majority less one.*

8.   Permanent Mortgage by the Sponsor of Portions of the Residential
        Condominium's Common Elements or Association-Owned Units

The use of this type of mortgage (a mortgage on an apartment for on-site staff, recreation room, or other property of the association) is another form of the below market
lease referred to at paragraph 5 above. This can be a beneficial device if used to
finance "front end costs" such as the cost of the recreation room. Raising funds in this
manner should reduce the per unit price as it spreads the payment for this capital item
over a period of time. Such mortgages must be disclosed so that a purchaser can
understand the "total cost of his unit and future monthly assessment."

(a) Required Disclosure

*Prior to the first sale of any unit, such mortgage is permissible if (i) it is
disclosed in the statement required at paragraph 1 above, (ii) it is fully
amortized over the term of the loan, and (iii) it contains a "prepayment
without penalty" clause.*

(b) Consent Required after Sale of Units

*After the sale of the first unit, such a mortgage is permissible only with
the consent of 75 percent of the individual unit owners and purchasers.*

9.   Expandable Condominiums

(a) Time Limit

*Additional units may be added to a condominium project in accordance
with a "plan" contained in the initial declaration, but all additions must
be made within seven years of recording the declaration. The right to*

continue to "expand" may terminate earlier if the sponsor fails to meet the terms of the plan.

(b) Certain Exceptions to Other Time Limits

For an "expandable" condominium, the time limits of paragraphs 3 and 7 above are extended by an additional four years, provided, however, that if the right to expand is terminated for failure to comply with the plan, then such limits are cut off as of such termination.

(c) Special Rule for Control

For "expandable" condominiums the provisions of paragraph 7(b) concerning the individual unit owners' right to elect one condominium board member shall be effective after 25 percent of the units built in the first phase are sold and closed.

(d) Special Rule for Warranties of Quality

The time limit applicable to 6(a)(ii) above shall be applicable to the common elements as they are built in phases, the warranty on each phase being treated as if each phase was a separate condominium. However, the right of actions shall be in the individual unit owner members of the condominium association board who may enforce the warranty in the name of the association.

10.　　　Conversions

(a) Notification of Tenants

A notice of the formation of a residential condominium must be given to each tenant.

(b) Termination of Occupancy by Landlord—Clearly, a landlord cannot terminate a tenant's right of possession if there is a lease. The rule under this paragraph assures the tenant a minimum of 120 days to move, with or without a lease. If there is a lease affording longer possession rights, its provisions will be honored. The financing of this type of project prohibits prolonged periods of delay in "completing the conversion." The interest rates usually charged between the time of purchase of the building and closing of the unit sale is on the basis of a construction loan rate and not at the rate of a loan secured by an income-producing property, often a difference of up to five percent. The longer the period of these "interim" loans, the higher the ultimate cost to the purchasers.

Notwithstanding that there is no lease for all or any part of the 120 days subsequent to the notice above, the tenant's possession may not be terminated during that period, except for failure to pay rent, waste or conduct disturbing other tenants or occupants, and the sponsor shall continue to provide services during that period to the tenants on the same basis that services were furnished prior to the conversion.

(c) Furnishing of Services and Payment of Rent

For the 120-day period above, the landlord must continue to furnish services to the tenant on the same basis as was done prior to the notice, and the tenant shall continue to pay the same rent as prior to the notice.

(d) Option to Purchase

Each tenant will have the option to purchase his apartment for a period of 90 days from the notice required above on the same terms or better than the apartment will be offered to the general public.

(e) Showing of Apartments to Prospective Purchasers

Notwithstanding lease provisions to the contrary, the tenant's apartment will not be shown to prospective purchasers without the tenant's permission until the expiration of the tenant's option to purchase or 90 days prior to the end of the term of the tenant's lease, whichever is the later to occur.

11.   Use of Earnest Money Deposits

   (a) Trust Accounts

   All earnest money shall be held in separate trust accounts to be designated and shall not be pledged, assigned, or used otherwise by the sponsor.

12.   Suit by Condominium Association on Behalf of Unit Owners

At this time, in several jurisdictions, it is unclear whether the condominium association may sue for damages or an injunction in matters affecting the individual units of a residential condominium. Hence, in a zoning case concerning a parcel adjoining a residential condominium project or a situation where the sponsor has breached his warranties of quality in all or some of the units but not the common elements, all of the several unit owners affected would need to sue in their own names, each hiring a lawyer, etc. The law generally recognizes the concept of a "class action" and an analogous rule should be encouraged for condominium use, where appropriate, to simplify and make available the benefits of joint effort which is the foundation of the condominium concept.

   (a) A residential condominium association may sue on behalf of the individual unit owners in those cases where more than one individual unit owner is or shall be affected or has or will be damaged by the same party and arising from the same or similar wrong, breach, or act.

   (b) Upon filing such an action, notice thereof by certified mail shall be given to all the unit owners on whose behalf such action was filed and any individual unit owner may withdraw from the action provided, however, the defendant may request that the rights of any such individual unit owner shall be determined in that action.

   (c) Any award resulting from such an action shall be held for the benefit of those individual unit owners on whose behalf the action was brought after deduction of the costs and expenses of the case. In the event some unit owners seek or request that the condominium association file an action on behalf of those owners and others similarly situated and the costs and expenses of such action exceed the award made, those owners making such request shall bear those costs and expenses. However, in those cases, where none of the affected individual unit owners request that such action be brought on their behalf and the costs and expenses of any such action brought by the condominium association exceed the award made, unless expressly agreed otherwise, such amount shall be treated as an expense of the entire condominium association.

13.   Mechanic's Lien

   In the event a mechanic's lien affects two or more units of a residential condominium, whether such lien attached prior to or after the formation of the condominium or recording the declaration, the owner of any unit so affected may remove the unit and the applicable percentage of the common elements from such lien by payment or posting a bond for that portion of such lien affecting such unit and common elements based upon the percentage of common elements involved.

14.   Actions among the Unit Owners and/or Condominium Association

   In actions brought by unit owners against other unit owners or the condominium association or by the condominium association against some or all of the unit owners, wherein the party defendant prevails, upon a finding that such action was brought without substantial cause or that it was brought in bad faith, the court may award the cost of reasonable attorneys' fees to the defendant.

DIVISION II—SPONSOR'S RIGHTS

1.   The efficient completion of the project and "sell out" are, in many respects, more important to the individual unit owners than to the sponsor. Hence, the condominium association or individual unit owners should not hinder or interfere with the program of the sponsor.

The sponsor may reserve the right to maintain sales offices, signs, and model units until all units are sold and in addition thereto an easement to complete construction of the condominium and to fulfill warranty obligations.

DIVISION III—CONDOMINIUM FORMATION

1.   Common Elements

(a) Percentage Asssigned to Each Unit

Any reasonable formula determined by the sponsor based upon square footage or values or a combination thereof should be permitted.

2.   Leaseholds

(a) Permissible

The formation of a condominium of a leasehold estate should be permitted.

(b) Special Rules for Residential Condominiums

(i) The essential information of the lease provisions such as length of term and rent must be disclosed.

(ii) The leasehold must provide that any individual unit owner may pay his separate rent so that his rights are not dependent on the payment of rent by other units or the association.

3.   Statutory Short Form Document

For basic provisions, a statutory form of declaration and bylaws should be available to aid in simplifying the examination of these basic documents.

4.   Time Sharing

(a) Definition—A time share is an interest in real estate and should be regulated as such. Time sharing should be exempted from laws regulating the sale of securities. Registration of those who practice the buying and selling of time sharing should be subject to the real estate laws where the property is located. For purposes of legislation time sharing shall consist of five or more separated time intervals over a period of at least five years. Additionally, legislation should not place a limit on the various forms which time sharing may take.

(b) Enabling Legislation—Enabling legislation should be created which would provide for legal recognition and regulation of time sharing. Required disclosure must comply with the laws and regulations of the jurisdiction where the time sharing takes place.

(c) Taxation—Each time share estate constitutes, for purposes of title, a separate estate or interest in real property except for taxation purposes.

DIVISION IV—CONDOMINIUM ASSOCIATION

1.   Board Organization

(a) Number of Members

The number of members sitting on the board shall be five but no more than seven.

(b) Meetings

All board of directors meetings should be open and notice should be posted at least ten days prior to the meetings.

(c) Personal Liability of Individual Unit Owner Board Members—Individual residential condominium unit owners are basically home owners living cooperatively. Any owner contributing his time to the affairs of all should be held to a reasonable standard of care. Clearly, good faith and honesty should be demanded but otherwise a board member should not be expected to exercise his duties with any greater expertise or diligence than he would apply to managing his home. This standard is in contrast to the high standard of care imposed on trustees under the "prudent man" rule.

A member of the board of directors in performing his duties shall act in good faith exercising the same care as he would in the conduct of his own affairs.

(d) Officers and Directors Liability Insurance

Such insurance should be a required expenditure of the association.

2. Budget Responsibility

(a) Board to Oversee

The board shall vote the annual budget which shall remain effective until such a budget is reduced by action of the association at a membership meeting, special or regular. The action of any such meeting shall expressly set forth the budget under which the condominium shall operate and must be passed by at least a 66 2/3 percent vote of the unit owners. Notwithstanding any other provision of the bylaws on calling meetings, by a written petition, holders of five percent of the votes shall have the right to have such a meeting called within 30 days after such petition is delivered to the chief executive officer of the association.

3. Meeting of Members

(a) Annual Only

The unit owners, except for special cause, should not have a regular meeting more frequently than annually.

(b) Voting

For a "residential condominium," each unit should have one vote to cast on issues to be presented to the unit owners. For units having more than one owner, the owners should designate one of their number as the "voter" for their unit.

(c) Cumulative Voting—To give voice to the few, the concept of cumulative voting has been employed not only in business corporations in some jurisdictions, but also in the election of some public officials.

In elections for the association board, the bylaws may provide that the unit owner may cumulate votes and cast as many votes for one candidate as the number of offices to be filled multiplied by the number of votes of the unit owner or to distribute such votes on the same principle to as many candidates as the unit owner may decide.

DIVISION V—INSURANCE

1. Individual Condominium Unit Policies

The "Homeowners No. 6" or broader form of protection should be made available in all jurisdictions.

2. Other Insurance

Associations should purchase, if available, the following forms of coverage: (a) Workmen's Compensation, and (b) liability for motor vehicles used by the association that are owned, rented, or non-owned.

DIVISION VI—UNIT MORTGAGES

1. Priority

The regular assessments of the condominium association should have priority over all other liens and encumbrances on a unit except (1) liens and encumbrances recorded before the recordation of the declaration, (2) mortgages and deeds of trust on the unit securing first mortgage holders and recorded before the due date of the assessment or the due date of the first installment payable on the assessment, and (3) liens for real estate taxes and other governmental assessments or charges against the unit. To the extent of the common expense assessments due during the six months preceding institution of an action to enforce the lien, the lien should have priority over the mortgages and deeds of trust described in clause (2) above.

DIVISION VII—BANKRUPTCY AND RECEIVERSHIPS

1. Priority of Assessment

    In the event the sponsor or any individual unit owner, voluntarily or involuntarily, is within the jurisdiction of the bankruptcy court, the assessments, regular and special, must be paid even if other creditors, except the U.S. government, are prejudiced.

2. Receiver

    In the event a receiver or trustee is appointed by a court to act under court supervision for the units owned by the sponsor, the condominium association may request that such receiver or trustee act in behalf of the condominium association for the administration of the common elements.

3. Association Not Acting

    In those cases where the condominium association fails in a material respect to administer the common elements in accordance with the condominium documents, 25 percent of the individual unit owners may request a court to appoint a receiver to perform the functions of the association under court supervision.

(Editor's Note: Condominium Legislation—Recommended Criteria was developed by the Condominium Committee of the NATIONAL ASSOCIATION OF REALTORS® to provide guidelines for drafting state condominium legislation. The criteria originally were approved by the Board of Directors of the NATIONAL ASSOCIATION OF REALTORS® on May 6, 1975. Additions subsequently were approved on November 11, 1975, February 10, 1976, May 2, 1977, November 16, 1977, and April 29, 1980. The criteria will continue to be subjected to regular scrutiny, and modifications and/or additions made to reflect changes in and a greater awareness of the condominium form of ownership.)

APPENDIX C:
ABOUT THE
CONTRIBUTORS

The Institute of Real Estate Management (IREM) of the NATIONAL ASSOCIATION OF REALTORS® is an organization of professional property managers that certifies property managers who have distinguished themselves in the areas of education, experience, and ethical conduct. IREM offers both property managers and the public an expansive program of courses, seminars, books, periodicals, audiovisual kits, and other educational activities and materials. *The Owner's and Manager's Guide to Condominium Management* has been prepared as part of this educational program.

The objective of this book is to present the processes and procedures involved in effectively managing a condominium and running a condominium association. To achieve this objective, it was necessary to solicit the participation of a number of real estate professionals who long have been involved with condominiums of all sizes. The following people served as contributing authors or editorial consultants:

Joseph T. Aveni, CPM®, president of HGM Hilltop Management Company in Cleveland, Ohio, a firm active in the management and development of condominiums, apartment buildings, office buildings, and shopping centers. In addition to being the 1977 president of IREM, Aveni has served the Institute in a variety of other capacities, including regional vice president, chairman of the Experience Exchange Committee, chairman of both the Membership Services and Communications Division Councils, and, from 1979 through 1984, IREM representative to the NATIONAL ASSOCIATION OF REALTORS® Executive Committee. A past president of the IREM Cleveland Chapter, Aveni received that chapter's 1973 Manager of the Year award. He also is a recipient of the Cleveland Apartment Homeowners Association's Man of the Year award and served as president of that association for three years.

Steven P. Bloomberg, a law partner with Moss and Bloomberg, Ltd., which practices law in DuPage, Will, and Cook counties in Illinois. As a specialist in municipal law, corporate law for profit and not-for-profit corporations, and condominium and homeowners association law, Bloomberg represents more than 80 condominium and homeowners associations and 17 municipal districts in the Chicago area. He has written and lectured on various areas of condominium law and has been a member of committees concerned with drafting and reviewing condominium legislation. After graduating from DePaul University Law School and prior to forming Moss and Bloomberg, Ltd., Bloomberg worked in the Illinois Attorney General's office, first as Assistant Attorney General and head of the Litigation Division of the Consumer Fraud and Protection Division and later as Special Assistant Attorney General assigned to major cases by the Attorney General.

R. Bruce Campbell, CPM®, CRE, PCAM, president of Wallace H. Campbell & Company, Inc., a management and investment property consulting firm that manages over 40 community associations in the Baltimore, Maryland, area. The firm has been involved with condominium associations since the first one was formed in Baltimore in 1967, and is active in various local and national organizations whose goal is to improve condominium living through legislative and management changes. In addition to being a member of IREM's national faculty, Campbell was the 1979 president of IREM's Maryland Chapter and received that chapter's 1980 Manager of the Year award. He also has served as local president of the Home Builders Association of Maryland

Apartment Council and second vice president of the Baltimore Chapter of the Building Owners and Managers Association (BOMA).

Aaron M. Chaney, CPM®, managing director of Chaney, Brooks & Company, a Honolulu firm which manages condominiums and cooperatives as well as apartment buildings, office buildings, resorts, and single-family detached homes throughout Hawaii. Chaney was the 1973 president of IREM and also has served as president of both IREM's Hawaii Chapter and the Honolulu Board of REALTORS®. He has lectured on property management throughout the United States, as well as having been a member of IREM's national faculty. In addition to this service, Chaney has been vice president of the National Association of Real Estate License Law Officials and chairman of the Hawaii Real Estate Commission. His articles on real estate have appeared in numerous publications, and his newsletter on the management of condominiums and cooperatives, started in the early 1960s, now has a circulation of more than 17,000.

Michael Cousins, CPM®, FRI, president of Sterling Property Management, Inc., in Willowdale, Ontario, Canada, a Toronto-area firm which specializes in the management of condominiums and apartment buildings. Cousins was the 1982 chairman and a 1981 regional vice president of IREM Canada, and has served IREM in both Canada and the U.S. in a number of other capacities, including Governing Council member, faculty member, course board director, and member of various committees. He has also been active in the IREM Greater Toronto Chapter, serving as its president for three years and receiving its 1979 Manager of the Year award. In addition to this service, Cousins is the 1984 governor of the Real Estate Institute of Canada.

John N. Gallagher, CPM®, assistant vice president and director of community management with Shannon & Luchs Company, a full-service real estate firm in Washington, D.C., which manages more than 7,000 community association units. Gallagher has been involved in most facets of the condominium form of ownership, including conversion of multifamily rental property to condominium ownership, development of land into new condominium homes, and all phases of association management and maintenance. Gallagher is a member of IREM's Governing Council and serves as a course board director on IREM's national faculty. He is 1984 president of the Greater Metropolitan Washington Chapter of IREM and is a past president of the Property Management Association of America (PMAA). Gallagher is the author of *Purchasing a Condominium*, published by PMAA, and a contributor to *The Condominium Home: A Prospective Owner's Guide*, published by the NATIONAL ASSOCIATION OF REALTORS®.

Richard M. Goldberg, CPM®, vice president of property management with IRE Financial Corporation, a Miami firm active in the management of a large number of community associations in South Florida. A licensed real estate broker, Goldberg has concentrated on the management of residential and commercial properties since the early 1970s. Goldberg serves on IREM's Governing Council and several national committees, and was the 1983 president of IREM's South Florida Chapter. He is also active in the South Florida Chapter of CAI as well as the Builders Association of South Florida and the Miami Board of REALTORS®. In addition to teaching "Management of Condominium and Homeowners Associations" at Dade Community College, Goldberg has been a guest speaker on property management at Florida Atlantic University, local chapter seminars, and CAI regional workshops.

R. Don Larrance, CPM®, vice president of Perry & Co., a full-service real estate firm in Denver, Colorado, engaged in the management of condominium associations and conversion of rental properties to condominium ownership, as well as the management of all types of income properties. Long active in IREM, Larrance is a member of the Governing Council, has been senior vice president of the Membership Admissions Division and the ACCREDITED RESIDENT MANAGER™ Division, has been a regional vice president, and has chaired the Chapter Activities Committee. He served two terms as president of IREM's Northern Colorado Chapter, which honored him with their 1976 Manager of the Year award. Larrance also serves on the faculties of both IREM and the University of Colorado.

Robert W. McLallen, president of Condominium Insurance Specialists of America, Inc., in Rolling Meadows, Illinois, an independent agency formed to serve associations and owners in the highly specialized areas of condominiums, cooperatives, and other community associations. McLallen was coauthor of the Chubb Insurance Company's unit owner contract in the mid-1970s and was instrumental in the development of the Fireman's Fund's national condominium program. In 1983, he was made chairman of CAI's newly formed Special Interest Committee on Insurance. McLallen is active in the development of educational programs on condominium insurance for both practitioners and insureds, and he and other members of his agency are frequent instructors for CAI.

Michael E. Packard, cpm®, pcam, president of Loomis Properties, Inc., in Oceanside, California, a firm specializing in the management, consulting, and brokerage of condominiums as well as apartment buildings, single-family detached homes, and commercial properties. Packard has been involved with community association management since the early 1970s. An active member of CAI, he is CAI's 1984 president, and he has spoken at several CAI conferences on community association management. Packard has also served as president of the San Diego chapters of both CAI and IREM.

W. Donald Sally, cpm®, president of Stonebridge Management Company in Dallas, Texas. A licensed real estate and insurance broker, Sally is past national president of CAI, as well as past chairman of the Chicago Real Estate Board's Property Management Council and past president of the Chicago Apartment Building Owners and Managers Association. He is a charter member of the Management Advisory Council of the National Housing Partnership in Washington, D.C., and a member of the College of Business Advisory Council for the University of Texas at Arlington. Sally has served IREM as a member of the Governing Council and as a member of the *Journal of Property Management* Committee and the *Journal's* Editorial Review Board. He twice has received the *Journal's* Author of the Year award and is a charter member of IREM's Academy of Authors.

Sally is active in the local chapters of both IREM and BOMA.

Thomas A. Scapillato, CPM®, president of TUSC Realty Investors, a real estate syndication and management firm based in Westmont, Illinois. Scapillato has been involved with the management, development, and sale of condominiums ranging in size from 36 units to 600 units and including projects in Florida, California, and Illinois. Prior to forming his own firm, he was a vice president of Balcor/ American Express, Inc., where he managed a real estate portfolio of 12,000 apartment units, 50 shopping centers, and 6 office buildings. Scapillato is a member of the national faculties of IREM and the Real Estate Securities and Syndication Institute, and has lectured at many colleges and professional seminars.

John J. Smolenski, CPM®, vice president of Baird & Warner, Inc., Chicago, and general manager of the full-service real estate firm's residential management division. Smolenski is responsible for the management of 8,000 units of housing in Chicago and northeastern Illinois, of which 4,500 units are condominiums representing 125 different associations and including high-rises, rehabilitated structures, and suburban garden complexes. Previously, he set up new associations, expanded the master homeowners association, and served as the liaison between the developer and homeowner boards for a planned unit recreational development of 1,250 units. Smolenski has been an instructor on maintenance management for CAI and a speaker on condominium and apartment management for IREM. He is frequently quoted in the daily press on condominium topics.

M. Vince Turner, assistant vice president, residential management department, with The Charles E. Smith Companies headquartered in Arlington, Virginia. Joining the Smith Companies in 1979 as a property manager specializing in condominiums, Turner now oversees both the condominium management and the new development management processes. His responsibilities include supervision of property managers, organization of ad hoc boards of directors and committees, new site plan review, 10-year budgetary forecasting, contract negotiation, and department liaison to IREM's CPM® program. Previously, Turner had gained more than a decade of experience in condominium management as well as in rental management and in new construction. Turner is a member of the board of directors of the Washington Metropolitan Chapter of CAI, chairman of that chapter's Public and Media Relations Committee, and a national instructor for CAI's Professional Management Development Program.

GLOSSARY

Accounting   System of gathering financial information and keeping a record of business transactions to prepare statements concerning assets, liabilities, and operating results.

ACCREDITED MANAGEMENT ORGANIZATION® (AMO®)   Designation awarded by the Institute of Real Estate Management to firms that prove themselves in compliance with certain standards, including organizational stability, management portfolio, and fiscal and operational reliability and education.

Accrual accounting   Method of recording expenses incurred and income due in the periods to which they relate rather than actual flow of cash.

Actual cash value   Amount of money that would be required to repair or replace existing building or improvement with another of like kind in the same condition, thereby taking into account depreciation; replacement cost less depreciation.

Additional living expense insurance   Coverage that would reimburse the insured for living costs in excess of normal living expenses if loss of or damage to property forced the insured to maintain temporary residence elsewhere.

Ad hoc committee   Special committee appointed to carry out a specific nonrecurring task and disbanded when that task is completed.

Adjourn   Officially dismiss or end a meeting.

Adjusted basis   Original cost or book value of an asset for income tax purposes.

Adjusted sales price   Amount paid or payable for an item less actual selling expenses and other expenses incurred to assist in the sale.

Administrative expenses   Cost of goods or services that can be attributed to the management of affairs of a condominium.

Agenda   Sequence in which issues are to be taken up in a meeting.

Agent   One who has the authority to act for or represent another; see **Insurance agent, Management agent.**

Agreed amount insurance   Policy under which coinsurance clause is waived if insured carries insurance of an agreed amount and under which insurer agrees to pay face amount on the policy in the event of total loss of property covered or upon occurrence of a stated contingency.

All-risk insurance   Policy under which a loss resulting from any cause other than those causes specifically excluded by name is considered to be covered.

Amend   Modify or change; under parliamentary procedure, modify a motion by adding, deleting, or substituting words.

Amendment   Revision of a governing document or, under parliamentary procedure, a motion.

Amenity   Facility that is part of common areas and increases physical comfort, such as a swimming pool or tennis court.

Amenity rental fee   Fixed charge paid by unit owner or guest for use of common facility and/or limited common area.

AMO®   See **ACCREDITED MANAGEMENT ORGANIZA-TION®.**

Annual membership meeting   Once-a-year assemblage of unit owners required by governing documents to conduct association business, such as electing a board of directors.

Appraisal   Survey of a property and estimate of its value by an expert in property analysis.

Architectural restrictions   Standards and restrictions that limit what unit owners can do to change the outward appearance of their units and outline procedures unit owners must follow to make changes to the exterior of units.

Articles of incorporation   Formal document that, when filed, sets up an association as a corporation under the laws of the applicable state.

Assembly   Group of persons gathered for some common purpose.

Assessment   Amount charged against each unit owner, based on percentages of budgeted common expenses, to fund the operation, administration, maintenance, and management of a condominium.

Asset   Item that has purchasing power, often because it can be converted into cash; *pl.*, entries in a balance sheet listing these items or properties.

Association   See **Condominium association.**

Association insurance policy   Written contract combining liability and property protection into one package and designed to cover common areas of a condominium, usually including the structure, and take precedence over unit owners' policies; also called master insurance policy.

Audit   Examination of financial records and accounts to verify their accuracy and determine if financial statements adequately reflect an association's financial status.

Automobile nonownership liability insurance   Protection against loss arising out of an association's legal responsibility and as a result of an association employee or officer having an accident while on association business in an automobile neither owned or hired by the association.

Balance sheet   Financial statement that indicates the financial status of an association at a specific time by listing its assets, liabilities, and members' equity.

Ballot   Paper used to cast secret vote.

Basis   See **Adjusted basis.**

Best's Key Rating Guide: Property–Casualty   An annually issued guide featuring comprehensive statistics on the financial condition, general standing, and transactions of property and casualty insurance companies throughout the United States.

Billing journal   Form used to chronologically record preparation of invoices.

Blanket fidelity bond   Contract covering loss of association money or real or personal property when such a loss is due to dishonesty of an employee.

Board of directors   Official governing body of a condominium association elected by members of the association; also called board of managers or board of trustees.

BOCA   See **Building Officials and Code Administrators International, Inc.**

Bodily injury liability insurance   Protection against loss arising out of insured's legal responsibility and as a result of injury, illness or disease, or death of another person.

Boiler Pressure tank in which water is heated and from which it is circulated either in the form of steam or as water.

Boiler and machinery insurance Property and liability coverage for loss arising out of the operation of pressure, mechanical, and electrical equipment.

Budget Estimated summary of expenditures and income for a given period.

Building Officials and Code Administrators International, Inc. (BOCA) A nonprofit organization that set up a model building code used widely in United States municipalities.

Bylaws Secondary laws of an association that govern its internal affairs and deal with routine operational and administrative matters; also called code of regulations.

CAI See **Community Associations Institute.**

Call a question To move to bring a question to an immediate vote.

Call for orders of the day Require an assembly to conform to prescribed agenda.

Capital expenditures Funds spent for additions or improvements to physical plant or for equipment.

Capital gains tax Fee levied on profit realized on the sale of a capital asset, including an owner-occupied dwelling, such as a house or condominium unit, or land.

Capital reserves See **Replacement reserves.**

Captions Notice that material underscored or treated in a special way in a document has no greater importance than items not treated in that way.

Cardiopulmonary resuscitation (CPR) A basic emergency procedure for life support consisting of artificial respiration and manual external heart massage.

Cash accounting Method of recording revenue when actual cash is received and expenses when actual cash disbursements are made.

Cash disbursements journal Book of original entry for chronologically recording all checks issued.

Cash flow statement Report that indicates actual inflow and outgo of cash and its related sources and uses in a given accounting period.

Cash receipts journal Book of original entry for chronologically recording all cash taken in from all sources.

CERTIFIED PROPERTY MANAGER® (CPM®) Designation awarded by the Institute of Real Estate Management to professional property managers who have met standards of performance, experience, education, and ethical conduct.

Certified public accountant (CPA) Accountant who has met certain state legal requirements.

Chair Person who presides over an assembly, meeting, committee, or board.

Chart of accounts System of coding by number each classification used in a budget and financial statements.

Coinsurance Insurance policy under which insured shares losses if property is insured for less than a certain percentage of its value.

Commingling of funds Combining or mixing monies.

Commit Send an issue to committee for study or action and resubmission to an assembly at a future time.

Committee Group of people officially delegated to perform a function, such as investigate, report, act on a matter.

Common areas Property owned jointly by all condominium unit owners that ordinarily includes land and structure or portions of structure not otherwise described as units; also called common elements.

Common expenses Costs of managing, maintaining, administering, repairing, replacing, and operating a condominium.

Communications program Organized method of transmitting information.

Community association. Type of compulsory association membership including, but not limited to, condominiums, cooperatives, timesharing, planned unit developments, and homeowners associations.

Community Associations Institute (CAI) Independent nonprofit research and educational organization formed in 1973 to develop and distribute guidance on condominium and homeowners associations.

Completed operations and products liability insurance Protection against loss arising out of insured's legal responsibility as a result of alleged injury from manufactured products or workmanship.

Condominium Form of ownership in a multifamily housing development that combines exclusive ownership of a dwelling unit and joint ownership of common areas.

Condominium association Private, automatic, usually nonprofit organization responsible for the total operation of a condominium community; also called council of owners, council, or association of co-owners.

Condominium management agreement Formal contract between a property management firm and a second party, either an association board or a developer, to manage a condominium in exchange for a stated rate of compensation.

Condominium unit That part of a condominium development, probably a space of air or three-dimensional area located within the walls, floor, and ceiling of a condominium structure, privately owned and independently and exclusively used by a unit owner; also called condominium apartment.

Contingency Event that may occur but is not necessarily expected.

Contingency reserves Funds set aside to cover unanticipated emergencies or major expenditures not included in the current fiscal year operating budget.

Contract Voluntary and legally binding agreement between parties calling for them to do or not do some specific thing for some consideration, usually monetary.

Contractors' protective liability insurance Protection against loss arising out of insured's responsibility and as a result of new construction or extensive repairs undertaken by the association.

Conversion Transfer of multifamily rental development to condominium form of ownership through sale of individual living units; multifamily dwelling whose ownership has been so transferred.

Cooperative Corporation that holds real estate, specifically a multifamily dwelling, shareholders in which have the right to live in one of its units; also called a co-op.

Corporate surtax exemption Release from obligation to pay additional tax levied on the amount by which a corporation's net income exceeds a certain sum.

Corporate tax rate Proportionate fee levied against the net income of corporations.

Countersignature Second or confirming signature.

CPA See **Certified public accountant.**

CPM® See **CERTIFIED PROPERTY MANAGER®.**

CPR See **Cardiopulmonary resuscitation.**

Cross liability endorsement Attachment to an insurance policy that provides protection for an association should a unit owner be awarded damages as a result of an accident in common areas.

Cumulative voting System by which votes are amassed to allow unit owner to cast as many votes as there are offices to fill.

Custodial maintenance Upkeep of an area through performance of cleaning, policing, and related routine housekeeping chores.

Damages Money paid or ordered to be paid as compensation for injury or loss.

Debate Discussion of a question pending before a deliberative body.

Declarant board The first board of directors appointed by the developer; also called the developer's board.

Declaration Legal document that, when filed, commits land to condominium use, creates a condominium association and serves as its constitutional law, physically describes a condominium, defines the method of determining each unit owner's share of the common areas, and outlines responsibilities and restrictions; also called declaration of codes, covenants, and restrictions or master deed.

Deductible Specific amount to be subtracted from a loss and written into an insurance policy as a means of effecting a decrease in premium.

Default Failure to fulfill or live up to terms of an agreement.

Deferred maintenance Upkeep that may be scheduled at a future date without allowing a minor problem to become a major one.

Delinquency Overdue assessment payment.

Depreciation Decrease in value of property because of physical deterioration resulting from wear and tear, functional inability to serve its use as well as a new property designed for the same purpose, or locational obsolescence resulting from external and environmental factors.

Developer One who converts a tract of land or other property to a specific use.

Direct loss Physical loss of or damage to property concerned.

Directors' and officers' liability insurance Protection against loss arising out of alleged errors in judgment, breaches of duty, and wrongful acts of a board of directors and/or officers in carrying out their prescribed duties.

Discharge a committee Remove a matter from a committee's consideration and put it before an assembly.

Division of a question Separate consideration of parts of a motion or an amendment to it.

Division of assembly Requirement that, in the event there is some doubt as to the accuracy of an announced voice vote or vote based on a show-of-hands count, a recount be taken by having members stand.

Easement   Right to use land owned by someone else for certain limited purposes, such as for party driveways, drainage, etc.

Emergency maintenance   Necessary repairs that cannot be predicted and require immediate attention.

Endorsement   Attachment to an insurance policy that in some way modifies its coverage.

Equity   Owner's interest in a property, usually determined by the value of the property less mortgage, liens, or other encumbrances against it.

Equity accrual   Buildup of an owner's interest in a property because of mortgage loan amortization or appreciation in its total value.

Errors and omissions insurance   Protection against loss arising out of an alleged error or oversight on the part of an insured professional while performing prescribed duties.

Escape provision   Clause in a contract that, under certain circumstances, allows either party to cancel the agreement prior to its expiration date.

Escrow   Agreement that something, usually money, given to a third party be held until certain conditions are met.

Estate   Nature of an owner's right or interest in his or her property and its use.

Expandable condominium   Development under condominium form of ownership designed to permit additional multifamily living structures to be built within it if the demand for them exists; also called an add-on or merging condominium.

Extended coverage insurance   Policy that extends basic fire policy to cover property loss caused by additional perils, usually including windstorm, hail, explosion, riot and civil commotion, aircraft, vehicles, and smoke.

Fair market value   Most probable selling price of property or item.

Fee simple absolute interest   Most complete type of private ownership of real estate which gives title holder the right to possess, control, use, and dispose of it at will.

Federal Home Loan Mortgage Corporation (FHLMC)   A private corporation authorized by Congress to purchase mortgages from savings and loan institutions; also known as Freddie Mac.

Federal Housing Authority (FHA)   Federal agency that functions as an insurer of mortgage loans.

Federal National Mortgage Association (FNMA)   A privately-owned, for-profit organization created by Congress that purchases and sells residential mortgages; also known as Fannie Mae.

FHLMC   See **Federal Home Loan Mortgage Corporation.**

Fidelity bond   Formal agreement under which an employer would be reimbursed for loss, up to an amount specified, that may result from a dishonest act of covered employee occupying a position of trust.

Fiduciary relationship.   Agreement based on trust in which one person or group of persons handles financial transactions for another or others.

Financial statement   Report that indicates certain information concerning financial position of an association.

Fiscal controls   Procedures for regulating and verifying financial activities.

Fiscal year   Twelve-month period for which an association plans use of funds.

Fixed expenses   Costs that remain relatively stable.

Fixture   Item of personal property that is annexed, attached, or affixed to or installed in real property, such as plumbing fixtures or wall-to-wall carpeting.

FNMA   See **Federal National Mortgage Association.**

Fraud   Deliberate deception practiced to secure unlawful gain.

Full agency management   A plan for handling all or designated aspects of the affairs of an association whereby a property management firm and/or its agent are contracted to perform a full range of administrative, maintenance, and operational tasks for an association.

Garagekeepers' legal liability insurance   Protection against loss arising out of insured's legal responsibility and as a result of damage to vehicles left in care, custody, and control of association.

Garden condominium   Multifamily dwelling under condominium owernship that usually is no more than three stories tall, has units arranged horizontally and vertically, and is built around a courtyard; also called low-rise condominium.

Gender   Notice that although a document refers to only one gender it applies equally to both.

General journal   Book of original entry to record miscellaneous entries that do not apply to other journals.

General ledger   Record to which all accounts in the form of debits and credits are transferred as final entries from the journals, thus indicating accumulated effects of transactions.

General maintenance   Upkeep that can be anticipated and performed on a regular basis or that is minor in nature.

Governing documents   Set of legal papers, filed by a developer with the appropriate local government office, that submit land to condominium use and create and govern a condominium association.

Graduate, REALTOR® Institute (GRI)   Designation awarded by state organizations of the NATIONAL ASSOCIATION OF REALTORS® to persons who have demonstrated competency in prescribed educational course material.

Ground rent   Payment for the use and occupancy of real property, according to the terms of a lease.

Hazard   Source or cause of a disaster, such as fire, flood, or worker's injury; also, perilous conditions that may create or increase the probability of loss.

Hearing   Examination, usually informal, of an accused person.

Heating, ventilation, air-conditioning system (HVAC)   The unit regulating the even distribution of heat and fresh air throughout a building.

High-rise condominium   Multifamily dwelling under condominium ownership that utilizes an arrangement of units placed one on top of the other.

HOA   See **Homeowners association.**

Hold harmless clause   Contractual provision that shifts liability inherent in a situation to another party; see **Indemnification.**

Homeowners association (HOA)   An organization of homeowners having individual lots as part of a development whose major purpose is to maintain and provide for the rights of owners to have easement in the use of common areas.

Horizontal property   Another name for a condominium.

Host liquor liability insurance   Protection against loss arising out of insured's legal responsibility as a result of an accident attributed to the use of liquor dispensed but not sold by an association and/or used in common areas.

House rules and regulations Guidelines related to day-to-day conduct in common areas and relationships between unit owners.

HUD See **United States Department of Housing and Urban Development.**

HVAC See **Heating, ventilation, air-conditioning system.**

Incidental motion Motion that involves question of procedure arising out of another motion and over which it takes precedence.

Income tax Charge levied by federal government against taxable income of an individual or corporation.

Indemnification Condition, usually contractual, of being protected against possible damage, loss, or suit; see **Hold harmless clause.**

Inflation Sharp and continuing rise in price levels due to an abnormal increase in available currency and credit greater than the proportionate increase of available goods.

Institute of Real Estate Management (IREM) Organization founded in 1933 to develop professionalism in the field of property management by setting standards of performance, experience, and ethics and making available to the industry educational courses and publications.

Insurance Protective measure that shifts risk of financial loss due to certain perils to an insurance company in return for payment of premiums.

Insurance agent Representative of an insurance company, licensed by the state, who negotiates and effects insurance contracts and services policyholders.

Insurance claim Sum of money demanded for a loss in accordance with the terms of an insurance policy.

Insurance inventory file A report listing all forms of insurance carried, the carriers, and expiration dates.

Insurance trustee Person or institution who administers recovery funds collected from insurance company.

Insured One covered by insurance; a policyholder.

Insurer One who provides insurance; an insurance company.

Interest Charge for a financial loan, usually based on a percentage of that loan.

Interim period Time during which unit owners are living in a condominium but developer controls the association.

Internal Revenue Code Laws that govern the filing of tax returns with the United States Treasury.

Investment   Outlay of money to realize income or profit in the future.

Investment summary   An attachment to the periodic financial summaries of operations that indicates the amount of investments held, the institution where invested, the rate of interest, and the maturity date where applicable.

Invoice   List of goods shipped or services rendered with an account of applicable costs; a bill.

Journal   Financial record book in which certain business transactions are recorded chronologically and for the first time.

Judgment   Court decree of indebtedness to another and amount of that indebtedness.

Leasehold interest   Position of a tenant in a leased property, including the right of use and possession for a definite and specific period of time in return for compensation.

Ledger card   Official record of a unit owner's assessment payments.

Lessee   One holding rights of possession and use of property under the terms of a lease; a tenant.

Lessor   One who leases property; a landlord.

Liability   Legal responsibility and obligation; *pl.*, financial obligations entered in a balance sheet.

Liability insurance   Coverage for damages arising out of insured's legal responsibility and resulting from injuries to other persons or damage to their property.

Lien   Claim or attachment, enforceable at law, to have a debt or other charge satisfied out of a person's property.

Limit debate   Place restrictions on the amount of time to be allowed for debate of an issue or the amount of time each speaker may debate an issue.

Limited common areas   Property that physically is part of a condominium's common areas but is reserved for the exclusive use of a particular unit owner or group of unit owners.

Line item budget   Format listing of expenses by type.

Loss   Amount of an insured's claim; amount of decrease in value of the insured's property.

Loss assessment insurance   Unit owner protection that would cover special assessments the owner may be obligated to pay because a loss incured by the association was not otherwise adequately insured.

Main motion   Proposal that brings business before an assembly for discussion or action.

Maintenance   Upkeep of property or an item in its proper and functional condition.

Maintenance program   Schedule of all repair, inspection, cleaning, lubrication, and other tasks necessary to keep something in proper working order.

Management agent   Representatives of a management firm.

Management agreement   See **Condominium management agreement.**

Management plan   Program for operating a condominium.

Master association   Organization of unit owners of more than one condominium created to maintain, operate, manage, and finance recreational facilities of which they share the use; also called common association or umbrella association.

Mechanical maintenance   Repair, inspection, lubrication, and cleaning of machines and tools to keep them in proper working condition.

Medical payments insurance   Coverage that voluntarily provides for payment of medical and similar expenses of persons injured in common areas regardless of the question of fault or legal liability.

Meeting   Assemblage of association members gathered to discuss issues and make decisions on them through motions.

Metes and bounds   Legal description of real property in which boundaries are defined by directions and distances.

Mid-rise condominium   Multifamily housing structure under condominium ownership that usually is 4 to 10 stories high and has a single front entrance and lobby and common corridors.

Minutes   Official record of proceedings of a meeting.

Mortgage   Temporary and conditional pledge of real property as security for a financial obligation.

Mortgagee   Lender in a mortgage loan contract, such as a bank or other lending institution.

Motion   Formal proposal put before an assembly on which action must be taken.

Mulch   Protective covering, usually organic, placed around plants to protect against weed growth and help soil retain moisture.

National Housing Act, Section 234   Passed in 1961, permitted Federal Housing Authority of the Department of Housing and

Urban Development to insure loans made by private lenders for construction, rehabilitation, and/or purchase of single-family or multifamily housing for rent or ownership, thereby extending mortgage insurance to condominiums.

Newsletter Printed periodical report devoted to news of and for a special interest group, such as a condominium association.

Noncumulative voting Assignment of one vote per person.

Obtain the floor Be formally recognized by the chair of a meeting and given the exclusive right to speak.

Occupancy restrictions Limitations on who may and may not buy and/or live in condominium units.

On-site management Plan for managing a condominium association whereby a person is hired and works exclusively for the association and handles all or designated aspects of its affairs.

Operating expenses Costs incurred to maintain a property and keep it productive of services.

Operating reserves Funds set aside for the payment of an annual expense.

Organization meeting First meeting of an association at which directors are elected.

Ownership interest Legal share, expressed in percentages, each unit owner has in common areas.

Parliamentarian Adviser to presiding officer who acts as the authority on rules of conducting a business meeting.

Parliamentary procedure Established rules of parliamentary law and unwritten rules of courtesy used to facilitate the transaction of business in deliberative assemblies.

Partition Legal action brought by a unit owner to separate the owner's share, based on ownership interest, of a condominium's common areas or common monies.

Payroll expenses Costs of wages, vacation and sick pay, holiday pay, group medical benefits, and employee benefits.

Payroll journal Book of original entry for chronologically recording all salary and related transactions.

PCAM See **Professional Community Association Manager.**

Pending question Motion before an assembly that has not yet been put to a vote.

Peril Cause of a possible loss against which insurance may be obtained.

Period of transfer   Time during which the developer transfers control of an association to unit owners and during which they must learn to accept responsibilities for running a condominium.

Personal injury liability insurance   Protection against loss arising out of personal insults, such as slander, liable, or false arrest, allegedly delivered by the insured.

Personal property   Possessions that are temporary or movable, as opposed to real property which is fixed; personalty.

Physical maintenance   Repair, inspection, and cleaning of a physical plant to keep it in proper condition.

Planned unit development (PUD)   A form of development that usually includes a mixture of open space, single-family homes, townhouses, condominiums or cooperatives, rental units, and recreational and commercial facilities within a defined area and specifically zoned arrangement.

Plat   Survey plan or map and descriptions of a tract of land showing property lines, easements, etc.

Point of order   Demand that chair enforce parliamentary rules which are being violated.

Police   Regular patrol of an area, keeping it neat in appearance.

Policy resolution   Formal statement submitted to an assembly for a decision; subsequent to passage, outline of plan of action.

Postpone definitely   Delay action on a pending question until some future time.

Postpone indefinitely   Kill a main motion for the duration of a meeting by forestalling vote on it.

Preamble   Introduction to a contract that identifies its purpose and establishes its legality.

Premium   Compensation to insurer for accepting risk of loss; cost of insurance.

Preventive maintenance   Program of inspection and regular care that allows potential problems to be detected and solved early or prevented altogether.

Previous question   Demand to close debate and vote immediately on an issue.

Privileged motion   Motion with highest authority that interrupts consideration of other matters and relates to urgent or special subjects.

Professional Community Association Manager (PCAM)   The professional designation conferred by the Community Associations Institute on individuals who have met certain minimum levels of experience, education, and participation in the profession of association management.

Program budget Format of listing expenses according to program or activity for which they will be disbursed.

Property damage liability insurance Protection against loss arising out of insured's legal responsibility as a result of damage to or destruction of another's property.

Property insurance Protection of insured's real or personal property against loss or damage caused by specified perils.

Property tax Fee levied by local governments against real estate, business equipment, and inventories.

Prorate Divide, distribute, or assess in proportionate shares.

Proxy Authorization given to one person to vote in place of another.

PUD See **Planned unit development.**

Question Matter being considered by an assembly.

Question of privilege Interruption of pending business to state an urgent request or make a motion on an immediate problem.

Quorum Minimum number of members that must be present or votes that must be represented in person or by proxy at a meeting in order for business to be transacted legally.

Real estate Land and all permanent improvements on it; realty.

Recess Short break in a business meeting.

Reconsider Bring a motion before an assembly as if it had not been considered previously, thereby cancelling the effect of the earlier vote.

Recording secretary An assistant to the secretary of the board of directors who takes the minutes at a board meeting.

Record of original entry Financial record of initial transaction of business; a journal.

Recreational lease Long-term agreement under which a developer retains ownership of a condominium's recreational facilities and allows unit owners to use them for a specified time in exchange for compensation in the form of rent.

Refer See **Commit.**

Rent Compensation given in exchange for the use of space or real property.

Replacement cost Amount of money rerquired to repair and replace an existing property with property of the same material and construction without deducting for depreciation.

Replacement reserves Funds set aside for probable repair and replacement of common area components at some future time.

Request for proposal (RFP) Information such as governing documents, budgets, and contracts provided by an association to a property management firm upon which the firm will base its bid for managing a property.

Rescind Cancel or nullify a previous action by an assembly.

Reserves Funds set aside for special purposes, specifically, to enable an association to meet nonrecurring and/or major expenses.

RFP See **Request for proposal.**

Risk Chance of a loss from a hazard.

Robert's Rules of Order Recognized formal guidelines for conducting a business meeting.

Second Indication from a second member that he or she agrees a certain motion warrants consideration of the membership.

Secondary motion Motion that relates to a main motion or involves emergency or procedural questions.

Self-insured retention That portion of a risk or potential loss assumed by the insured in the form of a deductible, self-insurance, or the lack of insurance.

Self-management Plan of running a condominium whereby unit owners carry out policy decisions of and handle affairs for an association.

Service contract Formal agreement that certain work necessary for the continuing operation of a condominium be performed in exchange for specified compensation.

Single-deed estate Real property covered by one title.

Single-family house Detached dwelling designed for occupancy by one family.

Special assessment Fee levied against unit owners to cover unexpected expenses.

Special meeting Unscheduled meeting called by board or membership to discuss urgent business.

Sprinkler leakage insurance Protection against loss caused by accidental discharge of water from an automatic fire prevention sprinkler system.

Standing committee Group of people formed to handle ongoing business on a certain subject.

Statement of income and expense Financial report that indicates how much income has been earned and what expenses have been incurred over a certain period of time and compares budgeted and actual figures for the period in question and year-to-date.

Statement of members' equity   Financial report that indicates vested interest of unit owners, or value of their property after all liabilites have been deducted, on a specific date.

State the question   Restatement of a motion by chair, thus opening it to debate.

Subcommittee   Subordinate committee composed of members appointed from a main committee to handle a specified task within the main committee's responsibilities.

Subrogation   Legal process of substitution by which an insurance company seeks from a third party, who may have caused a loss, recovery of the amount paid to the policyholder.

Subsidiary motion   Motion that takes precedence over main motions and affects the way a main motion is handled.

Suspend the rules   Set aside parliamentary procedures in order to take up a matter in such a way as to otherwise be in violation of them.

Table   Temporarily set aside a pending question when a more urgent matter arises; lay on the table.

Taxable income   That portion of revenue that is subject to taxation.

Tax exemption   Freedom from liability on taxes that apply to others.

Timeshare ownership (TSO)   A form of ownership, usually in resort or vacation condominiums, in which owners buy a specific period of time to occupy a unit in that development.

Title   Ownership of property and instrument that is evidence of that ownership.

Tort action   Legal filing of civil suit arising out of a wrongful act, damages, or injury involving liability.

Townhouse condominium   Multifamily dwelling under condominium ownership that utilizes an arrangement of units attached side by side, often rowhouses with individual entrances; also called zero lot line houses.

Trustee   See **Insurance trustee.**

TSO   See **Timeshare ownership.**

ULI   See **Urban Land Institute.**

Umbrella liability insurance   Protection against losses in excess of amounts covered by other liability insurance policies.

Underwriter   Employee of insurance company who reviews

applications for coverage, decides if it should be given, and determines appropriate rates.

Undivided interest Ownership that is inseparable and cannot be divided or severed, such as a condominium unit and its share of common areas.

Unit See **Condominium unit**

Unit deed Legal instrument that, when filed, transfers title of a condominium unit and its undivided portion of common areas from one owner to another.

United States Department of Housing and Urban Development (HUD) An agency of the United States government responsible for the administration of government housing and urban development programs.

Unit owner Person or persons, corporation, partnership, or other legal entity that holds title to a condominium unit and its undivided interest in common areas; also called apartment owner or co-owner.

Unit owner insurance policy Policy specifically designed to provide property and liability coverage to meet needs of owners of condominium units.

Urban Land Institute (ULI) Independent nonprofit research and educational organization incorporated in 1936 to improve the quality and standards of land use and development.

Use restrictions Rules and regulations, often prohibitive in nature, that regulate human behavior in common areas and between neighbors.

Utilities Community services rendered by public utility companies, such as gas, electricity, and telephone.

VA See **Veterans Administration.**

Veterans Administration (VA) An agency of the United States government that administers benefit programs for veterans, including the guarantee of loans to veterans.

Waiver Surrender of a right or privilege.

Watercraft liability insurance Protection against loss arising out of legal responsibility as a result of accident involving boats.

Water damage insurance Protection against property loss caused by water, with certain exceptions.

Workers' compensation Provision, required by state law, to cover cost of medical care and weekly income payments to injured workers or their dependents for industrial injuries or diseases, regardless of blame.

INDEX

establishment, 159
functions, 85, 159
goal, 85
membership, 85–86
procedure, 85
standards, 85, 160
Architectural control review committee,
160
ad hoc, 54
Architectural controls, 159–61
approval of changes, 159–60
enforcement problems, 161
log of violations, 161
necessity of, 159
review process, 160
standards, 85, 160
Architectural limitations, 17
Architectural restrictions, 42–44
function, 43
Architectural standards, 85, 160
Articles of incorporation, 21, 24, 27–28
administrative guidelines, 37
contents, 27
function, 27
indemnification clause, 27
master association, 28
Assessments
billing methods, 189–91
collection procedures, 38, 104, 189–91
delinquent, 88, 104–5
procedures for handling, 190–92
determination of, 39
discount incentives, 192
end-of-financial-period refund, 87
income source, 181
interim period practices, 51–52
need to increase, 154–55
negative incentives for payment, 192
overdue, 105
payment handling procedures, 190–91
recording procedures, 189–91
reduction, 87
special (*See* Special assessments)
suppression by developer's
subsidizing common expenses, 52
understatement, 52
Association insurance policy (*See*
Insurance coverage)
Association (*See specific types*)
Attitudes, changes in, 1–3
Attorney's services, use of, 57
Audits, 41, 57, 88, 183–84, 193–95
considerations in choosing auditor, 194
costs as administrative expenses, 174
definition, 193–94
report of, 194–95
copy sent to unit owners, 195

scope of, 194
Automobile hired and nonownership
liability insurance, 209

Balance sheet, 185
Balloting, 64–66
Banking accounts, 105
Best's Key Rating Guide: Property–Casualty,
215
Billing journal, 186, 189
Blanket fidelity bonds, 99, 140, 213
management agent, 116
Board meetings (*See* Board of directors)
Board of directors, 37, 59–69
annual membership meeting, purpose
of, 63
appointment of committees, 83
authority that can or cannot be
delegated, 38
balance of responsibility with on-site
manager, 101
bonding of members, 88
chain of authority, 44–45
changes in house rules and
regulations, 42–43
communication, establishing lines of,
148–50
communication plan, 155–56
delegation of duties, 62–63
delegation of management needs, 103
elections, 63–67 (*See also* Elections of
board of directors)
filling vacancies, 66–67
first, 49, 56–58
attorney hired by, 57
certified audit of financial
condition of association, 57
date of election, 55
election of, 55
problems confronting, 58
progressive reserve,
establishment of, 57
review of insurance coverage,
57
task of, 57–58
first annual meeting, 55
grievance procedures, 148, 156–58
guidance of association committees by,
92–94
hearings, 62
insurance protection of, 211–13
insurance responsibility for common
areas, 41
invitation to run for, 64
leadership qualities of members, 59
maintenance program, 117–18

maintenance standards, 106
meetings, 62, 75–77
  agenda format, 76–77
  annual membership, 63
  first annual, 55
  location, 75–76
  notification procedures, 75
  open, 75
  quorum requirements, 76
  regular, 75–76
  regularity of, 76
  room for, 76
  special, 76
  time, 75–76
  voting rules, 76
members, 59–60
  annual meeting, 63
  bonding, 88
officers selected by, 67–69 (*See also*
  Officers of association)
policies, 61–62
policy resolution, 61–62
removal from, 66–67
request for proposal to management
  firm, 109
reserves, establishment of, 178
resolutions, 61–62
responsibilities of, 60–63, 167
rules and regulations enforcement,
  procedures for, 148
selection of management agent, 108
special assessments, 39
staggered terms of office, 66
terms of office, 66
transition, 52–53
understanding of accounting
  principles, 168
Board of managers (*See* Board of
  directors)
Bodily injury insurance, 207–8
Boiler and machinery insurance, 203
Boiler maintenance, 129–31
Bomb threats, 145
Bonds (*See* Blanket fidelity bonds)
Budget, 40, 168–82
  advanced planning, 169–70
  approval, 169
  committee assistance, 170
  data required for, 170–71
  definition, 168
  drafting responsibility, 170
  estimating expenses, 170–71
  examination of past records and data,
    171
  exchange of financial experience with
    other condominium associations,
    171

expense section, 169
fiscal year preparation, 170
function, 168–69
hearing, 170
income, determining and itemizing
  sources of, 181–82 (*See also* Income,
  sources of)
itemizing expenses, 172–78 (*See also*
  Expenses)
line item classification of expenses, 172
master list of account categories, 172
notification, 169
participation of association members,
  170
period of, 168
preparation, 104, 169
  scheduling, 169–70
program classification of expenses, 172
reserves, 178–81 (*See also* Reserves)
revenue section, 169
Budget and finance committee, 87–88, 170
  ad hoc, 54
  budget preparation, 104
  functions, 87–88
  recommendations, 87–88
  review of employees' salaries and
    benefits, 89
Budgetary process (*See* Budget)
Budgeting techniques (*See* Budget)
Building fire code, 144
Building operations, 117–45 (*See also*
  Maintenance *and other specific topics*)
  maintenance program, 134–37
  maintenance service contracts, 138–41
  mechanical and building systems
    maintenance, 129–33
  physical maintenance, 117–29
  recreational-amenity maintenance, 134
  security and life-safety systems,
    141–45
Building Owners and Code
  Administrators International, Inc.
  (BOCA) code, 144
Building systems maintenance, 129–33
  (*See also* Maintenance)
Bundle of rights of buyer, 3
Business meetings (*See* Meetings)
Buying housing, attitudes toward, 2
Bylaws, 21, 24–26
  administrative procedures, 36
  amendment, 25–26
  assessment collection procedures, 38
  audit requirement, 88
  changes in, 89
  contents, 38
  declaration distinguished, 24–25
  drafting, 26

financial management provisions, 25
function, 24
house rules and regulations, 164
insurance requirements, 25, 41
items normal to, 25
items typically found in, 24–25
living guidelines, 42
miscellaneous items, 26
officers of association, 67
procedures for changing, 26
procedures to be taken against delinquent owners, 38
reserve funds, 39
special assessments, 39
terms of office of board of directors, 66
transfer of control, 44
use restrictions, 42
Bylaws committee, 89 (*See also* Rules and regulations committee)

Capital gains tax, 228–29
Capital reserves, 39
Cardiopulminary resuscitation (CPR) techniques, 144
Careers, attitudes toward, 2
Carpets and rugs, 127–29
Cash/accrual disbursements journal, 186
Cash/accrual receipts journal, 186
Cash flow projections, 40
Cash flow statement, 185
Cash method of accounting, 182–83
Casualty loss deduction, 226–27
CERTIFIED PROPERTY MANAGER® (CPM®), 63, 110
Certified public accountant (CPA), 183
Chain of authority, 44–45
Chart of accounts, 187–88
Checking account, 105
Checks
assessment payments, 190
countersignatures, 193
procedure for issuance, 193
Checks and balances, system of, 188–95
Choice to be made, 12–17
Closed-circuit television, 143
Coinsurance clause, 204–5
Collection of assessments and delinquent assessments (*See* Assessments)
Committee chairs, guidelines for, 93–94
Committee members, guidelines for, 94
Committees, 83–94
ad hoc (*See* Ad hoc committees; Ad hoc interim committees)
appointment of, 83
architectural control, 85–86

architectural control review, 160
budget and finance, 87–88, 170
community relations, 158
covenants, 92
guidance of, 92–94
guidelines
committee chair, 93–94
members, 94
insurance, 88
landscape and grounds, 86–87
maintenance, 88–89
newsletter, 91
nominating (*See* Ad hoc nominating committee)
renter's, 165
rules and regulations, 89–90
social/recreation, 90–91
special, 83, 92
standing (*See* Standing committees)
welcoming, 91
Common areas, 3–5
definition, 3–4, 33–34
final acceptance of, 53–54
identification in management agreement, 112
injuries in, 211
insurance responsibility, 41
interest of condominium owner in, 4, 36
limited, 34, 112
maintenance, 126–29
transfer of ownership, 53
undivided interest in, 4
Common expenses, 35
Communication (*See also specific topics*)
assessments increase, 154–55
assignment of responsibilities, 156
channels of, 148, 155
coordination of all forms in program, 155–56
establishment of lines of, 148–50
formality of means of, 150
forms of, 108
house rules and regulations, 161–62
importance of program, 156
management agent, 108
meetings, 153–54
newsletter, 151–53
overall plan, 155–56
personal contact, 149–50
special problems, 154–55
welcoming committee, 150–51
Communications committee, ad hoc, 54
Communications coordinator, 155–56
Community associations, 7–10
condominiums, 7–8
cooperatives, 8–9

homeowners, 10
planned unit developments, 9–10
timesharing, 9
Community Associations Institute (CAI),
11–12, 63, 110
Community relations committee, 158
Community rooms, maintenance of,
126–27
Complaints, 156–58
renters, 165
Completed operations and products
liability insurance, 140, 208–9
Comprehensive general liability
insurance, 207–8 (*See also* Liability
insurance)
Condominium Act, 21
Condominium association
certififed audit of financial condition
of, 57
creation, 22, 24, 27
definition, 19–20
developer's initial control of, 49
drawbacks, 16–17
establishment by developer, 21
federal tax status, 219–25
governing documents, 19–45 (*See also*
Governing documents)
insurance policy, 199–216 (*See also*
Insurance coverage)
interim period, 47–55
managing the human element, 147–65
master, 27–28
officers, 67–69 (*See also* Officers of
association)
owners' membership in, 20
period of ongoing governance, 48
period of transfer, 47–48, 55–56
purpose, 20
real life of, 55
responsibilities of, 20
three stages of development, 47–48
traditional house or, 15–17
umbrella, 27–28
unit owner's automatic membership
in, 47
Condominium management agreement
(*See* Management agreement)
Condominium managment and rental
management, 108–9, 112–13
Condominium owner (*See also* Unit
owners)
bundle of rights, 3
common area, interest in, 4
Condominium unit, 3–5
definition, 4, 33–34
Condominium unit ownership, 3 (*See also*
Unit owner)

drawbacks, 14
single-family home ownership
distinguished, 4
Condominiums
advantages, 12–17
cooperative or, 14–15
definition, 3
federal tax status
electing tax exemption, 220–22
tax exempt or corporate status?
222–25
formation, 21
popularity of concept, 12
reasons for incorporating, 27
rental unit or, 12–14
state law creation, 3
types, 7–8
types of buildings, 5
Contingency reserves, 39, 181
Federal Housing Administration
recommendation, 181
Contractor's protective liability insurance,
209–10
Contractors to provide services, 97–98
Contractual liability insurance, 209
Conversion of rental properties, 5–7
advantages, 6
definition, 5
occurrence of, 5–6
primary reason for 6
problems created by, 6
public offering statement, 29
risk, 6
social problems for tenants, 6
statistics, 6–7
transfer of control of new
condominium distinguished, 55–56
Cooperation, need for, 148
Cooperatives, 8–9
benefits, 15
condominiums or, 14–15
definition, 8
disadvantages, 14–15
physical form, 9
Corporate status, 222–25
Correspondence of management agent, 108
Corridors, maintenance of, 126, 128
Cost of housing, 16
Council of co-owners, 20
Council of unit owners, 20
Country club membership, 9
Covenants, enforcement of, 165
Covenants committee, 92
ad hoc, 54
importance of, 92
rules and regulations committee as
adjunct to, 92

---

operating, 39–40
progressive, 57
replacement (*See* Replacement
    reserves)
savings account for, 105
working capital, 39–41
Residential associations, 3
Resolutions, 61–62
copies to members, 62
policy, 61–62
Responsibilities
board of directors, 60–63, 167
condominium association, 20
developers, 49–51, 56–57
maintenance, 32, 37–38
management agent (*See* Management
    agent)
on-site manager, 101
ownership, 1
unit owners, 14
Restrictions, 32, 42–44 (*See also* House
    rules and regulations)
Resurfacing paved areas, 122
Resurfacing tennis courts, 134
Retired persons, 2
Revival of condominium concept, 10–11
Right-to-use agreement, 9
Robert's Rules of Order, 64, 77, 81
Roman concept, 10
Roof maintenance, 123–24
Rubbish removal costs, 175
Rules and regulations committee, 89–90
    (*See also* House rules and
    regulations)
adjunct to covenants committee, 92

Sale of unit, tax consequences of, 228–29
Savings accounts for reserves, 105
Secret voting, 64–66
Secretary of condominium association,
    67–69
Security expenses, 175
Security of occupancy, 13
Security systems, 16, 141–43
alarms, 143
closed-circuit television, 143
elevator lockouts, 142–43
guards, 143
intercom, 142
lighting, 142
Self-management, 95–100
advantage of, 99
attributes required of members, 98–99
blanket fidelity bonds, 99
choice of, 98–100
contracting for services, 96–97

contractors to perform services, 97–98
cost factor, 99
employees to carry out duties, 97
full agency management with, 103
legal implications, 99
maintenance program, 138
officers' and directors' liability
    insurance, 99
professional approach, 98, 100
size of development as factor, 99
supervision, 99
volunteers to perform maintenance
    tasks, 98
Service contracts (*See* Maintenance service
    contracts)
Sick pay, 173
Sidewalk maintenance, 122–23
Single deed estate, 21
subdivision into multiple single deed
    estates, 21
Single-family home ownership and
    condominium unit ownership
    distinguished, 4
Single-family house groups, 8
Singles (*See* Unmarried persons)
Small families, 2–3
Snow removal, 121
Social disadvantages, 158
Social interaction, 16
Social interdependence, recognition of, 148
Social obligations and restrictions, 17
Social/recreation committee, 90–91
activities planned by, 90
ad hoc, 54
functions, 90
interest areas, 90–91
recreational facilities supervised and
    operated by, 90
fees for, 90–91
Soffits and shutters, maintenance of,
    124–25
Special assessments, 39
explanation to justify, 87
income source, 182
prevention of future need for, 52
Special committees, 83, 92 (*See also*
    Committees)
Sprinkler leakage insurance, 202
Stairways, maintenance of, 126–28
Stairs, maintenance of, 123
Standing committees, 53, 83–93 (*See also*
    Committees)
appointments, procedure for, 84
areas of, 84
creation, 83–84
function, 83
size, establishment of, 84

U.S. Income Tax Return for Homeowners Association (Form 1120-H), 220
Unmarried persons, attitudes of, 2–3
Urban areas, 16
Urban Land Institute (ULI), 110
Use restrictions, 42–43
User fees as taxable income, 221
Utilities costs, 171

Vacation club license, 9
Vacation homes, 9
Vacation pay, 173
Vandalism insurance, 202
Vehicle insurance, 139
Veterans Administration financing, 31
Vice president of condominium association, 67–68
Violations of rules (*See* Enforcement of rules and controls)
Volunteers to perform maintenance tasks, 98
Voting procedures, 64–66
Voting rights, 24
Voting rules, 73–74, 76

Waiver of subrogation, 210–11
Water and sewage costs, 175
Water damage insurance, 202
Water line maintenance, 132–33
Water Tower Place, Chicago, Illinois, 7
Watercraft liability insurance, 209
Watering grounds, 118, 120–21
Weed and pest control, 118–20
Welcoming committee, 91, 150–51
    activities planned by, 91
    ad hoc, 54
    function, 91
Windows, maintenance of, 126, 128, 138
    operating expense, 175
Wiring maintenance, 133
Workers' compensation, 25, 116, 139–40, 213–14
Working capital
    forecasting, 40
    initial, 40
    reserves, 39–41
Working couples, 2–3

Zero lot line houses, 8